TO BE OR NOT:
AN E-PRIME ANTHOLOGY

To Be or Not:
An E-Prime Anthology

Edited by
D. David Bourland, Jr.
Paul Dennithorne Johnston

INTERNATIONAL SOCIETY FOR GENERAL SEMANTICS

San Francisco

© 1991 International Society for General Semantics
All rights reserved
Printed in the United States of America

INTERNATIONAL SOCIETY FOR GENERAL SEMANTICS
P.O. Box 2469
San Francisco, CA 94126

Library of Congress Cataloging in Publication Data

To be or not: an E-prime anthology / edited by D. David Bourland, Jr., Paul Dennithorne Johnston.
     p.   cm.
   Includes bibliographical references.
   ISBN 0-918970-38-5
   1. English language—Composition and exercises—Study and teaching.   2. English language—Rhetoric—Study and teaching.
3. English language—Semantics.   4.English language—Reform.   5. English language—Verb.
I. Bourland, D. David (Delphus David), 1928- .
II. Johnston, Paul Dennithorne, 1942- .
PE1404.T59   1991
808'.04207—dc20   91-29865
                                               CIP

CONTENTS

Dedication *vii*

Acknowledgments *viii*

Foreword *ix*

Introduction$_1$ *xi*

Introduction$_2$ *xvii*

Part One E-Prime in Action

Discovering E-Prime   3
ELAINE C. JOHNSON

Getting Rid of the *To Be* Crutch   7
RUTH S. RALPH

Escape from a Frozen Universe:
Discovering General Semantics   15
PAUL DENNITHORNE JOHNSTON

Writing that Works   21
DEWITT SCOTT

Toward Understanding E-Prime   23
ROBERT ANTON WILSON

Coping with Semantic Problems
in System Development   27
KAREN L. RUSKIN

Working with E-Prime:
Some Practical Notes   37
E. W. KELLOGG III AND D. DAVID BOURLAND, JR.

Part Two   Epistemological Foundations of E-Prime

A Linguistic Note: Writing in E-Prime   59
D. DAVID BOURLAND, JR.

The Semantics of a Non-Aristotelian Language   67
D. DAVID BOURLAND, JR.

Is-Less and Other Grammars   75
ROBERT IAN SCOTT

Speaking in E-Prime:
An Experimental Method for Integrating General Semantics into Daily Life   87
E. W. KELLOGG III

To Be or Not To Be:
E-Prime as a Tool for Critical Thinking   101
D. DAVID BOURLAND, JR.

Part Three   Further Applications of E-Prime

Labels: A Short Story   125
PAUL DENNITHORNE JOHNSTON

A Non-Aristotelian Paradigm for Linguistics   135
D. DAVID BOURLAND, JR.

*Dedicated to the memory of
Alfred Korzybski*

ACKNOWLEDGMENTS

We wish to thank the authors who have generously allowed us to publish their work herein: Elaine C. Johnson, E. W. Kellogg III, Ruth S. Ralph, Karen L. Ruskin, DeWitt Scott, Robert Ian Scott, Robert Anton Wilson. Our thanks to those who have contributed their creative and evaluative skills—Earl Hautala, June Johnston, Russell Joyner, Emory Menefee, Jerry Snider, Debra Ryll—and to Steve Allen for providing the foreword.

THE EDITORS

FOREWORD

IN A RECENT BOOK, *Dumbth,* I called attention to the pervasive, aggressive ignorance, poor thinking, and consequent inefficiency we now see on all sides. In an attempt to help, I offered eighty-one different suggestions that could reverse this distressing state of affairs by improving the ability to reason.

For many years I have had an interest in the general semantics movement, and have suggested that others become involved with it (my Suggestion #81). General semantics, as elaborated by Alfred Korzybski and his numerous followers, encompasses a number of insights, techniques, and devices for improving the way we deal with ourselves, others, and the world around us. This book concerns one of those techniques, startling in its simplicity: the removal of the verb "to be" from our written and spoken utterances, which produces the subset of English known as E-Prime. Like a lever that can open a container of precious things, E-Prime provides an entrance to the large and wonderful world of general semantics.

When most people encounter the notion of E-Prime, they begin to bristle with questions—Why? How? So what? David Bourland and others have spent years addressing such questions, and this volume contains the results.

STEVE ALLEN

Paul Dennithorne Johnston **INTRODUCTION[1]**

WHAT IF the word *is* didn't exist? Words give us mental tools to apprehend our environment. The use of words for creating and storing knowledge distinguishes humans from other species. Yet language, the tool that makes us human, can also hurt us, if it corrupts our ability to make accurate evaluations. When tool tolerances go awry, we can fine-tune. Those who use E-Prime, a recent version of fine-tuned English, drop the verb *to be* in order to put people back in control of the language they use.

We "make sense" of the universe by collecting information through sight, hearing, touch, taste, smell, then processing it consciously and unconsciously. This goes on from day one as we build up unconscious assumptions about the structure of the world. Our senses provide data. So does language. But language also interprets this data because, immersed in a language-using species, we cannot avoid filtering our perceptions through the logic of our inherited language. We often don't realize we've made assumptions. We call our unconscious and conscious belief-structure *knowledge* of what *is*.

Language shapes how we view the world. How we view the world shapes language. Use of E-Prime interrupts this cycle of cognitive looping, giving new life to perception and evaluation.

We know that language has the power to define reality. Benjamin Lee Whorf studied languages, including those of the Mayan and the Hopi, and concluded that language does influence perception. Some scholars say we won't perceive things our culture doesn't name. Conversely, language can delude us into believing that its *internal* relationships also hold true in the world *out there*. *To be* verbs (*be, been, were, was, am, are, is*) play a powerful role in setting up the logic of such delusional evaluations.

Little words with a mighty clout, *to be* verbs dictate how you think and what you know. These apparently unassuming verbs subvert your intellect and your perceptions because they *assume* the validity of *being* as a conceptual tool for accurately describing the universe. The idea of *being* legitimizes itself with and perpetuates the assumption that *things stay the same.*

To be verbs say that things have a predetermined fixed structure. When such verbs determine relationships, they set your world in concrete. Sometimes *is* makes God-like assertions: "That *is* the truth." Sometimes *is* says a thing *is* its name: "This *is* X."

In ordinary English, with its abundance of *is* definitions, we *know* that certain things *are* true. *Steel is steel. A thief's a thief. He is lazy. You are a genius. Life is tough.* In such conceptual anarchy, anything goes. Parents, teachers, priests, politicians, and bosses tell you how it *is*, and *truth* belongs to the enforcer of the highest *is*-quotient. "He *is* a bad son." "You *are* no good at math." "Lust *is* a sin." "This war *is* just." "You *are* worth five bucks an hour."

If we accept the proposition that *we* give form to our perceptual universe, we may call a chair or other "structure" an event, an area of wave-particles that we perceive as "solid." Conventional English grabs events and "objects," slices up their space-time, freezes the pieces, and leaves the user with chopped up, containerized fragments of reality. How often do these chunks usefully represent life? By the use of the passive voice, we separate action from doer. Our verbal gymnastics split mind from body, space from time, production from environment, thinking from feeling, conscious from unconscious, sex from emotion, action from responsibility, human blood from "surgical" war. Elementalistic thinking, with its roots in the artificial linguistic fragmentation of actions or entities, causes human misery and death. "It was polluted"—in life, you cannot split polluter from polluted, or murderer from victim, and make things right again.

In accordance with current scientific knowledge, we conceptualize "space" and "time" together: space-time. We have also learned that the observer affects the observed. Each of us, as human participant-observers, occupies a unique and continually changing point-of-view in space-time, one that we may describe as our individual *space-time-view.*

At any point in time, language lags behind the current scientific understanding of reality. For example, in physics we regard Einstein's contribution to relativity theory as a useful map for scientific exploration. But in language—our primary tool for communication and thought—we often use ancient logic based on the notion of *being* and its assumption of stasis. As a result, we believe in absolutes, we overlay old perceptions onto present perceptions, and we freeze present evaluations for future use. We put our semantic space-time-view on hold, then try to negotiate our way through a world we perceive as *basically always the same*. We hoard a handful of motion-picture frames, while the movie keeps on running. Meanwhile our space-time-view, like the tide, never stops.

Paradoxically, we seem to need to cram our knowledge into freeze-frames in order to have it at all. To "understand," we simplify, reduce, abstract, leave out some of the pieces of the jigsaw puzzle. How do you define things that keep changing in a universe of countless facets? You can devise methods that remind you to regard your knowledge as provisional, as the best "working knowledge" currently available, subject to verification, fine-tuning, change.

Today, many intellectual disciplines recognize that knowledge created by human nervous systems has limitations imposed by the limitations of the systems that create it. Robert Anton Wilson wrote, in *Quantum Psychology*: "Uncertainty, Indeterminacy and Relativity appear in modern science for the same reason they appear in modern logic, modern art, modern literature, modern philosophy and even modern theology. In this century, the human nervous system has discovered its own creativity, and its own limitations."

General semantics founder Alfred Korzybski, horrified by war atrocities he'd seen, framed his investigations into language and the nervous system in terms of his profession, engineering. Why, he asked, do we have such success engineering a long-lasting bridge, and such failure when we "engineer" a peace treaty? His studies led him to conclude that the language of science and engineering accurately portrays the structural relationships of the mechanical world. But the language of discourse has inherent logical problems that cause a structural disparity between words-cum-ideas and the phenomena they attempt to represent.

Korzybski saw a wide gulf between the world (the territory) and the language-thoughts-feelings (the maps) we use in observing, discussing, and understanding that world. In his major work, *Science and Sanity*, Korzybski wrote: "To achieve adjustment and sanity . . . we must study structural characteristics of the world *first* . . . then . . . build languages of similar structure, instead of habitually ascribing to the world the primitive structure of our language."

Korzybski said, in effect, that we make up our world in words, then delude ourselves that the external world fits our definitions. We think the map *is* the territory. To avoid this delusional behavior, we must go beyond the two-valued bipolar logic of Aristotle, which says that something either *is* or *is not*; e.g., night-day, all-nothing, true-false, yes-no, is-isn't. Comprehension of a highly complex world requires a many-valued logic. In a non-Aristotelian logic, we would think in terms of degrees and probabilities: night-predawn-dawn - - →sunrise-day, all-most-many-some-few-one - - →none, true-undetermined-? - - →false, yes-probable - - → perhaps-no.

Korzybski isolated two forms of *is* that encourage map-territory confusion: the *is-of-identity* (Sam *is* a dog), and the *is-of-predication* (the signal *is* red). By confusing the general with the particular, identification truncates knowledge, sometimes dangerously. For example, if, thinking all dogs *are* lovable, you reach out to pet Sam, a trained attack dog, you may lose a hand. Similarly, predication oversimplifies a complex reality. The signal may look red to you, but does it warn a color-blind driver of the danger ahead?

Such usage also ignores human selecting and labeling because it implies that God or the universe makes definitions and categories.

A method for reducing *is*-generated misevaluation came from linguist D. David Bourland, Jr. He knew that Korzybski had urged abandoning the *is* of identity and the *is* of predication, so when, at the Institute of General Semantics, he heard the suggestion that we stop using *to be* altogether, he tried it in a paper in preparation for a General Semantics Congress. (He later said the experience gave him a severe intermittent headache for a week.) He felt that such a discipline improved his writing by removing the passive voice (it *was* done), by forcing the doer into view (*Sam* did it), and by deleting stigmatic labels (he *is* a thief).

Bourland named the system "E-Prime." In one paper, he wrote: "The basic fallacy of the 'is' of predication has to do with its expressing a 'partial identity' . . . since the quality becomes fallaciously projected onto the object, situation, person, etc., in a denial of the projectional and transactional process involved."

As articles about E-Prime appeared, the idea caught on. English teachers, a writing consultant, therapists, a self-esteem teacher, among others, found that the use of E-Prime improved thinking, writing, self-image, and evaluation skills. Researchers, designers, and systems analysts reported that E-Prime, by bringing in the *doer*, exposed errors and omissions.

Passive statements obscure *whodunit*, or, in the case of system omissions, who didn't. E-Prime includes the actors. We must accept responsibility for our actions and transactional perceptions, because we cannot imply that the gods, Fate, or some Other Circumstance did it.

By excluding *A-is-B* logic, E-Prime challenges the conventional notion that subject-predicate relationships provide a sound basis for knowledge. This makes it necessary to develop workable alternatives, such as conceptions of knowledge in terms of experience, multiple characteristics, probabilities, growth, change, dynamic forms instead of static forms, etc.

E-Prime changes the logical structure of thought and language. The new logic, by its very structure, must holistically encompass space and time and view.

Space: Although they may appear identical, phenomenon$_1$ occupies a different space than phenomenon$_2$. Space$_1 \neq$ Space$_2$.

Time: We can't conceive of space without time. We can't attribute permanence because space-time means change through movement on the space-time continuum. Time$_1 \neq$ Time$_2$.

View: With passive statements overruled, we must include a participant-observer. We can't define a view without defining a point in the space-time matrix: space-time-view. We each have a unique view in the matrix, so we can only make relative comparisons. We don't verbally separate observer from actor, so we regard viewing as an active, projectional, transactional process. Space-time-view$_1 \neq$ Space-time-view$_2$.

I first heard about E-Prime from Dr. E. W. Kellogg III. The idea fitted with some notions I'd just heard on the relationship between words and health.

Kellogg said to me, "Why not say *I feel sick* instead of *I am sick*, or *I feel hungry* instead of *I am hungry*?" Doing this, he said, describes experience and eliminates the stranglehold of fixed states.

When I decided to try E-Prime, I found that it improved my self-image. You can't say, "I'm a failure," although you can say "I failed to achieve such-and-such." You can't identify rigidly with your perceived personal characteristics or social role. You must move closer to experience and understand yourself in terms of changing feelings, thoughts, and actions. You no longer have to live up to old "I am" labels.

As with physical exercise, you don't have to use E-Prime all the time to benefit from it. With some people, selected areas of use will encourage a critical awareness that improves conceptual health as well as thinking and communication skills. With others, only a deep commitment to using E-Prime will satisfy the need for epistemological clarity.

The discipline of E-Prime can make an important contribution to our linguistic tool kit. If we seek to think and communicate more clearly, to grow and change, to take control of our own lives, to feel more tolerance of difference and less fear of change, we may thank Bourland for bringing to light such an effective tool for making better maps.

In E-Prime, we can't ask questions such as "What kind of person am I?" We can't define ourselves concretely, forever. E-Prime helps us escape the prison of an *is-world* and travel in a universe free of such linguistic self-restrictions. We can stop asking unanswerable questions such as "what is love?" because, instead of defining love in terms of *is*, we seek dynamic definitions for understanding both the ongoing processes in our personal relationships as well as the changing feelings of emotional growth and developing maturity.

Myth says Procrustes would force travelers to fit into his bed by stretching their bodies or cutting off their legs. Instead of trying to force reality into the Procrustean Bed of fixed definitions, let us seek living descriptions that grow as we grow. Let us journey through a process world, a wonderfully rejuvenating adventure, as we explore the invaluable tool of E-Prime.

PAUL DENNITHORNE JOHNSTON
San Francisco, February 1991

D. DAVID BOURLAND, JR. ***INTRODUCTION$_2$***

WHEN I sat down at the Institute in Lime Rock, Connecticut, in the spring of 1949 to rewrite a paper without using the verb "to be," I had no idea what that activity would lead to. Well, the famous headache passed after a week, and eventually I decided to write all my "important" papers on general semantics topics in this same way. I did not say anything about this discipline to others for years, believing that to do so would stimulate unwanted criticism. I felt that serious students of general semantics should follow the basic Korzybskian directive and studiously avoid using the verb "to be" in the ways known as Identity and Predication. So if one simply (simply?) avoided *all* uses of that verb, one just applied rigorously some key tenets of general semantics, right?

By the middle 1960s my friend and colleague Charles H. Chandler had convinced me that others might find it interesting to learn about this technique, which by then I had exercised in several papers. To have a handy label for the procedure of doing without the verb "to be," I coined the term "E-Prime." The first paper in part 2 of this anthology contains the initial effort to bring this matter to the attention of the general semantics community. Please note that, from the very beginning, I have seen E-Prime as an additional extensional device (*Science and Sanity,* fourth edition, page xlviii), a device offered to join the application of indexes, dates, etc., quotes, and hyphens, as proposed by Korzybski. The noble purpose of the extensional devices, as Korzybski stated in his seminars, consisted of providing the means for "changing the [semantic] structure of our language, without changing the language itself." And why, one might ask, should we wish to change the semantic structure of our everyday language?

Such an effort makes little sense, as long as one insists on taking

xvii

a superficial attitude toward language and its use by humans.

Life becomes more interesting, more complex, more challenging when one begins to reflect on the deeper aspects of the creation and consequences of utterances. Korzybski directed our attention to such matters through what he referred to as neuro-linguistic and neuro-semantic processes. From a neuro-semantic viewpoint, by applying the extensional devices one may provide opportunities for a higher degree of cortico-thalamic integration—the "balanced" neurological interacting of the "higher" and "lower" centers of the brain. In *Science and Sanity* Korzybski emphasized extensively the need for delaying briefly one's reactions in order to allow the desired cortico-thalamic integration to function. He saw this delay as a beneficial consequence of applying the extensional devices, maintaining silence on the objective level, exercising a consciousness of abstracting, etc., fostered by training with the Structural Differential. Korzybski had the following to say about the "psycho-physiological delay":

> No matter how small, it serves to unload the thalamic material on the cortex. In a number of clinical cases, Dr. Philip S. Graven has demonstrated that the moment such a delay can actually be produced in the patient, he either improves or is entirely relieved. The precise neurological mechanism of this process is not known, but there is no doubt that this "delayed action" has many very beneficial effects upon the whole working of the nervous system. It somehow balances harmful semantic reactions and also somehow stimulates the higher nervous centers to more *physiological* control over the lower centers. (*Science and Sanity*, p. 424.)

One may produce a "delay," as described by Korzybski, in various ways. He referred to the daily life wisdom of "thinking twice," "counting to ten," etc. Korzybski pointed out, however, that despite the sound psycho-physiological basis for such procedures, *their effectiveness can become vitiated by the Aristotelian semantic structure of our language*—"a language involving the 'is' of identity," which must lead to confusion in orders of abstraction. (*Science and Sanity*, p. 425.)

A delayed reaction of the kind advocated by Korzybski, set in a very favorable semantic environment, can result from *listening in E-Prime*, as practiced by Dr. E. W. Kellogg III. See our paper "Working with E-Prime: Some Practical Notes" in part 1 of this volume for his comments on his experiences along these lines. The procedure, as Kellogg describes it, amounts to translating the statements of others as necessary into E-Prime as they speak, and then responding to this E-Prime version. Here one obviously has the

Introduction 2

delayed reaction and a possible reduction in Identification and other neuro-semantically undesirable processes.

Once again we have a neuro-semantic procedure easy to describe, but somewhat difficult to apply. And yet . . . the consequences seem outstanding. So far we have the following:

1. Write, speak, "think" without using the verb "to be."
2. Translate the speech of others into E-Prime *as they speak* and respond to the E-Prime version.

In my opinion, *listening in E-Prime* promises to produce more benefits than any other aspect of this subset of English.

Another consequence of using E-Prime—the near elimination of the passive voice—deserves attention. In her paper in this anthology, "Coping with Semantic Problems in System Development," Dr. Karen Ruskin placed particular importance on this aspect of E-Prime. So did Dr. Robert Ian Scott in "*Is*-less and Other Grammars," and Dr. Ruth S. Ralph in "Getting Rid of the 'To Be' Crutch." Writing and journalism teachers will find this method very useful because it forces the writer to find alternatives to the passive voice.

Paul Dennithorne Johnston points out in his "Introduction₁," the inherent elementalism of the passive voice: the separation and usual suppression of a key part of the agent-action situation. Once again, I feel that I must point out that while E-Prime certainly does not destroy *all* the identification mechanisms in English, and it does not do away with *all* cases of elementalism through making the passive voice awkward, *it does in fact remove major pathways to those two semantic problems*. Sounds like good general semantics to me!

For some time now serious students of Korzybski's methodology have discussed "internalizing general semantics," and have even commented on whether others "really have general semantics in their guts." I never felt that I understood what those expressions meant, or how to go about accomplishing the obviously worthwhile goal of internalizing general semantics. Now I finally do: write/speak/think/listen in E-Prime. For starters.

D. David Bourland, Jr.
Wichita Falls, Texas
February 1991

Part One

E-PRIME IN ACTION

Elaine C. Johnson   **DISCOVERING E-PRIME**

L IKE MANY of my colleagues, I entered the English classroom woefully unprepared to teach students how to write clearly. I didn't know what to say to them when I read over their thin, voiceless prose. Nevertheless, I forged ahead, assigning writing, reading it with attention, responding always to what struck me as honest, authentic. Over time, I observed that the best student writers used language vividly, as all fine writers do, and gave strength to their writing, in part, by using a variety of verbs.

One day I read a paper I found particularly flat and dull. I reread the first paragraph, and noticed that all the verbs came from the verb "to be." I drew little boxes around every form of that verb I came to in that student's paper and wrote in the margin, "Vary your verb choices." When I sat down with the student to go over the paper to show her how to make the writing more effective, I helped her change the sentences to accommodate other verbs. We eliminated the passive voice. She seemed skeptical, but could see that her writing had improved, just by tinkering with the verbs she had used. Notice the difference:

> BEFORE
>
> Dear Miss Havisham:
>
> You and I are two different people and for this reason I don't at all agree with the way you've chosen to live your life. I can only imagine how hard it was for you when the groom didn't show up at your wedding, but that was no reason to lock yourself up. The damages you created could have been less if you hadn't been so selfish. I believe that your involving other people made the situation much worse than it could've been.

Elaine C. Johnson teaches English at Tamalpais High School, Mill Valley, California. Originally published in *Et cetera* 45, no. 2 (Summer 1988).

AFTER
Dear Miss Havisham:
   In many ways we differ from each other and for this reason I don't agree with the way you've chosen to live your life. I can only imagine how horrible you must've felt when the groom didn't show up for your wedding, but why did you need to lock yourself up? The damage you created could have lessened if your selfishness hadn't taken over. I believe that involving other people with your problems made the situation much worse.   [Christofani Wicks, age 16]

As a teacher, I had experienced a major breakthrough in learning what to say to students to help them improve: "Vary your verb choices!" Note what another student did in her revision:

BEFORE
   Anyway, here we all were sitting around the swimming pool, talking. Of course when one's whole family is sitting around, one does not talk about the gorgeous guy sitting in the blue lounge chair on the other side of the pool or the fact that one is able to see Bart's boxer shorts through his dress whites, particularly in the presence of company. Especially when the company was to be one's in-laws. So conversation went on to cover dinner plans for tomorrow night, wedding plans for next month, and plans about Bart's next assignment. [This particular subject was dominated by both fathers and lasted for a *very long while.*] All of these topics were of no interest to me, so I continued watching the cute guy across the pool.

AFTER
   Anyway, there we sat around the swimming pool, talking. Of course when one's whole family sits around, one does not talk about the gorgeous guy in the blue lounge chair on the other side of the pool or the fact that one can see Bart's boxer shorts through his dress whites, particularly in the presence of one's future in-laws. So conversation went on to cover dinner plans for tomorrow night, wedding plans for next month, and plans about Bart's next assignment. [Both fathers dominated discussion of this particular subject.] I had no interest in any of these topics, so I continued watching the cute guy across the pool.
                                                            [Lori Vinskey, age 17]

Years went by, and I encouraged students to use "vivid verbs," to "show" in their writing, rather than "tell." I never had cause to go further with this until last fall. I encountered a student who wouldn't settle for my weak explanations as to why his writing improved when he sought active verbs and eliminated forms of the verb "to be." He wanted to know *why* I made such a fuss over verbs, "to be" in particular. I realized I had no solid theoretical base from which to make my arguments, so turned to a colleague, our resident semanticist, Ruth McCubbrey.

"What reason do I give to students for eliminating/minimizing forms of the verb 'to be'?" I asked her.

"Tell them it ties their language closer to experience, that using other verbs forces them to take responsibility for their statements. You know: 'I liked the film' instead of 'The film was great.' I have an article I'll give you," she responded.

Later that day, my colleague handed me a reprint of E. W. Kellogg's "Speaking in E-Prime: An Experimental Method for Integrating General Semantics into Daily Life" [*Et cetera* 44, no. 2, Summer 1987]. To say it changed my life wouldn't exaggerate my reaction by much. I read it and reread it, amazed and delighted by what I found in Kellogg's piece. Much of it validated what I had struggled with for years, but hadn't understood, the *why* of E-Prime. Kellogg defines E-Prime as English without forms of the verb "to be." Korzybski concerned himself with the "is of identity" and the "is of predication" only—thus allowing "to be" as a helping verb and as a synonym for existence—but I have adopted Kellogg's definition, finding it a greater challenge! I learned something about why certain people angered me and stopped conversation cold when they spoke in English absolutes ("The play was wonderful!") I realized something very important: When I wanted to express myself very clearly, or make a very important point, I always spoke in E-Prime! I thought back on classroom situations, heated arguments, and saw the pattern repeated over and over. I thought, if he can do it, if he can speak and write consistently in E-Prime, so can I.

I had the privilege of working last year with a group of able seniors. I read an enormous amount of their writing, and, after I read Kellogg's article, shared with them some of the insights I had gained from him, insights that supported the comments they had found, some of them over and over again, on their papers. My colleague held my hand during this process, warning me of the arguments students voiced to the best thinking on the subject. They complained that their writing seemed to lack force when they tried to eliminate "to be" verbs. I referred them to Kellogg's points about mirroring their own experience through what they wrote, rather than setting down a series of assertions. Many of them took what I said to heart, and worked hard to rid their writing of forms of the verb "to be." They spoke to each other of E-Prime and seemed to regard it as a toy, a puzzle to solve. They eliminated the passive voice from their writing. I read and graded twenty-three research papers and found about five uses of the passive in all of them. That must set some sort of a record for research-based writing on the high-school level.

   I have not used the term E-Prime with my other classes, but have found ways to explain why I consider careful verb choice so important. My freshmen can compose general statements without using "to be" verbs ("I found the movie more rewarding than the novel"), and my juniors and seniors know that if they rely too heavily on that verb, I will box in every instance, and pressure them, not too gently, to improve their writing by substituting other verbs. I say again and again that eliminating "to be" verbs forces me to vary my sentence patterns, to say what I want to say more responsibly, to speak honestly to myself and others, to see the world as flexible rather than static. Using E-Prime makes me a better writer, and a better person.

GETTING RID OF THE "TO BE" CRUTCH

Ruth S. Ralph

THE LITTLE VERB *to be* serves as an all-purpose crutch for users of English. Grammarians, linguists, and writers, besides general semanticists, recognize the pervasiveness of *to be* and many of the ways it can lead us astray. Nevertheless, one English sentence in two employs some version of *to be,* and most paragraphs have at least a dozen.

What would happen if we threw *to be* out of the English language altogether? Could we still speak and write? A brief unit consisting of two or three one-hour lessons in E-Prime (English minus the verb *to be*) for adult professionals will provide unexpected bonuses.

Besides making students use a wider selection of action verbs—besides making their sentences livelier and more interesting—E-Prime also calls the students' attention to the psychological and philosophical implications of their addiction to *to be.* The E-Prime unit helps explain why Alfred Korzybski worried so much about the "ises-of-identity and predication." These lessons apply equally well regardless of the course title—general semantics, technical writing, creative writing, or business English.

Recently, I taught the E-Prime unit at the U.S. Department of State to my class in Effective Writing for Managers, composed of twenty employees rated GS-12 to GS-17. Most of these students had graduated from college, and several held advanced degrees. They responded enthusiastically to the unit. But not all students of E-Prime need such advanced credentials. I have also presented this unit to ordinary high school seniors.

Ruth S. Ralph teaches at the American University, Washington, D.C., and works actively in the new national organization Plain Talk, Inc. In 1971 she wrote her doctoral dissertation on "The Effects of Training in General Semantics."

Reprinted from *Classroom Exercises in General Semantics,* International Society for General Semantics, San Francisco, 1980.

Before getting into the unit itself, I usually find it helpful to examine the various ways we use *to be* in English: as an auxiliary to form the progressive tense, as a copula or equals mark, and as the essential auxiliary to form the passive voice.

In the first usage, as an auxiliary for the progressive tense, *to be* doesn't do much damage. We can say, "Josie is dreaming" or "Archie is running for office." People who like to identify grammatical relationships can have some fun with these, because the participle (in the above examples *dreaming* and *running*) acts like an adjective in a Subject-Linking Verb-Adjective (S-LV-Adj) basic sentence pattern. But they can also interpret it so that the whole phrase (*is dreaming* or *is running*) becomes the verb in a Subject-Verb pattern. In either case, *to be* doesn't confuse the meaning since these verbs translate easily into the present tense (*dreams* or *runs*). If *to be* acted in this way only, we would need have no concern about it. But in its two other uses, *to be* really causes trouble.

In a sentence like "Reginald is absent," the verb links or couples the subject to the predicate adjective to state a fact. Hearers recognize that Reginald might come in late at any moment. But the sentence "Reginald is stupid" uses the same grammatical structure. This sentence, unlike the first, does not state a verifiable report. Instead it presents the opinion of an agent who hides outside the sentence. A more forthright statement would be "*I think* Reginald is stupid." Clearly, in this case, Reginald, the innocent victim, may have done nothing to earn himself the bad label he got stuck with. Equally obvious, anyone who hears the statement "Reginald is stupid" tends to believe that he has less intelligence than the average; and more important, that next month or next year, Reginald will remain just as dumb as today.

A similar confusion arises with the usage "Mr. Landers is my supervisor," compared with "Mr. Landers is a cornball." In both, the verb *to be* undiscriminatingly relates the subject and the predicate noun, implying that they equal one another. Because we tend to accept the S-LV-N pattern as a factual report, we do not often differentiate when the same grammatical structure presents not a fact, but an unsupported opinion that belongs to Mr. Nobody.

In this way, the S-LV-Adj pattern produces the "is of predication" and the S-LV-N pattern gives us the "is of identity"—serious problems that concerned Alfred Korzybski. Simply dealing with the philosophy and psychology of these "ises" justifies our E-Prime experiment. But the next problem demands even more concern.

The third use of *to be* brings home the really bad effect it can have

Getting Rid of the "To Be" Crutch

as the auxiliary to form the passive voice. The big problem here lies in the passive usage itself. Style manuals, probably without exception, advise writers to avoid the passive and use the active voice whenever possible, for a number of very good reasons.

Passive usage takes the agent out of the subject position and puts him or her back into the sentence, if at all, as the object of an adverbial prepositional phrase tacked onto the end of the sentence. The original object must then move into the subject position, and we get, for example, "The water was spilled by Hortense." Like all passive subjects, the water does not act. An agent must drink it, splash it, use it, or spill it. Passive sentences crawl and drag along, lacking directness and liveliness. Each contains at least two more words (*was* and *by*) than its active voice counterpart. For these reasons among others, writing instructors urge their students to avoid the passive voice.

A more complicated problem arises when a writer selects for the subject of a passive sentence neither a person nor an object (as the innocent victim) but rather an abstraction coined from what would normally have been the verb of the sentence with a suffix such as "tion" or "ment." Verbs like *use, arrange, consider,* and *suspect* turn into *utilization, arrangement, consideration,* and *suspicion,* preempting the subject position and leaving the verb position blank. Then "smothered verbs" must use a form of *to be* to take their place. So we get sentences like "Utilization of the proposed arrangement *is* effectuated" or "Consideration of your unfounded suspicion *is* responsible for unnecessary delays in the completion of our project." We can see that such sentences do not contain any agent and, because *to be* doesn't take an object, can't have an object either. Who does what? Does anybody know? Surely such sentences have no referents in the real world.

I call sentences that start like these examples "subjections" because the subject so often ends in "tion." And I advise my pupils to shun the "tion." Although it may sound profound and high class, it actually conveys little or no meaning. Ordinarily, I would expect bright professionals with good ideas to stay away from "subjections." But, ironically, I find that business, technical, legal, and academic writing overflows with these agentless, objectless, and meaningless passives. They occur pervasively in the mountains of paperwork that choke professional offices and sharply reduce their effectiveness. And none of this could happen without that sneaky little verb *to be*.

In the real world, action and change always go on, producing constant variety and nothing identical. Besides the individuality of every *thing,* every *person* sees with unique eyes, and feels, hears, smells, and tastes with one-of-a-kind sensors. He or she processes sensations through an individual brain and nervous system, and responds uniquely to an environment seen from only one shifting point of view.

General semantics requires that we remain aware of abstracting—the process with which each person selects a few things to pay attention to in the environment, and ignores most others. The notion of abstracting further asserts that people's brains provide names with which people refer to objects of experience, and, in turn, their brains give out more words with which they refer to and categorize the original names. General semanticists call these "higher level abstractions." The Korzybskian formulation of intensional reasoning means that people's brains may generate verbal concepts or ideas spun out of other ideas, without reference to external objective reality.

Therefore, when we say that something *is* something, we dishonestly, although probably unconsciously, suggest that what we *think* must really exist. This hides the fact that we use *to be* to make judgments and to put people into pigeonholes by describing them with a single adjective or noun. E-Prime results in better writing because it comes closer to describing what really goes on "out there."

To start the E-Prime unit, I ask the class, "What would happen if we decided to prohibit anyone from using *to be* for a single hour, or from writing it in any letter or report for a day?" Students usually respond that the idea *is* absurd, that English without *to be is* bound to sound funny, that nobody would *be* able to do it, and that it just *isn't* practical. This article itself, written entirely in E-Prime except for quoted examples and references to *to be* by name, demonstrates, I hope, that E-Prime need not sound peculiar.

I next suggest that E-Prime can eliminate confusion, head off misunderstandings, cut out lies, clarify relationships, and deal a solid blow to gobbledygook. With all these claims going for it, I ask, why not give it a try?

The idea of E-Prime originated with D. David Bourland, a student of Korzybski's. The E-Prime unit demonstrates that students don't really need *to be* nearly as much as they think. Conversely, getting rid of some of their "ises" helps students see that E-Prime can help their writing in other ways—by making them select better subjects, more active verbs, and fewer flowery modifiers.

I start the E-Prime unit by passing out copies of an article, "The Unisness of Is," which I paraphased from an old article in *Time*. I include a copy at the end of this paper for any teachers who want to copy and use it. This article reports an interview with David Bourland in which he explains the rationale of E-Prime. I assign this for overnight reading because it accords Bourland the credit he deserves for inventing E-Prime, and at the same time it gives the students ammunition for a lively class discussion at their next session.

When the students next convene, they usually sound skeptical. Most of them, having looked at how much they rely on *to be*, realize they would have a hard time getting along without it. On the other hand, I point out that English has thousands of other verbs, both action and linking, and that surely bright people can find substitutes for just one verb.

Some students object that E-Prime has no practical application. To this, I truthfully reply that Dr. Albert Ellis, the well-known psychologist, considers *to be* such a serious threat to mental health that he has rewritten many of his books in E-Prime as his contribution to sanity. Incidentally, I add, Dr. Ellis's books don't sound funny at all.

Regardless of whether or not my students seem convinced that E-Prime will cure all their writing problems, I exercise my authority and insist that each student write for the next assignment an essay of about three hundred words in E-Prime, on any subject he or she likes. In case they don't remember all the parts of *to be*, I tell them to consult the dictionary. I also remind my students that the verbs *to do* and *to have* as well as the auxiliaries *can, may, might, will, would*, etc., do not belong to *to be*, so they can freely use them in their essays.

Students often leave this session of the class grumbling that their teacher *is* crazy. But by the next class session I usually find that their attitudes, at least about E-Prime, have changed. Most of the students, having accepted the challenge of E-Prime, quickly become its advocates. They see all kinds of values they didn't anticipate. One student told me rather bemusedly, "I can't believe it. I've been thinking in the passive all my life!"

Picking up on the enthusiasm of the moment, I invite the students to read their essays aloud to one another, taking turns. As each one reads, the others listen carefully, smiling at the strategies the writer has used to avoid the *to be* trap, and marveling at the way E-Prime produces livelier, more tightly constructed expression. I always admire the variety of subjects the students have chosen. And along with them, I note that some subjects fit the E-Prime format better than others.

Students who try to describe the Library or Congress or the King Tut exhibit, essentially passive inanimate subjects, have more trouble than those who write about sports, family adventures, or accidents, in which *I, we, he, she,* or *they* supply realistic agents for action verbs.

But no matter what subject they have chosen, writers who have always relied heavily on the passive voice and the "is of identity" find E-Prime much harder going than their less pompous classmates. Some students write delicate descriptions, while others deal with earthier events in blunter language. But regardless of the theme, each essay sparkles with action verbs that enliven the writing at the same time they cut down on the need for extra adverbs.

Of course, neither I nor my students believe that we should necessarily give up *to be* forever. David Bourland may speak and write exclusively in E-Prime, but for most of us, just cutting down on our reliance on *to be* will suffice. We've seen how E-Prime can give us a shortcut to understanding the passive voice and the "ises of identity and predication," all of which interfere with lively description, clear writing, clear thinking, and honest expression. I usually suggest that students come back to E-Prime every few weeks, just to check up on themselves.

In any event, an E-Prime unit serves as an eye-opener for both students and teacher. For a two- or three-hour project, most of my students agree with me that E-Prime really pays off. After all, I couldn't have written this paper without it.

The Unisness of Is

A *Time* magazine article furnished the basis for the following report. Some years ago a reporter talked with D. David Bourland, a computer systems analyst, about his project of scrubbing from his speech and writing all forms of the verb *to be*. The first time he tried to do this, Bourland recalls, "it gave me a headache. But after practicing for a while, I found that it comes easily."

Would writing in E-Prime, as Bourland calls English minus the verb *to be*, sound funny? Bourland answers: "People seem impressed by the clarity of my expression and the ease with which they can understand me."

"For example," he continues, "in a case where most people might judge themselves harshly by saying, 'I'm no good at math,' I would advise them to say instead, 'I got poor grades in sixth grade arithmetic,' or 'I did better in other subjects than I did in math.' With this sentence structure, I feel that people will not condemn themselves forever to fail at problems that require mathematical skill. Rather they will recognize that they simply report on past experience, without predicting that the same thing will inevitably, or even probably, happen again. In this way, we can avoid the 'self-fulfilling prophecy.' "

Bourland's interest in language and its effects on behavior and thought stems from his experiences as a young man in the 1940s when he studied at the Institute of General Semantics in Lakeville, Connecticut. There he attended lectures by Alfred Korzybski, whose theories form the basis of the general semantics movement. Korzybski believed that the verb *to be* causes serious communications disturbances and other psychological problems for modern man. In his book *Science and Sanity*, Korzybski referred to these problems as the "is of predication" and the "is of identity." In both, he blamed the verb *to be* for misleading people into making untrue and unwarranted assumptions.

Going his teacher one better, David Bourland heads up a crusade for the adoption of E-Prime.

"General semanticists," Bourland explains, "object to *to be* for philosophical as well as psychological reasons. To start with, we reject an axiom of classical logic: the principle of identity. For that reason, we call ourselves advocates of 'non-Aristotelian logic.' Heraclitus, a Greek philosopher who lived before Socrates, insisted that 'everything changes.' He saw this as the basic truth of existence. Time moves inexorably, and in the fraction of a second you need to describe a thing, it has already begun to alter.

"For example, sentences like 'A rose is a rose,' 'the law is the law,' and 'a man ain't nuthin' but a man' do not really say what they seem to. The first rose has wilted a tiny bit before you get to the next one. In the second example, identical words mean different things. One translation of 'the law is the law' might read, 'You must obey a jaywalking ordinance or take your chances on getting a ticket if they catch you.'

"Even more clearly," continues Bourland, " 'A man ain't nuthin' but a man' might translate to, 'You can't expect any man to behave more honestly, strenuously, forcefully, etc., than the average person.' You should notice that we could make many other translations for these sentences, so that what appears as a simple 'truth' in these sayings can actually mean almost anything anyone wants it to mean. Along with that belongs the idea that a speaker has no assurance that his listener will get the same message he sends.

"I believe firmly that language affects thought and behavior," Bourland goes on. "People don't realize how much everything changes because the verb *to be* gives them an illusion of permanence. Our language remains the language of absolutes and this very usually causes it. The spurious identity it so readily connotes perverts our perception of reality.

"A pair of common enough sentence structures employ *to be* to tempt man into mistaken value judgments. Korzybski called the Subject-Linking Verb-Adjective sentence pattern the 'is of predication' and the 'Subject-Linking Verb-Noun' pattern the 'is of identity.' "

A sentence like "Robert is stupid" exemplifies the first, while "Marcia is a genius" demonstrates the second. "Actually," explains Bourland, "both limit in a similar manner our ability to see Robert and Marcia as whole persons, or to accept the idea that they may develop different characteristics in the future. This makes us always see them as stupid or brilliant now and forever after."

Besides keeping us from falling into the errors he described, Bourland says, E-Prime has certain advantages over conventional English. For one, unanswerable questions like "who am I?—why was I born?—was man created to suffer?—who is the ruler of the universe?" do not arise because without *to be* nobody can ask them.

People who take refuge in waffling statements based on unprovable or unproved evidence cannot say in E-Prime, "It is established . . . " or "Of course, that is common knowledge. . . ."

In a sense, Korzybski argued that every time we use "is," we lie. Even though certain "to be" statements tell facts (i.e., Mr. Thomas is my boss), they still prevaricate in that the sentence directs our attention away from all the other aspects of Mr. Thomas's personality. It makes us believe that Mr. Thomas's "bossness" takes precedence over anything else about him.

According to David Bourland, "Using E-Prime can improve a person's outlook on life. Once you realize that every time you say *is* you tell a lie, you begin to think less about a thing or person's 'identity' and more about its function. I find that E-Prime makes me stay honest."

ESCAPE FROM A FROZEN UNIVERSE: Discovering General Semantics

PAUL DENNITHORNE JOHNSTON

WHY DID THEY confuse me? For years I listened, occasionally with acute distress, as people voiced conflicting views—each claiming to describe social reality and moral necessity. With my discovery of general semantics came an explanation for this frustrating disparity of "knowledge" as propounded by different individuals and a method of interpretation for solving many problems of the social world and the self.

Why does one person tell me one thing *is* fact, or truth or right, and another tell me exactly the opposite? Lacking reliable information, how can one negotiate a complex society without repeatedly making mistakes? General semantics has helped me come to terms with these discouraging riddles.

When at fifteen I first sold a short story, I decided I had to *be* a writer. At that time, our family lived on a schooner in the Bahama Islands. We had moved there from the Massachusetts countryside in my ninth year. I grew up isolated from urban society and did not experience city life until leaving home at seventeen. Subsequently, I often felt confused by the social world and its diversity of cultural values. Although I had difficulty establishing common ground with the reading public, I continued to try to *be* a writer.

Publishers bought my short stories but rejected my first ten novels. I despaired of earning a living writing fiction and thought I *was* a failure. As a reporter or editor, I could earn a living, but, according to my idea, that did not constitute *being* a writer. Therefore I had failed to *be* what I had set out to *be*. With hindsight, I see that general semantics would have eased my burden by helping me view differently the idea of *being*, to see *being* as a kind of epistemological problem, instead of a notion of a fixed state of existence

Reprinted from *Et cetera* 46, no. 2 (Summer 1989).

Copyright © 1989 by Paul Dennithorne Johnston. All rights reserved.

finally achieved, a logical construct having unfortunate real-life repercussions on my self-image and my happiness.

Like many English-speaking people, I had learned an Aristotelian system of reasoning with which I perceived the world in terms of opposites: a thing *was*, or it *was not*; I thought in terms of black–white, beautiful–ugly, good–bad, dead–alive and so on. My parents had given me values mostly from the nineteenth-century romantics: "Truth," "Beauty," "Art," "Culture," "Knowledge," etc. I had read voraciously, and I tended to see the world through the eyes of English literature. At home I had learned absolute good-bad dichotomies, for example: GOOD: literature, originality, individuality, abstinence; BAD: television, mass production, conformity, drunkenness. According to my logical system of polar opposites, which inherently followed Aristotle's law of the excluded middle, either *I am a writer* or *I am not a writer*. My statement "I am a writer" seemed fraudulent to me because I had to earn a living doing other things. My on-off logic allowed no middle way, no *degrees of being a writer*.

I got my first job in Nassau, a city where the "decadence" of night clubs, bars, brothels, and casino gambling shocked my innocent sensibilities, as the materialism and disrespect for "culture" that I saw conflicted with my idealized picture of reality. Meanwhile, I felt some contempt for the "respectable" class because it practiced conformity. Attempts to rebel against my sheltered upbringing, my going to parties, bars and night clubs, often produced conflicting feelings: guilt and a desire to break free of puritanical inhibitions.

A few years later, to develop my writing skills, I worked as a reporter in England. There, in a country where one's native accent apparently decided one's financial and social status, I also perceived confusing messages on how life should *be*, particularly from that war of values between the classes. Attitudes between upper and lower classes seemed quite "racist," all the more bewildering to me because the "races" (social classes) had the same color skin. While employed varnishing rowing sculls at an elite boarding school, I observed an elderly white lower-class male kowtow to an upper-class white schoolboy, a child of under ten: avoiding eye contact, the old man hung his head obsequiously, touched his forelock and muttered "Sir." Observation of this event left me stunned with disbelief.

At thirty-three, after jobs as clerk, bookkeeper, reporter, editor, railway porter, farm worker, carpenter, and so on, I went to college in London. I thought if I could learn the *truth* about reality, my confusion would disappear. Studying sociology, psychology, and philosophy felt like I had found a supermarket of Truths, every Truth the *Real* Truth, and every one different.

I learned about Truth as a relationship, not a thing. At last I had found the truth about Truth! *If objective truth does not exist, we view the world subjectively. We negotiate the truth. The most powerful negotiator wins.*

I learned that language "bewitches" people.(1) One asks, "Is it the truth?" and searches for "the truth" as if it exists. The structural logic of language tricks one into thinking a thing exists when it does not. My conclusion: Knowledge does not equal truth and reality. Disciplines, doctrines, and philosophies might have internal truth, as closed formal systems, yet still remain essentially meaningless. *We experience life autistically, deluded that we communicate.*

In my search for definitions, I had written news stories, plays, humor, essays, articles, poetry, short stories, novels. I had belonged to an institution that gave its own slant to the truth and called it news. Although academics and philosophers had more sophisticated ideas, they also looked through their own spectacles, and said this *is* this and that *is* that, without agreement among themselves.

Words do not speak truth; words create the brand of truth required. Words exhort, persuade, categorize, define. Words lie. So I felt.

I still wanted a universal truth, mediator, designer, etc. I wanted the world to "make sense."

I still felt that words and meaning had great significance; I thought if I could see through cultural bias and discover how *we know what we know*, I would find *the* answer. I enrolled for postgraduate study of the sociology of knowledge at the University of Wales, departed London, and bought a small-holding in Wales, five acres, a house, and barn. However, when the university term began, I chose to remain on the farm and continue writing. My pursuit of Truth had led nowhere. The tautological basis of knowledge meant that nobody knew anything. I might as well stay at home and milk the goats.

A few years later in California, Dr. Ed Kellogg told me about E-Prime, an English variant that eliminates the use of the verb *to be* in all its forms. He showed me his manuscript of an article about E-Prime and we discussed the subject at length.

E-Prime excited me because it offered an escape from the tyranny of the "is of identity," a way of *being* that translated a dynamic universe into a frozen condition which meant no growth, little joy in learning experience, and fear of change. For example, a person who *is* a writer must live up to a preconceived notion of *being* and *continue to exist as such*, or fail. Conventional logic allowed me no escape from the frustration of not being what I should *be*. However, eliminating the verb *to be* increased my freedom to experience both the world and the self as *process*. In addition, one obtained increased freedom from the tendency to force living experience into static conceptual boxes, a paradoxical need rarely satisfied because life-experience consists of endless change.

Later, Dr. Kellogg gave me a copy of *Et cetera* with his E-Prime article in it.(2) I read every article in that *Et cetera*, and mailed my application for International Society for General Semantics membership.

As I read more about general semantics, my enthusiasm grew. Korzybski's model of *abstracting* explained to me that people "know" different realities as they *abstract different pieces of a vast dynamic universe*, and it explained why people of equal intelligence, education, and ability hold such different beliefs.

The problem of conflicting realities had long troubled me. In this article, I use the term *realities,* rather than *value-system*, to suggest that most people possess little awareness of their immersion in a particular system. To them (and to me) there appears no choice of viewpoint, values, or "fact"; *it is the way it is*. My early reality I learned from my family. I valued certain abstractions: nature, "good" taste, self-control, thrift, work, individualism, literature, art, etc., and distrusted others: artificiality, vulgarity, materialism, hedonism, waste, laziness, conformity, crowds, "the system," etc.

In Nassau, in my late teens, I had found new "rules." People took pride in their ability to have a good time. A few years later, when I moved to England, I saw another set of realities, conflicting rules between the classes and within classes. The middle class valued abstractions of refinement, proper behavior, good character, honor, justice, fair play, respectability. The working class seemed to hold in contempt many middle-class ideals, and to value, on the one hand, independence and "being clever" rather than education or infrastructure, and, on the other hand, security through loyalty to their "betters."

I heard working-class people use a vocabulary of absolutes, often spoken with great conviction, a vocabulary of *it is*. By contrast, middle-class speakers often used the relativistic terms "rather," "perhaps," "as it were," etc. Nevertheless, "correct" middle-class attitudes and behavior had the importance of a moral imperative: "It isn't done," "It's not proper," etc.

Not thoroughly schooled in the reality of either class, I sometimes did not know what to think or do. I felt trapped by the absolutisms of my upbringing and by those of my new environment, and I could imagine no escape.

One profound difference between my reality and the British reality lay in the attitude toward individual potential. In an American elementary school I had learned the democratic ideal; I recall my first-grade teacher telling us, "Anyone can grow up to be president." My ancestors left Britain and Ireland to escape the personal and economic oppression of a stratified society. In Canada, my grandfather took his family west to homestead virgin territory. The "pioneering spirit" permeated my own experience of our family's move to isolated islands in the Bahamas. With my North American belief in individuality, I could not accept the English view that a person should never try to "rise above his station."

Thus, the general semantics theory that we abstract *what we think we know* explained to me the source of conflicting realities and removed many doubts about my own ability to perceive the social world. As I studied, I sought to remain aware that my own perceptions come from abstracting. I began using general semantics principles in my daily life, including the "tools for thought": *So far as I know, Up to a point, To me, the What, When, and Where indices.*(3) I saw *knowledge* as an abstraction, no longer a holy grail.

I built a physical model of Korzybski's structural differential to remind me of the many levels of abstracting. Some time passed before I gained a broader understanding of the phrase *the map is not the territory*. At first, I visualized geographical maps, later verbal maps (words), eventually maps of the silent level (mental pictures, abstract notions, stereotypes, vague idealizations, values, fears, hopes, etc.).

My conclusions resulted in some liberation from an oppressive set of rules about reality. Released from the *is of identity*, I no longer had to *be* anything: writer, husband, etc. I could apprehend and experience life as process, not a series of oughts and shoulds. The Aristotelian logic of polar opposites, thinking in terms of *right–wrong*, and seeking the *right* answer, had forced me into one logical dilemma after another. The vocabulary of an ongoing process improved my understanding of behavior and experience. My "failures" had arisen from inadequate tools for thought. Non-Aristotelian logic gave me more effective tools.

Although I have only begun seriously studying general semantics, I think I have learned useful methods for dealing with some practical problems of daily life. For example, I can often avoid signal reactions—those immediate responses and snap judgments in which one reacts like a "bull to a red flag"—and therefore accept events more calmly, with less argument. I get angry far less than in the past, as I try to remain aware that the abstractions of others have a validity of their own. I find it easier to make decisions because I can to a greater degree separate values and assumptions from "facts." I often see that apparently conflicting situations only seem that way because of conflicting abstractions. Reviewing the abstractions in view of the overall experience often resolves the conflict. One may view "mistakes" as feedback, which redefines knowledge. Self-reflexive knowledge changes, grows, evolves.

As I endeavor to put general semantics theory into practice in daily life, I often find myself rudely reminded of the difficulties involved in breaking life-time evaluational habits. I do not see general semantics as a panacea; certain experiences remain beyond its scope.

Nevertheless, I expect my new tools to continue to make my life more interesting and harmonious, with increasing freedom from the frozen universe of fixed states.

NOTES AND REFERENCES

1. E. R. Emmett, *Learning to Philosophize* (London: Longmans, 1964; Pelican Books, 1968; reprinted 1969).
2. E. W. Kellogg III, "Speaking in E-Prime," *Et cetera* 44 (1987):118–28.
3. Kenneth S. Keyes, Jr., *How to Develop Your Thinking Ability* (New York: McGraw Hill, 1950 and 1979). Reprinted as *Taming Your Mind* (Coos Bay, Ore.: Love Line Books, 1975).

FOR FURTHER READING

Absolutisms

Alan Walker Read, "Language Revision by Deletion of Absolutisms," *Et cetera* 42 (1985):7–12.

E-Prime

D. David Bourland, Jr., "A Linguistic Note: Writing in E- Prime," *General Semantics Bulletin* 32-33 (1965/66):111–14.

D. David Bourland, Jr., "The Semantics of a Non-Aristotelian Language," *General Semantics Bulletin* 35 (1968):60–63.

J. Samuel Bois, *Art of Awareness* (Dubuque, Iowa: Wm. C. Brown, 1966), 292–93.

Elaine C. Johnson, "Discovering E-Prime," *Et cetera* 45 (1988):181–83.

DeWitt Scott **WRITING THAT WORKS**

WHILE READING business writing, much of it thin and voiceless, I often think of Elaine Johnson, an English teacher at Tamalpais High School in Mill Valley, just north of San Francisco. When she found a student's writing particularly flat and dull, she reread the first paragraph and noticed that all the verbs came from the verb *to be (be, is, am, are, was, were)*.

She began encouraging her students to use "vivid verbs," to "show" in their writing instead of merely "telling." When one asked why she made such a fuss over verbs, *to be* in particular, Johnson turned to a semanticist for an answer and discovered "E-Prime." It means English without forms of the verb *to be*. E-Prime changed Johnson's life. Now, when students ask why eliminating forms of the verb *to be* improves writing, she gives the semanticist's answer: "It ties your language closer to experience. Using other verbs forces you to take responsibility for your statements: 'I liked the movie' instead of 'the movie was great.'"

Some tips on writing in E-Prime: Take an *is* statement and bring it down to earth: Instead of "Mary is smart" say "Mary scored 160 on an IQ test."

Replace the *is* with an action verb: Instead of "David is a bad driver" say "David darted in and out of traffic."

Say what you mean: Instead of "Is Mary there?" say "May I speak with Mary?"

Change from the passive to the active voice: Instead of "The experiment was conducted" say "Mike conducted the experiment."

An editor with the *San Francisco Examiner,* DeWitt Scott also serves as a writing consultant to business and industry.

Reprinted with permission from *Pacific Bell Business Digest,* August 1989. Also printed in *Et cetera* 46, no. 4 (Winter 1989).

A semanticist, Dr. E. W. Kellogg III of Ashland, Oregon, sometimes translates the words of others into E-Prime. "I can often smooth out arguments in my vicinity simply by interjecting E-Prime translations of key statements into conversation," he says. "For example, if someone says 'That's a stupid idea!' I might reply 'What don't you like about it?' rather than 'It is not!' Principally because of this tactic, I haven't had a real argument in years."

I experiment with E-Prime. It can't cure all the problems in our rich and convoluted language. But removing the supreme irritant, *to be,* forces me to express myself in straightforward statements and come out of the clouds.

The next time somebody asks you to "tell it like it is" or says, "this is what it's all about," you can say, "Let me tell you the way it looks to me, *now.*"

TOWARD UNDERSTANDING E-PRIME

Robert Anton Wilson

E-Prime, abolishing all forms of the verb "to be," has its roots in the field of general semantics, as presented by Alfred Korzybski in his 1933 book, *Science and Sanity*. Korzybski pointed out the pitfalls associated with, and produced by, two usages of "to be": identity and predication. His student D. David Bourland, Jr., observed that even linguistically sensitive people do not seem able to avoid identity and predication uses of "to be" if they continue to use the verb at all. Bourland pioneered in demonstrating that one can indeed write and speak without using any form of "to be," calling this subset of the English language "E-Prime." Many have urged the use of E-Prime in writing scientific and technical papers—Dr. Kellogg exemplifies a prime exponent of this activity. Dr. Albert Ellis has rewritten five of his books in E-Prime, in collaboration with Dr. Robert H. Moore, to improve their clarity and to reap the epistemological benefits of this language revision. Korzybski felt that all humans should receive training in general semantics from grade school on, as "semantic hygiene" against the most prevalent forms of logical error, emotional distortion, and "demonological thinking." E-Prime provides a straightforward training technique for acquiring such semantic hygiene.

To understand E-Prime, consider the human brain as a computer. (Note that I did not say the brain "is" a computer.) As the Prime

---

Robert Anton Wilson has published science fiction, historical novels, poetry, and futuristic sociology, and he has two plays published.

An earlier version of this article appeared in *Trajectories*, no. 5, the newsletter published by Robert Anton Wilson. Reprinted from *Et cetera* 46, no. 4 (Winter 1989).

Law of Computers tells us, GARBAGE IN, GARBAGE OUT (GIGO, for short). The wrong software guarantees wrong answers. Conversely, finding the right software can "miraculously" solve problems that previously appeared intractable.

It seems likely that the principal software used in the human brain consists of words, metaphors, disguised metaphors, and linguistic structures in general. The Sapir-Whorf-Korzybski Hypothesis, in anthropology, holds that a change in language can alter our perception of the cosmos. A revision of language structure, in particular, can alter the brain as dramatically as a psychedelic. In our metaphor, if we change the software, the computer operates in a new way.

Consider the following paired sets of propositions, in which Standard English alternates with English-Prime (E-Prime).

1A. The electron is a wave.
1B. The electron appears as a wave when measured with instrument-1.
2A. The electron is a particle.
2B. The electron appears as a particle when measured with instrument-2.
3A. John is lethargic and unhappy.
3B. John appears lethargic and unhappy in the office.
4A. John is bright and cheerful.
4B. John appears bright and cheerful on holiday at the beach.
5A. This is the knife the first man used to stab the second man.
5B. The first man appeared to stab the second man with what looked like a knife to me.
6A. The car involved in the hit-and-run accident was a blue Ford.
6B. In memory, I think I recall the car involved in the hit-and-run accident as a blue Ford.
7A. This is a fascist idea.
7B. This seems like a fascist idea to me.
8A. Beethoven is better than Mozart.
8B. In my present mixed state of musical education and ignorance, Beethoven seems better to me than Mozart.
9A. That is a sexist movie.
9B. That seems like a sexist movie to me.
10A. The fetus is a person.
10B. In my system of metaphysics, I classify the fetus as a person.

The "A"-type statements (Standard English) all implicitly or explicitly assume the medieval view called "Aristotelian essentialism" or "naive realism." In other words, they assume a world made up of block-like entities with indwelling "essences" or spooks—"ghosts in the machine." The "B"-type statements (E-Prime) recast these sentences into a form isomorphic to modern science by first abolishing the "is" of Aristotelian essence and then reformulating each observation in terms of signals received and interpreted by a body (or instrument) moving in space-time.

Relativity, quantum mechanics, large sections of general physics, perception psychology, sociology, linguistics, modern math, anthropology, ethology, and several other sciences make perfect sense when put into the software of E-Prime. Each of these sciences generates paradoxes, some bordering on "nonsense" or "gibberish," if you try to translate them back into the software of Standard English.

Concretely, "The electron is a wave" employs the Aristotelian "is" and thereby introduces us to the false-to-experience notion that we can know the indwelling "essence" of the electron. "The electron appears as a wave when measured by instrument-1" reports what actually occurred in space-time, namely that the electron when constrained by a certain instrument behaved in a certain way.

Similarly, "The electron is a particle" contains medieval Aristotelian software, but "The electron appears as a particle when measured by instrument-2" contains modern scientific software. Once again, the software determines whether we impose a medieval or modern grid upon our reality-tunnel.

Note that "the electron is a wave" and "the electron is a particle" contradict each other and begin the insidious process by which we move gradually from paradox to nonsense to total gibberish. On the other hand, the modern scientific statements "the electron appears as a wave when measured one way" and "the electron appears as a particle measured another way" do not contradict, but rather complement each other. (Bohr's Principle of Complementarity, which explained this and revolutionized physics, would have appeared obvious to all, and not just to a person of his genius, if physicists had written in E-Prime all along. . . .)

Looking at our next pair, "John is lethargic and unhappy" vs. "John is bright and cheerful," we see again how medieval software creates metaphysical puzzles and totally imaginary contradictions. Operationalizing the statements, as physicists since Bohr have learned to operationalize, we find that the E-Prime translations do not contain any contradiction, and even give us a clue as to causes of John's changing moods. (Look back if you forgot the translations.)

"The first man stabbed the second man with a knife" lacks the overt "is" of identity but contains Aristotelian software nonetheless. The E-Prime translation not only operationalizes the data, but may fit the facts better—if the incident occurred in a psychology class, which often conduct this experiment. (The first man "stabs," or makes stabbing gestures at, the second man, with a banana, but many students, conditioned by Aristotelian software, nonetheless "see" a knife. You don't need to take drugs to hallucinate; improper language can fill your world with phantoms and spooks of many kinds.)

The reader may employ his or her own ingenuity in analyzing how "is-ness" creates false-to-facts reality-tunnels in the remaining examples, and how E-Prime brings us back to the scientific, the operational, the existential, the phenomenological—to what humans and their instruments actually do in space-time as they create observations, perceptions, thoughts, deductions, and General Theories.

I have found repeatedly that when baffled by a problem in science, in "philosophy," or in daily life, I gain immediate insight by writing down what I know about the enigma in strict E-Prime. Often, solutions appear immediately—just as happens when you throw out the "wrong" software and put the "right" software into your PC. In other cases, I at least get an insight into why the problem remains intractable and where and how future science might go about finding an answer. (This has contributed greatly to my ever-escalating agnosticism about the political, ideological, and religious issues that still generate the most passion on this primitive planet.)

When a proposition resists all efforts to recast it in a form consistent with what we now call E-Prime, many consider it "meaningless." Korzybski, Wittgenstein, the Logical Positivists, and (in his own way) Niels Bohr promoted this view. I happen to agree with that verdict (which condemns 99 percent of theology and 99.999999 percent of metaphysics to the category of Noise rather than Meaning)—but we must save that subject for another article. For now, it suffices to note that those who fervently believe such Aristotelian propositions as "A piece of bread, blessed by a priest, is a person (who died two thousand years ago)," "The flag is a living being," or "The fetus is a human being" do not, in general, appear to make sense by normal twentieth-century scientific standards.

COPING WITH SEMANTIC PROBLEMS IN SYSTEM DEVELOPMENT

KAREN L. RUSKIN

IN HIS PAPER "General Semantics as a General System Which Explicitly Includes the System-Maker," Robert Pula stated: "Unconsciousness of the multiordinality of terms readily leads to confusion and therefore conflict in daily life. More important for us, lack of awareness of this mechanism can lead to confusion in system building."

I wish to describe to you several instances in which unconsciousness of multiordinality, plus several other key formulations of general semantics, hampered the development of a large computer-based information storage and retrieval system that I participated in recently. I ask you to restrain such curiosity as you may possess relative to precisely *which* computer company performed work on this project, and precisely *which* system this work concerned. Let it suffice to say that the effort involved over one hundred programmers and systems analysts, and that (if this means anything to you) we automated an AUTODIN switch.

More specifically, I wish to describe to you how I found it helpful in coping with system development problems to employ the orientations of consciousness of abstracting, Alfred Korzybski's extensional devices, multi-valued aspects of terms, multiordinal aspects of terms, and the semantic tool of E-Prime.

Karen L. Ruskin, who has worked in operations research and computer studies, holds an A.B. from the University of California, Riverside, a Licenciatura in English linguistics from the Universidad de Costa Rica, and an M.D. from Ross University, New York. She currently studies medicine in New York City.

Reprinted from *Coping with Increasing Complexity,* edited by Donald E. Washburn and Dennis R. Smith; copyright © 1974 by Gordon and Breach Science Publishers Inc.

27

Whereas most of the contributions to this conference have dealt with the basic issues of general systems theory and general semantics on comparatively high orders of abstraction, this effort more modestly provides some extensional examples of the formulations of general semantics operating in an environment more frequently considered the province of general systems theory.

E-Prime: A Semantic Tool

I have written this paper in the language of E-Prime, a subset of the English language and differing from ordinary English only in that it contains no form of the verb "to be." Invented by D. D. Bourland, Jr.,(1) and described by him here in another paper, E-Prime has a plethora of general semantics formulations inherent in it.(2) Its use requires more acute awareness by the user of his own speech patterns, written or vocal, increases his awareness of the speech patterns of others, and seems to facilitate consciousness of abstracting. It tends to force one initially to describe situations on comparatively low orders of abstraction (by specifying role players) before sweeping on to summarizing higher orders of abstraction.

Why Not Use E-Prime?

In the process of developing technical documents, I have found that I frequently need to include lists of items labeled "Tables," and sketches and diagrams of items labeled "Figures." Since I write in E-Prime, when I refer to a table or a figure in the text material, I ordinarily write: "Table I contains a description of . . . ," or "Figure 1 shows. . . ."

Readers of text written in this way have stated: "I think you should express it as 'A description of . . . is contained in Table I,' and ' . . . is shown in Figure 1'." To such comments I can only respond: "Why *not* do it my way?" So far, no one has come up with a valid reply.

Journalists have long endorsed writing in the active voice "because it makes better copy." Another journalistic rule pertaining to news stories requires the writer to state "who, what, why, when, where, and how" in the leading paragraph of the article. Some personal journalistic experience and a recent visit to the School of Journalism at the University of Missouri at Columbia lead me to note that, however pragmatically useful, these journalistic techniques have no underlying methodology; as "gimmicks" these methods simply "work." The journalists at the University of Missouri seemed fascinated to discover a methodology, E-Prime, backing up the newspaper tradition of writing in the active voice "because it makes 'better' copy."

E-Prime and a Real-Time System

Not only in newspaper stories does E-Prime make better copy. Obfuscation becomes very difficult when one uses E-Prime in varied writing contexts. In this paper I have chosen to describe some of the benefits that ensued from persistently using E-Prime in the development of a large, complex, real-time computer system.

Visualize a scenario of the operational environment of a project staffed by computer professionals: people seated at desks, file cabinets and bookcases placed near the lucky, an occasional semi-wall partition, with a computer room down the hall. I have a centrally located desk, a file cabinet, and a typewriter (the only member of the professional staff to have one). On a typical day another project member brings a sheaf of papers to my desk, saying: "This is the system initialization description." I quickly scan the front page, finding only the title "System Initialization." In a tactful way I ask something to the effect of: "Have you just written this, or do you know who wrote it?" "I just wrote it," responds the donor. "Thank you for bringing this to me," say I, "and I may call on you later with questions." I immediately write on the cover page, "Received from [name of donor] on [that day's date]."

Subsequently I review the material, etc., but most importantly for purposes of this paper, I have indexed and dated the system initialization papers on an impetus that I ascribe to the awareness of abstraction enforced by vigilant use of E-Prime. If a junior programmer has prepared the system initialization description, I would have to view it as potentially imperfect. If the programming manager has brought the description I would consider it (potentially even more imperfect, but probably) much more authoritative. At this point I know several of the journalist's requisites for a news story's lead paragraph: *who*—programming manager; *what*—system initialization description; *why*—integral part of the basic makeup of the system, hence important to document; *when*—that day's date, as written on the cover page; *where*—in the project environment; *how*—not yet determined. Later I will have to ask the programming manager on what sources he had based his write-up. Had he designed these procedures himself? Had he made a few modifications to a standard procedures package? To assure optimal legitimacy of the system initialization information, I would need to learn at least these things.

This example provides just one context in which I found E-Prime an invaluable eliciter of questions, resulting in obtaining answers to at least some of the questions, and knowing important questions that remained unanswered.

Credentials of the Map Maker

E-Prime often forces one to express oneself in the first person, or at least to ascribe a source or basis for an assertion. One might call this "naming the map maker." I see in this process an addition to Korzybski's classic three-stage "map-territory" analogy, which in E-Prime becomes:
1. A "map" belongs to a "level of abstraction" different from that of the "territory" it represents.
2. A "map" does not contain all the structural characteristics of the "territory" it represents.
3. A "map$_1$" may self-reflexively contain a "map$_2$" of higher order that shows the relation between the "territory$_1$" of "map$_1$" represented in some detail to the surrounding "territory$_2$" of "map$_2$."
4. One needs to know as much as possible about the "map maker" (and when he made the "map") in order to evaluate properly the credibility of the "map."

It *matters* to know who made the map for any given territory, as the map maker includes in his map the product of his particular background. Hence, if a marketeer gives me information (a map) supposedly describing some equipment or systems capability (the territory described by the map), I would probably check at least another source to verify the correctness of the marketeer's map. Reasons for this become quickly apparent: The marketeer has selling as his principal goal; he does not necessarily care if he makes his sale by representing his product accurately, since his measure of effectiveness of success lies in making the sale, however he can. Responsible system developers have different measures of effectiveness, as their superiors or clients will probably judge them on the basis of timely, meticulous, professional work performed. A system developer's map and a marketeer's map of a given territory could, and probably would, differ significantly. I cite the case of marketeers, associated with the company responsible for the project discussed in this paper, assuring the customer that adding an optical character reader (OCR) to the computer system in the future would require no additional computer programming efforts. In fact, adding an OCR in the future would entail enormous, expensive new programming efforts.

Describing Computer Programs and Their Interaction

It pleases me to report that use of E-Prime in writing descriptions of computer programs and systems imposes clarity and specificity. In our multi-programming, interrupt-oriented processing environment, computer programs continuously gained and relinquished control of the core memory units in the central processor on a priority basis.

In this environment, if someone writes as a final description: "When Condition X occurs, Program A is called," we find ourselves missing a piece of crucial information; namely, we have to know *which* program out of the fifty possible "called" Program A. E-Prime makes such a quandary impossible. A writer must state instead something like the following: "When Condition X occurs, Program K calls Program A to assume control of the processing."

Using the structure described above (" . . . , Program A is called") makes it possible to omit extremely important information while using seemingly perfectly acceptable English. Any use of the "Is-of-Predication" (and its insidious counterpart, the "Is-of-Identity,"e.g., "This is the system initialization description") carries with it significant danger of expressing incomplete, misleading, or even unauthoritatively wrong information. However, this example shows how even the comparatively benign auxiliary use of "to be" can lead to unnecessary linguistic woes. Because of the structure of the English language, we have grown accustomed to the use of such linguistic forms, and undoubtedly most people accept them unquestioningly. Whether a person chooses to speak and/or write in E-Prime depends upon an individual intellectual decision. Despite how one chooses in that regard, knowledge of the availability of the linguistic tool of E-Prime makes possible a useful, more critical scrutiny of the meanings or lack thereof of oral and written English. Further, E-Prime "builds in" the consciousness of abstracting so strongly emphasized in Korzybskian general semantics.

Lexicographic Breakdown in Computer Terminology

The increasing rate of development of computer technology has provided our language with increasingly many new additions for our dictionaries. However, because of the paucity of lexicographers in the computer field, we have few of these new computer-oriented terms standardized and documented, with no consensus on the meanings for many terms. Instead, we have a sizable number of multi-valued terms that may mean many different things depending upon their users. Various computer installations carry with them characteristically unique terminologies. It appears that these terminologies differ radically from installation to installation. I found that it becomes extremely important to recognize this fact to "understand" what one reads and what one hears people say.

Examples of multi-valued, computer-oriented terms include the following: program, routine, subroutine, calling sequence, programming, module, [computer] word, block of [computer] words, file, table, software, etc. I will describe some meanings with which I have familiarity for one of the more commonly used multi-valued terms, the term "software." When I first encountered the word "software" in a major way in 1966, I worked for a company that dealt with "software" exclusively. The company brochures and promotional materials described it as a "software firm." In this early context, we used the term "software" to mean that we performed studies of various kinds, and that our *sole* product consisted of reports on the findings of the studies. We used the word "software" in the trade language, so to speak, to contrast it with the word "hardware." "Hardware" companies build airplanes or sell or manufacture nuts and bolts. You might have called a software company a "think tank."

Today, the word "software" has assumed varied, complex, and specific implications, depending upon its context. Table I contains a list of some of the different meanings that I have encountered for the term "software."

TABLE I

DEFINITIONS OF "SOFTWARE"

Software$_1$	=	non-hardware
Software$_2$	=	computer programs (only)
Software$_3$	=	computer operating system and "utility" computer programs; also known as "systems programming"
Software$_4$	=	computer programs and documentation for them, excluding any systems analysis

In the context of the project described in this paper, I "coped" with wide use of multi-valued terms by not using those terms. Given more time, it might have become practical to make a dictionary and attempt to achieve consensus among project members on meanings of some of these multi-valued terms. However, because of time constraints, I could not attempt such an undertaking.

Unconsciousness of Abstracting

As described above, developing computer-oriented terminology has resulted in multi-valued terms. In my computer system development project, the lack of documentation for words' multiple meanings created problems, and the lack of recognition of the existence of this multi-valued condition created even further problems for members of the project team. One might describe this as multiordinal misunderstanding.

The contractually required project specifications included several documents, among them the client's request for proposal document and the "winning" company's proposal. Correlating the information in these papers with real-world implementation became confusing due to a lack of differentiation between levels of abstraction.

Certain project members confused information in the project specifications with the quite different actual tasks that the programmers had already completed in developing working, end-product computer programs. The project members afflicted with unconsciousness-of-abstracting assumed that because the project specifications called for supplying Function A in a certain way, the responsible programmers had completed Function A in that specific way. This invalid assumption led to incorrect system descriptions; the persons unconscious of abstracting wrongly assumed that the words written on the paper of the project specifications represented real-world accomplishments of actual computer programs.

Applicability of Korzybski's Extensional Devices

I found Alfred Korzybski's extensional devices particularly useful as semantic tools, lending great support in ordering the large mass of written information that ensued from the project discussed in this paper.(3) Four of the extensional devices had significantly greater applicability in this instance than the remaining one: use of the term "etc." as a reminder that one cannot hope to know or say "all" about a given topic. The relevant four devices—indexing, dating, using quotation marks, and hyphenating—proved remarkably effective in ordering and expressing information in the clearest way possible, given constraints of time pressures and the great bulk of work requiring attention.

Indexing

In the strict Korzybskian sense, in order to use the extensional device called "indexing," one should apply consecutive numeric subscripts to the same term to express differentiation of each item in the string from its predecessor and its successor. In the context of my project, I could have made a chart identifying Programmer$_1$ as T. Watson, Programmer$_2$ as G. Dantzig, Programmer$_3$ as W. Zangwill, etc., which might have proven somehow useful—but I did not. Instead I wrote the name of a given programmer wherever necessary for identifying responsibilities or authorship for work complete, work in progress, work not yet begun, and so on. This relatively crude form of indexing contributed significantly to development of effective management tools for this project, used virtually invariably with an accompanying date as described below.

Dating

Coping with the complexities of the large, technically difficult project in which I participated and which I describe in this paper included use of the extensional device "dating." In practical application this involved putting the date of *that* day on every paper that I wrote or received. It became my practice to put my initials and the day's date, among other identifiers (such as "working paper"), on each page that I wrote, eventually amounting to somewhat more than three hundred pages of technically specific material, written mainly in E-Prime. I insisted on dating each page because in a developing project such as ours, document cannibalization occurred frequently; in this way it became relatively simple to discover if the material at hand remained current, or if some new version had superseded it.

My system of applying dates (and source of authorship) to *all* papers that I could affect made my project sector a deliberately enforced "process world," and we could differentiate the clearly labeled outdated versions of papers from the clearly labeled current ones. Without my insistence on the use of dates and labels (essentially "indexes" as described above), I feel almost certain that the entire project would have drowned in an ocean of anonymous working papers.

Using Quotation Marks

I found quotation marks helpful in clarifying the relationship of a part of a sentence to its context, but in this milieu—focusing on writing computer programming specifications—use of quotes seemed needed relatively infrequently.

Hyphenating

Hyphenation often helped clarify otherwise potentially muddled sentences. I include the following example as one of the more complex instances of hyphenation applied usefully:

> The send-interrupt, read-to-disk, check-for-end-of-message-indicator, thread-new-disk-sector-address, display-DD173-continuation-form, issue-FREAD, exit-to-dispatcher cycle continues until the routine "CRT" senses the end-of-message indicator.

Because of the preliminary nature of the particular document that included the above sentence, we had not yet assigned paragraph numbers; deprived of that standard method of referencing, we found that with the use of hyphens we could summarize a long, complex process relatively briefly.

Conclusion

I should like to mention that in my opinion the preceding comments provide explicit evidence in support of the contention that general semantics has immediate relevance for the development of complex computer systems. We really do not need to concern ourselves with whether we should regard general semantics as a special case of general system theory or conversely.

Indeed, in a manner conceptually similar to Gödel's famous proof that one cannot prove every theorem implicit in a set of postulates, Professor Dodd has shown that—provided we take a sufficiently broad approach—we must of necessity operate within a closed system.(4) Accordingly, we need not devote further energy to the matter of who has the most open system.

Perhaps we can use the time conserved as just described in developing more effective general systems and more effective general semantics.

NOTES AND REFERENCES

1. D. D. Bourland, Jr., "A Linguistic Note: Writing in E-Prime," *General Semantics Bulletin*, 1965/1966, nos. 32 and 33.
2. D. D. Bourland, Jr., "The Semantics of a Non-Aristotelian Language," *General Semantics Bulletin*, 1968, no. 35.
3. A. Korzybski, introduction to the 2d ed., *Science and Sanity: An Introduction to Non-Aristotelian Systems and General Semantics* (Lancaster, Pa.: International Non-Aristotelian Library Publishing Co., 1941).
4. Stuart C. Dodd, "On Producing the Epicosm Model Reiterantly—To Mirror the Cosmos to Men," in *Coping with Increasing Complexity*, ed. by Donald E. Washburn and Dennis R. Smith (New York: Gordon & Breach Science Publishers, 1974).

WORKING WITH E-PRIME: SOME PRACTICAL NOTES

E. W. KELLOGG III AND
D. DAVID BOURLAND, JR.

> To achieve adjustment and sanity and the conditions that follow from them, we must study the structural characteristics of this world first and, then only, build languages of similar structure, instead of habitually ascribing to the world the primitive structure of our language.
>
> Alfred Korzybski, *Science and Sanity*

LISTEN to almost any news program, and you'll hear reports of political, social, and environmental crises. These problems do not originate "outside" of us, but from the beginning have stemmed from the short-sightedness of human beings going about their daily tasks using a two-valued, true-or-false, Aristotelian orientation: an orientation that has proven itself woefully inadequate to solving the complex problems of the twentieth century. Threats of nuclear war, overpopulation, and ecological disaster hang over our heads, and if we wish to survive, the solutions to these problems must also originate from us.

The science of ecology teaches us that we need to see through non-Aristotelian eyes, and deal with the world as an interdependent whole of interconnecting parts. And yet the English language itself betrays us in this task, as its very structure trains us to use the old simplistic viewpoint we need so desperately to outgrow. Unless we learn to think and communicate differently and more effectively about our problems, we may soon find ourselves released from the necessity of having to think at all. The authors see E-Prime (English without the verb "to be") as a practical starting point in the development of such a non-Aristotelian language. We hope that our readers will find the information presented here useful should

---

Dr. E. W. Kellogg III presently serves on the executive committee of the International Society for General Semantics, and has published research in such fields as the biochemistry of aging and the phenomenology of lucid dreaming.

Reprinted from *Et cetera* 47, no. 4 (Winter 1990-91). Copyright © 1990 by E. W. Kellogg III and D. David Bourland, Jr. All rights reserved.

they choose to make E-Prime an integral part of their own lives.

Since the publication of Bourland's article, *A Linguistic Note: Writing in E-Prime*, in 1965,(1) numerous articles, books, even dissertations (see references 2–17) have appeared testifying to the effectiveness of E-Prime as a discipline that encourages, even forces, the user to write, speak, and think more clearly and accurately. On the surface, the term E-Prime refers to an English language derivative that eliminates use of the verb "to be" in any form (such as "am," "is," "was," "are," "were," "be," and "been"). E-Prime allows users to minimize many "false to facts" linguistic patterns inherent in ordinary English, and to move beyond a two-valued Aristotelian orientation that views the world through overly simplistic terms such as "true-*or*-false," "black-*or*-white," "all-*or*-none," "right-*or*-wrong."

E-Prime automatically eliminates the "is-dependent" overdefining of situations in which we confuse one aspect, or point of view, of an experience with a much more complex totality (see references 7 and 12 for more details). This overdefining occurs chiefly in sentences using the "is of identity" (e.g., "John is a scientist") and the "is of predication" (e.g., "The leaf is green"), two of the main stumbling blocks impeding a non-Aristotelian approach. E-Prime can also enhance creativity in problem solving, by transforming premature judgment statements such as "There *is* no solution to this problem" into more strictly accurate versions such as "I don't see how to solve this problem (yet)."

Although many people have found the idea of E-Prime intriguing, not many have attempted to put it into practice. Of those who have, some have mastered writing in E-Prime, and a few speaking or thinking in it. Whatever the virtues of E-Prime as a linguistic discipline, experience has shown that students can benefit markedly from the practical advice of their predecessors. In this article, the authors will answer the major questions about the theory and practice of E-Prime that they have heard over the years, and offer useful guidelines that will smooth the path for those determined to make the discipline of E-Prime their own.

You call E-Prime a "linguistic discipline." A linguistic discipline for what?

Within practical limits, users of E-Prime try to say exactly what they mean. When I (E.K.) say "almost always" I mean that and not "always." In my writing I almost always delete or modify such absolutisms, and in speaking I try to do so, but sometimes don't succeed. I try to qualify what I say to make it more accurate, avoiding the absolutistic point-of-view by using qualifiers such as "in my experience," "as I see it," "to me," etc.

As a discipline, E-Prime, like general semantics,(18) works to achieve a useful congruency between the verbal maps we make *of* experience, and the actual territory of experience itself. Although in the simplest sense E-Prime need only involve giving up any use of the verb "to be," in a practical sense it may also include other non-Aristotelian linguistic devices such as dating and indexing,(18) the avoidance of absolutisms,(19) etc. Thus, E-Prime$_k$ denotes an E-Prime that also makes use of the general semantics formulations Korzybski suggested.(18) My (E.K.) own preferred form of E-Prime (E-Prime$_p$), *aims* at a phenomenologically ideal language(20) that represents and communicates the territory of my experience both to myself and others as clearly and accurately as possible.

How does E-Prime work?

Although one could describe E-Prime simply as English without the verb "to be," such a definition misses the profound transformation in personal orientation resulting from such a change. *In essence, E-Prime consists of a more descriptive and extensionally oriented derivative of English, one that automatically tends to bring the user back to the level of first-person experience.* In his book, *Language, Thought and Reality,* Benjamin Lee Whorf gives numerous examples of languages and cultures that support his "principle of linguistic relativity" which states that the structure of the language we use influences the way we perceive "reality," as well as how we behave with respect to that perceived reality.(21)

For example, if you saw a man, reeking of whiskey, stagger down the street and then collapse, you might think (in ordinary English) "He is drunk." In E-Prime you would think instead "He acts drunk," or "He looks drunk." After all, you might have encountered an actor (practicing the part of a drunken man), or a man who had spilled alcohol on himself undergoing a seizure of some kind, etc. Instead of simply walking by, you might look more carefully and send for an ambulance.

Although E-Prime usually reduces hidden assumptions, it does not necessarily exclude them. For example, you may have seen a woman, or a robot, or an extraterrestrial, etc., that looked like a man and acted drunk. E-Prime fosters a worldview in which the user perceives situations as changeable rather than static, and in which verbal formulations derived from experience indicate possibilities rather than certainties.

Thus, removing the verb "to be" from English results in a language of a more phenomenological character,(20) in that this change can automatically reduce the number of assumptions in even simple sentences. Statements made in E-Prime almost always mirror first-person experience more adequately than the "is" statements they replace. E-Prime also greatly encourages one to use the active voice ("I did it," "Smith did it") rather than the often misleading, information poor, and even psychologically crippling passive voice ("It was done").(4)

If you can just translate a statement bristling with forms of "to be" from ordinary English to E-Prime, so what? Why bother?

In the first place, you can't. You simply cannot take a body of work written in ordinary "is" English, and by recasting it into E-Prime say "exactly the same thing."(16) Almost by necessity the writing will shift away from an Aristotelian towards a more non-Aristotelian language structure.(5) One cannot *rewrite* documents such as the Holy Bible, the United States Constitution, Shakespeare's plays, etc. in E-Prime; one can only *translate* them into E-Prime. Although I (D.B.) once translated the opening part of the Declaration of Independence as an illustration of the difference that E-Prime can make—(I prefer my version naturally)—we certainly have not called for a complete rewrite of everything into E-Prime. In the first place one can't rewrite these and other precious documents without changing their "meaning" as mentioned earlier. And in the second place, neither of us has the time even to begin such an endeavor, however much we might like to view the result!

Some languages do not have a verb exactly like "to be." Does this mean that native speakers of these languages think and communicate more clearly than do speakers of ordinary English?

The absence of the verb "to be" in a language does not necessarily confer any advantages to it. Rather than focusing on the absence of a verb that functions syntactically exactly like the English "to be," we need to address ourselves to the mechanisms of identity and predication used in a particular language. For example, Russian and Hebrew usually employ (in the present tense) simple juxtaposition for identity and predication structures. In a literal translation into English we would find, for example, "I farmer." Remedial procedures analogous to E-Prime for other languages will of necessity depend on the syntactic structure of the particular language involved. General semantics, and the discipline of E-Prime, address the semantic problems peculiar to *English*. In *Science and Sanity*, Korzybski (18) targeted three main semantic factors of the English language that he felt needed revision in order to make general adjustment and sanity possible: (1) the subject-predicate form, (2) the "is" of identity, and (3) the elementalism of the Aristotelian system (see note 1). E-Prime eliminates two of these factors *in one stroke*.

I want to use the "is of identity" in identifying and classifying. Surely the scientific method depends on determining what "IS" and "IS NOT" true. What harm can possibly result from using "to be" in this context?

Classification does not depend on "this is this and that is that," but on *scientists* labeling "this" (phenomenon) by "that" (label). Actually, one might claim that scientific progress depends on the unmasking of assumptions masquerading as scientific facts or as "universal" laws. E-Prime can work synergistically with the scientific method in exposing artifacts. For example a scientist would not say "This *is* true," but instead "The available evidence supports hypothesis X." Science doesn't depend on "common sense" but on the scientific method, which deals in probabilities and not certainties.

When scientists (or anyone else) forget that a label *is not* the thing *indicated* by the label, they can get into serious trouble. When I (E.K.) test an enzyme's activity in a spectrophotometer, I *assume* that all of my reagents have proper labels, I *assume* that the balance on which I weigh these reagents gives reasonably accurate readings, I *assume* I know the chemical reactions involved through my training and by inference, and I *assume* that the spectrophotometer works properly. However, I actually only *see* a pen making a line on a paper chart. I know from hard experience that any one of the assumptions I made could have, and on occasion indeed have, proved false and resulted in false readings. E-Prime can make one much more aware of such covert assumptions, and in making these assumptions overt can give the user the opportunity to correct for them.

Actually, users of the scientific method *cannot* prove that a hypothesis "*is* true," only that it "*is not* true." "Hypothesis" by definition means a "tentatively assumed proposition," which makes phrases like "This hypothesis is true" oxymoronic. One would need to look at *all* the crows in the universe to prove the proposition "All crows *are* black," but one needs only one white crow to prove it false. Many working scientists don't clearly understand this intrinsic limitation of the scientific method—that except in the case of the trivial (e.g., the validation of a specific fact—"This particular crow has black feathers") it can disprove a hypothesis, and cannot prove it. Instead, the method does allow scientists to judge a hypothesis as more or less probably valid, given the evidence available to them at a particular time and place.

Why eliminate ALL uses of the verb "to be"?

In principle, if not in practice, we agree that in some instances one could use forms of "to be" (in its auxillary, existence, and location modes) without causing appreciable "semantic damage." Even so, most English teachers would agree that most of us overuse and misuse the verb, and that even a 75% reduction in its use would improve our writing and speaking skills. But why go to the extreme of trying to eliminate it totally? Because for better or worse, it looks as if only an all-or-nothing approach to this problem works successfully. De Morgan, Santayana, Korzybski, and many general semanticists warned against misuses of the verb such as the "is" of identity, yet they continued to misuse it themselves!

We see the misuse and overuse of the verb "to be" by English speakers as a kind of linguistic addiction. It allows us to play God using the omniscient "Deity mode" of speech, as when we say, "That *is* the truth." It allows even the most ignorant to transform their opinions magically into god-like pronouncements on the nature of things. Its overuse allows one to communicate sloppily without unduly taxing the brain by trying to come up with more appropriate verbs.

Let's compare this linguistic "addiction" to one more mundane—cigarette smoking. Although reducing smoking from two packs to two cigarettes a day might reduce lung cancer to a level not significantly different from not smoking at all, no medical authority that we know of recommends this. And why? *Because it rarely, if ever, works.* Very few people can go from overuse to moderation in use—the temptation for old habits to reassert themselves proves just too strong. Although a less extreme form of E-Prime that allows for an occasional use of "is" would probably accomplish the same goals, we have yet to see anyone manage this. For those simply interested in writing only, a less drastic form of E-Prime (such as E-Prime mod) (15) might suffice. With word processing capabilities, one could easily edit and revise writing in accordance with non-Aristotelian and phenomenological principles, checking each individual usage of "to be" for possible misuses. Given the word processing technology available today (1990), self-proclaimed general semanticists no longer have any excuse for not ridding their prose of instances of the "is of identity" and the "is of predication." However, we ourselves have found it unnecessary to use the verb "to be" even in its more benign aspects—indeed, we have found that eliminating these usages has improved our writing style.

Perhaps most importantly, I (E.K.) very much doubt whether I could have learned to comprehensively eliminate misuses of "to be" in my speaking, and finally in my thinking, without the simple, and easily understood discipline that pure E-Prime requires. The simplicity of the basic rule allows me to make changes in real time, *while* speaking or thinking.

What about critics of E-Prime who, while admitting that E-Prime sounds like an interesting idea, claim that it can never work, and that eliminating all uses of "to be" from English damages the language in fundamental ways?

Criticisms of E-Prime often depend on theoretical arguments that have little validity in actual practice. In our experience E-Prime not only does not damage English, but, as we have already pointed out, it actually improves it in a number of interesting and significant ways. Still, does E-Prime have any disadvantages? Unfortunately, yes, and the prospective user will have to decide on their relative importance. First, you lose the helping verb function of "to be" indicating a continuous process. For example the statement "It is raining outside" translates to "It continues to rain outside," which indicates the progressive mode in another way. One also loses the use of "to be" implying a future condition, as in "She is coming." In E-Prime one could say, "She comes" (dramatic!), or "She will come later," or more specifically, "Anita said that she left the office fifteen minutes ago and should arrive any minute now."

In the context of poetry, the E-Prime user may lose some of the power of metaphor ("He is a tiger"), although one can compensate for this loss by using similes ("He acts like a tiger"). On the other hand, poets who use E-Prime will find themselves forced to vary their verb choices, a process that can add to the evocative power of a poem. E-Prime also forces a substantial reduction in the use of the passive voice ("It was done"), but except in special instances, such a reduction would usually prove beneficial rather than detrimental.

Of course, learning to write and speak in E-Prime involves the disadvantage that one has to devote a certain amount of time and effort to the task, especially in the early stages. Writing acceptably in E-Prime initially involves additional drafts, and even final versions may sound awkward until this new writing skill has developed. Overall, most criticisms of E-Prime in regard to its potential applications as a spoken or written language seem woefully premature, as it has not yet had time to grow and develop.

I have heard that if we learn to write, speak, etc. in E-Prime that we will AUTOMATICALLY reduce the level of dishonesty, bigotry, etc., in our lives. How does this come about?

First of all, it doesn't. Neither of us has ever made such claims for E-Prime, although I (D.B.) once had *Time* magazine attribute such views to me.(23) One can lie or express bigotry in E-Prime just as one can in ordinary English. For example you can say "I didn't take the money!" when you did, or "Members of the XYZ race smell like pigs," when they do not. While the *discipline* of E-Prime aims at reducing dishonesty and prejudice (prejudging) in our communications, the *technique* of E-Prime does in no way guarantee such a result. We have found that while E-Prime can facilitate honest communication, that as in any other language, the intention of the individual involved plays the predominant controlling role.

E-Prime does not cure or resolve all linguistic and behavioral problems. Sometimes, general semanticists feel called upon to point out this unfortunate situation to us, often as if to say something to the effect of, "Well, if E-Prime doesn't solve *all* of my problems, I really don't see any reason to bother with it!"

However, consider what this easily teachable technique *does* accomplish: (1) E-Prime can make communication clearer and more understandable by lowering the level of abstraction and bringing it closer to the level of first-person experience; (2) it resolves two of the main semantic problems that Korzybski educed in English; (3) it can improve self-esteem by providing immediate prophylaxis for those who tend "to live their lives in the passive voice"; and (4) it invites attention to the verbal excesses of those who enjoy speaking in the "Deity mode."

When I try to write in E-Prime my writing sounds awkward. I write much more easily in "is" English. I realize that eventually I will learn to use E-Prime more effectively, but how can I make it through this transitional period without losing my job?

We can tell you from personal experience that most of this awkwardness derives from the problems inherent in using any new language. The more you use E-Prime, the more your skills will improve. By simply following the rule (no forms of "to be") anyone can write in E-Prime, but it usually takes a great deal of practice and *creative* effort before a person can learn to write in it well. Over the years many people (who knew nothing of our idiosyncrasy) have complimented us on both our speaking and writing skills—but it took years of practice before this happened. As far as using E-Prime in work-related writing, it will probably seem better for the novice user to simply try at first to minimize instances of "to be" as much as feels "stylistically comfortable," with the aim of eventually writing professionally in 100% E-Prime as skill improves. Of course, we still recommend writing in 100% E-Prime in less critical areas (personal letters, diaries, notes, etc.) during this transition period.

Our skill in using E-Prime increases continuously, and we can honestly say that our stylistic limitations derive not from E-Prime as a language, but from limitations inherent in our present abilities. We do not speak in E-Prime as well as we write in it, and our skills in *speaking* E-Prime will probably remain several years behind our skills in *writing* in E-Prime, into the foreseeable future. Although we understand the difficulties facing a novice user, "this too shall pass," with time and practice.

When I try to write in E-Prime I tend to sound either "wishy-washy" or "spaced out"—most of my sentences include "seems" or "appears" instead of "is," and even my factual descriptions sound indefinite. How can I change this?

Novice writers in E-Prime often still write using "to be" sentence structures,(14) and often try simply to replace deleted "is's" with "seems" and "appears." Such sentence structures often use the passive voice, as in "It was done." At first one might translate this as

"It appears done," but by moving from the passive to the active voice one can proceed to a much less "wishy-washy," and more informative version, as in "Dan did it." Similarly, one need not translate "The rice is cooked" into "The rice seems cooked," but instead can redescribe the actual "event" more informatively, as in "Russell cooked the rice."

Forms of the verb "to have" can make useful alternatives for their "to be" counterparts during the early stages of learning to use E-Prime. Quite often they can substitute with minimal or no changes in many "to-be"-style sentence structures. For example, "The rice is cooked" translates as "The rice has cooked," "There is a store" changes into "They have a store," and so on. Because of its utility, however, beginners tend to overdo it, and lapse into a form of pidgin E-Prime. Unfortunately, overuse of the verb "to have" brings its own set of problems,(24) leading the user to map/see the world in terms of objects and possessions instead of dynamic processes ("I *have* a relationship to . . . " instead of "I relate to . . . "). As a verb, "to have" encourages the user to change action verbs into quasi-object nouns ("I *have* love" instead of "I love"), so we recommend that students of E-Prime minimize their use of "to have" as soon as possible, and release and make use of the trapped verbs instead.

In other instances, it helps to bring the "is" sentence back to the level of first-person experience, and to use verbs that directly tie into that experience. Thus, instead of saying "The music is good," or the weak E-Prime alternative "The music seems good" one might instead say, "The music sounds good." Other examples include "She looks beautiful" instead of "She seems beautiful," and "This food tastes good" instead of "This food seems good." Please don't misunderstand: "seems" and "appears" have their uses, especially in contexts where one wants to emphasize doubt. However, with practice you can learn to write in E-Prime without using them at all should you so choose, once you have learned more elegant alternatives to the "is style" sentence structures that require them as substitutes.

I feel that I use E-Prime fairly well for factual writing and reporting, but it just doesn't work when I want to express myself creatively or poetically. Does the inherent nature of E-Prime as a language make it unsuitable for artistic expression?

As a glance through any good poetry anthology will show you,(22) many major poets throughout English history, who could not possibly have heard of E-Prime, make very sparing use of "to be" in their work. In fact, with very little effort we have found complete poems written in perfect "E-Prime" by Shakespeare, Pope, Blake, Shelley, Keats, Emerson, Longfellow, Tennyson, Yeats, and Joyce. If anything, rather than hindering artistic expression, E-Prime might actually enhance it.

Imagine a third-year student in French who tries to write poetry like Baudelaire, fails, and then blames the French language rather than his or her current lack of skill for the failure. If you try to use E-Prime for tasks beyond your current level of skill, then fail, it makes little sense to blame E-Prime for the failure. Criticisms of E-Prime in regard to its potential for use in creative endeavors seem premature, as it has not yet had time to grow and develop. At present, to our knowledge no one (let alone an artistic genius) has ever tried to write a novel, or epic poem, in 100% E-Prime.

Who can say what novelists like William Faulkner or Ernest Hemingway might have written had they learned E-Prime as their native tongue instead of ordinary English? Again, can one judge the potential of French as a language by looking at the written works of a class of third-year French students? One might compare E-Prime at its present stage metaphorically to that of a seedling. E-Prime needs to grow and develop and one might hope that critics would refrain from criticizing it based on its current lack of "fruits," just as one would not criticize an apple seedling for not yet producing apples.

I've learned to write in E-Prime fairly well, and have even attempted to speak in it. I sounded awkward, and I had trouble holding even an ordinary conversation without leaving many sentences half-finished. Why should I make the effort required to speak in E-Prime?

Speaking in E-Prime confers a number of advantages to people seriously interested in training themselves in non-Aristotelian thinking. We have found speaking in E-Prime an efficient and effective discipline, as its use forces us to incorporate general semantic principles in an integral way almost every time that we open our mouths. I (E.K.) also frequently translate the speech of others into E-Prime, and this has served me well as a buffer against signal reactions in my own thinking and behavior, and in preventing signal reactions in others. I can often smooth out arguments in my vicinity simply by interjecting E-Prime translations of key statements into conversation. For example, if someone says "That is a stupid idea!" I might reply, "What don't you like about it?" rather than "It is not!"

Most importantly however, the discipline of speaking in E-Prime eventually forced me (E.K.) to learn to *think* in E-Prime. The simplicity of the rule (don't use any forms of "to be") allowed me to make changes in real time, *while* speaking and eventually while thinking. In learning a foreign language, beginning students continue to think in their native language, while they translate their thoughts as best they can into the language they hope to learn. *But experience has shown that in order to gain true fluency in a language a student must learn to think in it.* This point may sound trivial but it can have profound importance, as thoughts in one language may not have an adequate translation in another. And as we often see the world through the medium of the language we use, this shift can in fact change the way we experience the world.(21) Excluding "to be"—with its connotation of permanence, finality, and completeness—can bring one to experience the world more as a process, as a world that changes, rather than one defined by static ideas and permanent objects.(11) These days I habitually think in E-Prime, and although this took me years to achieve, I see the effort involved as trivial when I consider the value of the result.

When you begin speaking in E-Prime you may often find yourself half-way through a sentence before you find to your dismay that you have nowhere to go but "is." We suggest in such cases that you stop and rephrase the sentence into E-Prime. If you have already finished the sentence, reword it either aloud or silently. Often this happens when you used the passive voice and put the object, rather than the subject, of a sentence first. To avoid this, try beginning each sentence or clause with the subject, to make sure that you will not inadvertently leave it out. For example, change "The hike was held. .". . to "The Sierra Club held the hike. .". . Look for patterns in the sentences that you can see no way to complete. Once you have discovered the pattern (often old "is" sentence structures) look for alternatives that satisfy you. They do exist, but you may need to work hard to find them, because in order to see them you will have to break through your own habitual patterns of language use.

I find it difficult to use E-Prime versions or responses to colloquial expressions such as ''Who are you?,'' ''How are you?,'' ''Is X there?,'' and "Where is Z?" without sounding at least a little odd. How can I deal with standardized expressions like this?

In speaking E-Prime in a non-E-Prime world, I (E.K.) sometimes resort to "pidgin E-Prime" to avoid statements which, although they make better logical sense than their English equivalents, may sound slightly awkward. For example, if someone asks me "Who are you?," instead of replying "My friends call me Ed," I might simply say "Ed." Of course, I assume the questioner really meant to ask "How do you label yourself?," and not "With what verbal concepts do you identify yourself as an existential being?" Other languages (for example French and Spanish) do in fact ask questions about one's name in a more logical manner (*Comment vous appelez vous?, Como se llama usted?*). Instead of asking "How do you label yourself?" you might simply substitute a general request for more personal information, as in the imperative, "Tell me about yourself." Specific situations allow other E-Prime variations, such as: "Your name, please?" (great for hotel desk clerks or telephone operators), "Would you please introduce yourself? I don't believe we've met before." (good for formal social occasions), "What name do you go by these days?" (great with disciples of swamis who have changed their name, or bank robbers with a number of aliases), or even (for singles situations) "If I want to find your number in the telephone directory, what name should I look under?"

No matter how improved E-Prime versions of idiomatic English phrases appear from a general semantics point of view, they may still sound a little out of the ordinary to the unprepared listener. Instead of asking "How are you?" I might ask "How do you do?," or "How has life treated you lately?" or even a West Coast alternative such as "How goes it?" On the telephone, instead of asking "Is Julie there?" I'd probably ask "May I speak with Julie?" Rather than asking "Where is X?" I might ask "Where can I find X?" or more elegantly, "Would you please direct me to X?" In my experience, even colloquial expressions have socially acceptable E-Prime equivalents, although it might take a fair amount of time and effort on your part to find one in any given situation.

On the other hand, in the early days of trying to speak E-Prime I (D.B.) rationalized my use of polite, formula,"to be" dependent phrases in order to avoid the risk of sounding like a nut. Now I've decided to stick to E-Prime all the time, even if I do occasionally sound a trifle odd. Like my co-author, I also have found "pidgin E-Prime" useful during the transition period. Of course, we recognize that pidgin E-Prime can sound less than elegant, and condone its use only when necessary during the earliest phase. At this point, let me describe two devices I've employed to good advantage along these lines:

> 1. *Locate.* Any student of Spanish can tell you that English does not have a verb that corresponds to *estar*. By using "to locate" intransitively (and somewhat ungrammatically), and ignoring the durative aspect, we can come close to the meaning of *estar*. Instead of asking, "Where is X?" we can inquire "Where does X locate?" or "Where can I locate X?"
>
> 2. *Equals.* We can dramatically illustrate the pervasive use of "to be" by the pidgin use of "equals" instead. Let's consider one example in detail. Originally, we can assume that a sincere, thoughtful person wrote this bit of semantic gobbledygook. The reader may wish to convert each instance of "is" to "equals" to underscore the misery: "Because language is the symbolization of thought, and symbols are the basic unit of culture, speech is a cultural phenomenon fundamental to what civilization is."
>
> Now suppose we try to recast this assertion into E-Prime, and attempt to capture what the writer might have tried to express, but could not with all of those "is's" of identity gumming up the works. We believe that the author, whose name we've withheld to protect the guilty, might have meant something like this: "Because language depends upon the symbolization of thought, and because symbols define the basic unit of a culture, speech as a cultural phenomenon plays a fundamental role in civilization as we know it." (E.K.)
>
> Or this: "Semantic reactions provide the basis for the linguistic and, more generally, symbolic behaviors that constitute the basic unit of cultures. Hence we must recognize speech (in the broadest sense) as a cultural phenomenon fundamental to each specific civilization." (D.B.)

From our point of view, the original "is-of identity" version sounds rather trite and pompous, whereas the E-Prime versions at least have the virtue of providing the basis for further scientific/philosophical investigations.

I find it very hard to vent my emotions in E-Prime. I get much more satisfaction telling someone "You ARE an idiot!" than saying "You act like an idiot sometimes!" How can I overcome this deficiency?

Each of us routinely uses language to manipulate others, to get them to do what we want, and to provoke a physical or emotional response. In many ways "is" statements have much greater emotional impact than their E-Prime equivalents. "You are a #%&*!" can evoke an emotional reaction significantly greater than the E-Prime equivalent, "You act like a #%&* sometimes!" "Is of identity" statements have the ability to powerfully stimulate signal reactions, not giving the unprepared individual a chance to buffer the blow consciously. However, this "disadvantage" as such applies mainly to written E-Prime. Spoken language has an emotional impact not just through *what* you say but through *how* you say it. Voice tone, rhythm, and inflection can drastically change the perceived meaning of a sentence. An innocuous "Thank you" said sarcastically can provoke an explosive response ("Don't you use that tone of voice with me!"). In this sense, E-Prime only modulates and does not control the affective content of speech. Or to put it another way, if you really want to provoke someone to punch you in the nose, you can do it in E-Prime, with the time-honored "F&%k you!" But why would you want to?

What effect does E-Prime have on our semantic reactions?

Korzybski (18) proposed the non-elementalistic term "semantic reactions" to label more accurately the complex "cortico-thalamic," "psycho-physiologic" interplay typical of us as human beings and carried on uniquely by us as time-binders (see note 2). Research into this field has expanded greatly since Korzybski's time, and today (1990) scientists use terms such as psychosomatic, psychoneuroendocrinology, and psychoneuroimmunology in their investigations into the mechanisms by which almost every aspect of our complex mind-body systems affects almost every other aspect. Thus "thinking" does not exist in isolation, as the way you think affects the way you feel, which affects the physiological functions of the endocrine and immune system, etc. Words can, and do, profoundly affect many different aspects of the mental-emotional-physiological-biochemical-etc. complex that comprises our physical selves.

In our experience we've found E-Prime to have a significant impact on our semantic reactions. Although much of this impact occurs at "the silent level" (see note 3), we can at least point out how using E-Prime can reduce stressful reactions during daily life. If Ron tells me (E.K.) that "*Dick Tracy is* a great movie," and I translate this into "*Ron* liked *Dick Tracy*," I can avoid feeling angry with Ron later when I discover that *I* did not like it. In fact, I might not even attend the movie in the first place knowing how Ron's taste in movies differs from mine. In the moment, if someone says to me "You are a #%&*!," I now automatically translate such a statement into a more benign E-Prime form such as "You have made me very angry!" As a result I experience a reduced stress response (feeling upset, increased heart rate, cold hands and feet, adrenalin rush, etc.) Similarly, in communicating with others, I've noticed that E-Prime doesn't "push their buttons" in the way that ordinary English used to and that "heated" arguments rarely occur.

How can E-Prime improve creativity?

E-Prime can boost creativity in a number of ways, but let's look at just one. Problems that "are" unsolvable in ordinary English only *seem* unsolvable in E-Prime. This apparently subtle shift in attitude can make a great difference. When people say "That is impossible" they have in effect erected a mental brick wall by dismissing even *the possibility* of coming up with an answer to a particular question. If I (E.K.) say "That seems impossible," or "I don't see how to solve this problem (yet)," part of my mind continues working on the problem and often eventually finds one or more solutions to it.

Do you think E-Prime will ever come into general use?

Yes—at least in diluted form. We see E-Prime gaining acceptance in small stages where it has the most immediate advantages—as in the improved clarity seen in writing that reduces the use of *is, am, are, was,* and *were* to a minimum. This has already begun to happen. DeWitt Scott, a copyeditor for the *San Francisco Examiner* and a writing consultant, recommends E-Prime as a useful writing tool because it "forces me to express myself in straightforward statements and come out of the clouds."(14) If a practical newspaperman can see the benefits of E-Prime in news reporting, one can hope that other writers will not lag far behind.

What sort of practical program would you recommend for learning to write and speak in E-Prime?

As a first step, concentrate on using E-Prime in unimportant notes or letters and in your personal diary. After you have gained some facility in writing, begin to use E-Prime for more serious work. Although it works best to aim at a goal of 100% E-Prime for your final version, expect to have a few "to be" sentences in the text in cases where the E-Prime version sounds overly awkward, etc. Count any reduction in the incidence of "to be" in your written work

WORKING WITH E-PRIME 53

as an achievement in the right direction. With continued effort your expertise in writing in E-Prime will increase to the point where few, if any, readers will detect any abnormality of writing style: more than likely you will receive compliments on the clarity and improved quality of your finished work.

By the time you have learned to write easily in E-Prime, you will probably already have begun to occasionally speak in it. However, if you really want to reap the full benefits of the discipline, you will have to make a serious commitment to speaking in E-Prime *exclusively*, because *speaking* in E-Prime will force you to learn how to *think* in E-Prime. Just as with learning a foreign language, a time comes when you begin to think in the language rather than to merely translate sentences into it, so with learning to speak in E-Prime. Unfortunately this process usually requires total immersion in the language and culture and a serious commitment on the student's part. As we do not live in an E-Prime culture, this makes your own personal commitment to speak in E-Prime doubly important.

When first learning to speak in E-Prime, you may have to rehearse each sentence mentally before you say it. For a while people might find your conversation a trifle limited, but as many people like to hear themselves talk most of all, they probably will not notice your reticence. Nodding the head, looking intelligently interested and occasionally mouthing words and phrases such as "yes," or "perhaps," "I agree," "indeed," etc., will prove adequate for all but the rarest of conversations, where someone actually wants to talk *with* rather than *at* you. In such a case, if you take on an attitude of deep thought, even half-finished phrases and pidgin E-Prime may command respect! As mentioned earlier with respect to arguments, I have also found it valuable to practice translating the statements of others during conversations, and then feeding back the E-Prime statement to the original speaker. You will probably feel surprised at the difference this can make.

Some Final Words.

In our experience, writing and speaking in E-Prime has proven itself an effective discipline for integrating non-Aristotelian thinking and behavior patterns even into so-called habitual or even "unconscious" levels of the "mind-body." I (E.K.) not only write and speak in E-Prime, I think and even dream in it. Although E-Prime does not train one in *all* aspects of non-Aristotelian evaluation, it does a thorough job of training its students in some aspects, and facilitates the learning of many others. Learning to write and speak in E-Prime can constitute the heart of an effective system of self-training in general semantics, and deserves serious consideration from individuals committed to the integration of non-Aristotelian processing into their habitual thought and behavior. We believe that you will find the results well worth the effort, and we look forward to hearing from you. But please—do it in E-Prime!

NOTES

1. *Elementalism.* Korzybski pointed out a variety of general semantic mechanisms that characterized the Aristotelian orientation. Among these he found: (a) widespread identification, (b) allness, (c) a two-valued system of evaluation, (d) ignoring the multiordinality of many important terms, (e) an emphasis on an intensional rather than extensional definitions, and (f) elementalism. (See reference 18, pp. xl–xlii, for a more detailed summary.) Korzybski perceived elementalism as especially harmful because of its pervasiveness. He used the term "elementalism" to label the procedure by which we verbally separate one or only a few aspects of complex, interdependent dynamic processes, and then pretend to deal with them "objectively" as independent or separate. He saw examples of Aristotelian elementalism in discussions of "body" versus "mind," "feeling" versus "thinking," "space" as separable from "matter" and "time," etc.

   Korzybski encouraged a non-elementalistic, non-Aristotelian, approach to life problems: personal, social, and scientific. He originated the use of the extensional device of the *hyphen* as a symbolic tool to foster a more holistic approach, as in terms such as "space-time," "body-mind," and "psycho-logics," etc. At one time I (D.B.) tried to encourage the use of the non-elementalistic term, "socio-logics,"(25) to little avail as yet.

2. *Time-binding.* Alfred Korzybski's appearance on the intellectual scene began in 1921 with the publication of *Manhood of Humanity.*(26) In this work he defined humanity functionally as a time-binding class of life, labelling in this way the capability of human beings to pass on their intellectual accomplishments from generation to generation through symbolic means, usually spoken and written language. This accounts for the exponential growth of human knowledge, and explains the intrinsic anti-human bias of totalitarian regimes (of the right or the left) that characteristically prevent, or pervert, time-binding processes. Korzybski's analyses of the mechanisms of time-binding eventually led to the publication of his major work, *Science and Sanity* in 1933.(18)

3. *Silent Levels.* Korzybski's non-Aristotelian model, as illustrated by his Structural Differential, makes use of an Event Level, an Object Level, and a Symbolic Level composed of an indefinitely great number of orders of abstraction. He referred to the Event and Object Levels as the "silent levels" in which we basically "live our lives," despite the conscious human preoccupation with the Symbolic Level. With reference to the Structural Differential (see reference 18, pp. 386–411), Korzybski said of it in his seminars, "It came to me in a flash, and I have spent the rest of my life trying to understand it."

REFERENCES

1. D. David Bourland, Jr., "A Linguistic Note: Writing in E-Prime," *General Semantics Bulletin* 32–33 (1965/1966): 111–14.

2. D. David Bourland, Jr., "The Semantics of a Non-Aristotelian Language," *General Semantics Bulletin* 35 (1968): 60–63.
3. K. L. Ruskin, "Coping with Semantic Problems in System Development," in *Coping with Increased Complexity: Implications of General Semantics and General System Theory*, ed. by D. E. Washburn and D. R. Smith (New York: Gordon and Breach Science Publishers, 1975).
4. Albert Ellis and Robert A. Harper, *A New Guide to Rational Living*, 2d ed. (North Hollywood, Calif.: Wilshire Book Company, 1975); Albert Ellis, *How to Live with a Neurotic* 2d ed. (North Hollywood, Calif.: Wilshire Book Company, 1975); Albert Ellis, *Sex and the Liberated Man* (Secaucus, N.J.: Lyle Stuart, 1976; 2d ed of *Sex and the Single Man)*; Albert Ellis, *Anger: How to Live with and without It* (Secaucus, N.J.: Citadel Press, 1977); and Albert Ellis, *Overcoming Procrastination* 2d ed. (New York: Signet, 1977).
5. Robert Ian Scott, "*Is*-Less and Other Grammars," *General Semantics Bulletin* 38–40 (1976): 42–49.
6. Steven A. Elkind, *To Be or not to Be: An Investigation of Linguistic Relativity by Altering the Language of Encounter Group Members in a Manner Suggested by General Semantics Theory*, Ph.D. diss. (Los Angeles: California School of Professional Psychology, 1976).
7. E. W. Kellogg III, "Speaking in E-Prime: An Experimental Approach for Integrating General Semantics into Daily Life," *Et cetera* 44, no. 2 (1987): 118–28.
8. Ruth S. Ralph, "Getting Rid of the *To Be* Crutch," in *Classroom Exercises in General Semantics*, ed. by Mary Morain (San Francisco: International Society for General Semantics, 1980).
9. Bryon L. Cannon, *An E-Prime Approach to the Holy Bible*, M.S. diss. (Fort Hays, Kans.: Fort Hays State University, 1987).
10. Elaine C. Johnson, "Discovering E-Prime," *Et cetera* 45, no. 2 (1988): 181–83.
11. Paul Dennithorne Johnston, "Escape from a Frozen Universe: Discovering General Semantics," *Et cetera* 46, no. 2 (1989): 136–40.
12. D. David Bourland, Jr., "To Be or not to Be: E-Prime as a Tool for Critical Thinking," *Et cetera* 46, no. 3 (1989): 202–11.
13. Robert Anton Wilson, "Toward Understanding E-Prime," *Et cetera* 46, no. 4 (1989): 316–19.
14. DeWitt Scott, "Writing that Works," *Et cetera* 46, no. 4 (1989): 320–21.
15. William Dallman, "A Letter on E-Prime," *Et cetera* 44, no. 1 (1990): 77–78.
16. D. David Bourland, Jr., "To Be or not to Be: E-Prime as a Technique for Critical Thinking," in *Thinking Creatively*, ed. by Kenneth G. Johnson (Institute of General Semantics, 1990).
17. Robert Anton Wilson, *Quantum Psychology* (Phoenix: New Falcon, 1990).
18. Alfred Korzybski, *Science and Sanity* (Lakeville, Conn.: International Non-Aristotelian Library and Publishing Company, 1933). 4th ed., 1958.
19. Alan Walker Reed, "Language Revision by Deletion of Absolutisms," *Et cetera* 42 (1985): 7–12.
20. E. W. Kellogg III, "Mapping Territories: A Phenomenology of Lucid Dream Reality," *Lucidity Letter* 8, no. 2 (1989): 81–97.
21. Benjamin Lee Whorf, *Language, Thought, and Reality* (Cambridge: MIT Press, 1956). See also C. Weggelaar, "The Whorf Hypothesis: The Case of Dutch and English," *Et cetera* 39 (1982): 332–43.
22. See, for example, Helen Gardner, ed., *The New Oxford Book of English Verse: 1250–1950* (New York: Oxford University Press, 1972), or Joseph Auslander and Frank Ernest Hill, eds., *The Winged Horse Anthology* (New York: Doubleday, 1929).
23. *Time*, "Behavior," May 23, 1969, 69.

24. Erich Fromm, *To Have or to Be* (New York: Harper & Row, 1976).
25. D. David Bourland, Jr., "Preliminary Notes on 'Foci of Synthesis': General Semantics and the Principle of Least Effort," *General Semantics Bulletin* nos. 1 and 2 (1949–50): 17–21.
26. Alfred Korzybski, *Manhood of Humanity* (New York: Dutton, 1921). 2d ed. distributed by the Institute of General Semantics.

Part Two

EPISTEMOLOGICAL FOUNDATIONS OF E-PRIME

A LINGUISTIC NOTE: WRITING IN E-PRIME

D. David Bourland, Jr.

Introduction

MEN HAVE WARNED US for years of the dangers and inadequacies that can result from the careless, unthinking, automatic use of the verb "to be." Alfred Korzybski, Augustus de Morgan, and George Santayana have contributed outstanding warnings. It seems appropriate to reproduce here some of their more trenchant criticisms of this seemingly innocuous term.

Santayana stated, in *Skepticism and Animal Faith:*

> The little word *is* has its tragedies; it names and identifies different things with the greatest innocence; and yet no two are ever identical, and if therein lies the charm of wedding them and calling them one, therein too lies the danger. Whenever I use the word *is*, except in sheer tautology, I deeply misuse it; and when I discover my error, the world seems to fall asunder, and the members of my family no longer know one another.(1)

De Morgan, writing something over one hundred years ago, showed in *Formal Logic* the close connection between the verb "to be" and allness orientations:

> The most difficult inquiry which anyone can propose to himself is to find out what any thing *is:* in all probability we do not know what we are talking about when we ask such a question. The philosophers of the middle ages were much concerned with the *is*, or *essence*, of things: they argued to their own minds, with great justice, that if they could only find out what a thing is, they should find out all about it: they tried, and failed. Their successors, taking warning by their example, have inverted the proposition; and have satisfied themselves that the only way of finding what a thing is, lies in finding what we can about it; that

Reprinted from the *General Semantics Bulletin*, nos. 32 and 33 (1965/1966).

modes of relation and connexion are all we can know of anything; in short, the proverb "tell me who you are with, and I will tell you who you are," applies as much to the nature of things as to the character of men.(2)

As one might expect, Korzybski gave the clearest expression of the sociocultural issues involved in, and implied by, the verb "to be." The following two excerpts from *Science and Sanity* present his position:

> The little word "to be" appears as a very peculiar word and is, perhaps, responsible for many human semantic difficulties. If the anthropologists are correct, only a few of the primitive peoples have this verb. The majority do not have it and do not need it, because all their semantic reactions and languages are practically based on, and involve, literal identification. In passing from the primitive stage of human society to the present slightly higher stage, which might be called the infantile stage, or infantile period, too crude identification was no longer possible. Languages were built, based on slightly modified or limited identification, and, for flexibility, the "is" of identity was introduced explicitly. Although very little has been done in the *structural* analysis of languages in general, and of those of primitive peoples in particular, we know that in the Indo-European languages the verb "to be," among others, is used as an *auxiliary* verb and also for the purpose of positing false to facts identity. With the primitive prevalent lack of consciousness of abstracting, and the primitive belief in the magic of words, the *semantic reactions* were such that words were identified with the objective levels. Perhaps it is not too much to say that the primitive "psychology" peculiarly required such a fundamental identity. Identity may be defined as "absolute sameness in all respects" which, in a world of ever-changing processes and a human world of indefinitely many orders of abstractions, appears as a *structural* impossibility. Identity appears, then, as a primitive "over-emotional" generalization of similarity, equality, equivalence, equipollence, etc., and, in no case, does it appear in fact as "absolute sameness in all respects." As soon as the structurally *delusional* character of identity is pointed out, it becomes imperative for sanity to eliminate such delusional factors from our languages and *semantic reactions*. With the advent of "civilization," the use of this word was enlarged, but some of the fundamental primitive implications and psycho-logical semantic effects were preserved. If we use the "is" at all, and it is extremely difficult to avoid entirely this auxiliary verb when using languages which, to a large extent, depend on it, we must be particularly careful not to use "is" as an identity term. . . . (p. 400)
>
> For thousands of years, millions upon millions of humans have used a great deal of their nervous energy in worrying upon delusional questions, forced upon them by the pernicious "is" of identity, such as: "What *is* an object?," "What *is* life?," "What *is* hell?," "What *is* heaven?," "What *is* space?," "What *is* time?," and an endless array of such irritants.

> The answer, based on the human discrimination of orders of abstractions and so proper *human evaluation,* is definite, undeniable, simple, and *unique:* "Whatever one might *say* something '*is,*' it *is not.*" Whatever we might *say* belongs to the verbal level and *not* to the un-speakable, objective levels.
>
> Let me repeat once more that the "is" of identity forces us into semantic disturbances of wrong *evaluation.* We establish, for instance, the *identity* of the un-speakable objective level with words, which, once stated, becomes obviously false to facts. The "is" of identity, if used as indicating "identity" (structurally *impossible* on the objective levels), says nothing. Thus, the question, "What *is* an object?," may be answered, "An object *is* an object"—a statement which says nothing. If used in definitions or classifications, such as "Smith *is* a man," a type of statement used even in the *Principia Mathematica,* or "A *is* B or not B," as in the formulation of the law of "excluded third" in the two-valued Aristotelian "logic," it always establishes an *identity,* false to facts. The first statement expresses the *identity* of a proper name with a class name which must lead to the confusion of classes (higher order abstractions) with individuals (lower order abstractions). This confusion leads automatically to disturbed evaluation in life, because the characteristics of a class are *not* the "same" as, nor identical with, the characteristics of the individual. I shall not analyse in detail the "A *is* B," because, obviously, it *is not.* (pp. 408–409) (3)

In this paper the writer describes an approach toward this particular term that can produce semantically interesting results. If we represent the whole of the English language as E, and the linguistic element "to be" with all its inflectional forms by e, then this paper concerns the language E', defined as:

$$E' = E - e$$

This subtraction may appear trivial, but consideration will show that it introduces important structural changes. Grammatically speaking, we have given up most of the passive voice, much of the subjunctive mood, and some participial usages. More significantly, however, subject-predicate language (note 1) has become impossible, the "is" of identity cannot rise up to debilitate our statements, and we become *forced* to use actional, functional, straightforward statements.

Origin and Applications

I cannot claim credit for having made the suggestion that led to the formulation of the language E-Prime. Unfortunately I cannot name the person who did. While on a fellowship at the Institute of General Semantics in 1949, I saw a letter written by a man from some small town in Connecticut (Tollins?), which advanced an audacious suggestion. He recommended that we stop using the verb "to be" in any form.

At that time I had a paper in preparation for the Third Congress on General Semantics (University of Denver, July 1949). The suggestion seemed worth trying; it clearly constituted much more than a mere grammatical trick. Accordingly, I prepared the paper later published as reference 4, trying to avoid any use of "to be."(Note 2) This initial attempt to write in E-Prime resulted in a paper not necessarily stilted or awkward in phraseology, as one might expect.

I have also used E-Prime in references 5 and 6, plus the present paper. It has eventually become easier to write in E-Prime, even when treating rather extensive analytical material such as in reference 6. Of course, one would find it particularly difficult to *speak* routinely in E-Prime. However, one can use the E-Prime approach in key places of an oral analysis or discussion, to good effect. I have tried this on occasion and can recommend E-Prime as a good technique for bringing a discussion out of verbal clouds, onto orders of abstraction that tend to promote fruitful analysis and agreement. I recommend this approach particularly to teachers of general semantics who wish to help students become sensitive to mechanisms of identification, and to authors of serious articles in the field.

Some Properties of E-Prime

This section presents a discussion of the more important properties of the language E-Prime, certain questions that vanish, certain role-players that become evident, and some aspects of abbreviation.

1. *Vanishing Questions:* One simply cannot ask, in E-Prime, certain questions that have long plagued individuals in various ways. In addition to the questions posed by Korzybski in the second quotation given above, we can include the following ones:

   What is man?
   But is it art?
   What is general semantics?

I submit that the structure of those questions predisposes the ensuing discussion to areas of discourse in which the likelihood of useful information exchange becomes severely reduced (not *impossible*, mind you, but significantly *reduced*). This observation tends to lend further emphasis to the magnitude of the task accomplished by Korzybski in proceeding from such a question as "What is man?"

A Linguistic Note

to his time-binding definition of mankind, and thence to general semantics.

2. *A Matter of Abbreviation:* To a certain extent, the verb "to be" allows and, indeed, seems to force abbreviation or truncation in speech and writing. In the language of mathematics a goodly amount of abbreviation becomes sheer necessity; mathematicians even encourage one another to emphasize abbreviations in formal presentations in the name of "elegance." This seems appropriate, and serves as a matter of despair only for struggling students, since the language of mathematics contains precise definitions for the quantities, relations, operations, etc., involved in such elegant statements. In marked contrast to this, descriptions and assertions in our ordinary discursive languages usually contain extremely high order abstractions (e.g., "right," "the past") that require extensive elucidation rather than further abbreviations.

One example may illustrate further the desired point of this matter of abbreviation. Consider the following assertion, with which one really can have little quarrel (on the face of it): "We do this thing because it is right." The last three words potentially imply volumes of political, sociological, and theological discourse, as well as inspiration, disputation, etc. We could employ the statement as a whole in (at least partial) justification of actions that could range from seeming heinous to some, to those that seem unquestionably foreordained (and hence requiring no justification) to others. Of course, this raises questions about the nature of the information content of such an assertion. In any event, one may find it an interesting exercise to recast that statement in E-Prime, while preserving the presumed intent of the original statement. I suggest this as one possibility: "We do this thing because we sincerely desire to minimize the discrepancies between our actions and our stated 'ideals.'" That form obviously does not have the pithy snap of the original statement. Some would probably characterize that particular E-Prime variant as somewhat pedestrian. Even so, the E-Prime statement seems to admit openly the participation in the overall situation of some creed or set of beliefs, allegedly held currently by some humans and subject to change (although perhaps only after some considerable struggle).

3. *Return of the Role-Players:* Perhaps due in large part to the abbreviational aspects discussed above, a language whose structure allows (or encourages) incessant use of "to be" seems to suppress the presence or influence of some of the important role-players. E-Prime, in contrast to such suppression, tends to invite

particular attention to the agents involved. We become encouraged to reflect the fact that certain humans, still living or formerly living, as acted upon by beliefs about one another and the worlds about us, perform or performed the various activities under discussion. It becomes evident that some person wrote the given paper—it did not appear by some magic. One furthermore becomes aware of the implication that the person who prepared the given non-magical paper may have included some inaccuracies or misleading statements. Hence we may suggest that the use of E-Prime fosters the critical review of written material.

4. *A Disclaimer:* The use of E-Prime does not, by itself, preclude identification or other undesirable linguistic forms and reactions (such as confusion in orders of abstractions, elementalism, and ignoring the multiordinality of most key terms). It does, however, perform outstandingly in removing what one could call the "supreme irritant." The following statement by Korzybski provides a measure of what E-Prime has to offer:

> The subject-predicate form, the "is" of identity, and the elementalism of the Aristotelian system are perhaps the main semantic factors in need of revision, as they are found to be the foundation of the insufficiency of this system and represent the mechanism of semantic disturbances, making general adjustment and sanity impossible.(3, p. 371)

By adopting E-Prime, we accomplish the first two factors requiring revision called for by Korzybski, *at one stroke.* The following section comes to grips with the third factor called out.

A Beneficial Combination

Korzybski asserted in his last few seminars that one of his most important contributions consisted in revising the structure of our language, through the extensional devices (Note 3), without making it necessary to revise the language itself. Let us represent the result of transforming the structure of conventional English by the adroit application of the extensional devices as E_k. Then let us consider the proper subset of E_k consisting of the set intersection (or "join") $E_k \cap E'$. We may represent that join as E_k'.

This operation preserves the structural benefits that potentially accrue from the extensional devices that encourage our consciousness of abstracting (Note 4), which facilitate the construction of non-elementalistic formulations, and which warn against treating higher order abstractions loosely. The language E_k' supplies the linguistic assistance that results in improved formulations as discussed in the preceding sections. Furthermore, the basis for undeniably justified criticism of an occasional use of the *"is* of identity" in reference 3 becomes removed.

I suggest that the general semantics community explore the possibilities of E-Prime as well as the even more beneficial E_k'.

REFERENCES

1. George Santayana, *Skepticism and Animal Faith* (New York: Scribner, 1923).
2. Augustus de Morgan, *Formal Logic (1847)*, ed. A. E. Taylor (London: Open Court, 1926).
3. Alfred Korzybski, *Science and Sanity: An Introduction to Non-Aristotelian Systems and General Semantics* (Science Press, 1933); now distributed by the Institute of General Semantics, Lakeville, Conn.
4. D. David Bourland, Jr., "Introduction to a Structural Calculus: A Postulational Statement of Alfred Korzybski's Non-Aristotelian Linguistic System," *General Semantics Bulletin,* 1952, nos. 8 and 9.
5. D. David Bourland, Jr., "Semantic Construction: A Time-Binding Mechanism," *General Semantics Bulletin,* 1963/1964, nos. 30 and 31.
6. D. David Bourland, Jr., and Robert P. McManus, "A General Model for Information Transfer Systems," U.S. Navy Electronics Laboratory Technical Memorandum No. 804, May 21, 1965, unclassified.

NOTES

1. Logical or linguistic form in which an "entity" (the subject) has a property or "quality" (the predicate) assigned through an asserted "identity" relation, as in "Grass is green," "Beauty is truth," "John is a liberal." Some respectable philosophical, and even mathematical logical, circles continue to regard the subject-predicate form with approval.
2. This effort fell short in one instance. A glaring "was" spoils an otherwise perfect record (excluding quotations, of course). I fancy that a well-meaning editorial change *may* have done me in.
3. Indexes, chain indexes, dates, use of the et cetera, hyphens, and quotes.
4. The devices can also foster consciousness of semantic construction; see reference 5.

THE SEMANTICS OF A NON-ARISTOTELIAN LANGUAGE

D. David Bourland, Jr.

Introduction

IN AN EARLIER paper this writer invited attention to some of the characteristics of a subset of the English language he called "E-Prime."(4) This subset consists of standard English with the exclusion of all the inflectional forms of the verb "to be." It forms a language with some interesting properties.

The earlier paper covered the more prominent characteristics of E-Prime. The following items review the consequences of adopting E-Prime:

> Certain questions vanish. One cannot ask, in E-Prime, "What is life?" "What is Man?" etc. We regard these as poorly structured questions. These questions involve the use of what some critics have called the "is of identity."

> Some misleadingly elegant abbreviations become impossible, as implied in such statements as "We know this is the right thing to do." These abbreviations usually involve what some call the "is of predication."

> Some verbally suppressed, but nevertheless active, role-players return to the scene. Statements reflect the fact that some human originated, repeated, stated, etc., them. The frequency of such low content forms as "It has been found that . . . ," "It is known that . . . " goes to zero. E-Prime tends to invite attention to the agents involved in information transactions.

The use of E-Prime certainly cannot forestall all the mechanisms of identification, which of course go much deeper than mere verbalization. However, E-Prime does remove the "supreme irritant"

Reprinted from the *General Semantics Bulletin*, no. 35 (1968).

and, in the process, eliminates both the subject-predicate form and the "is of identity."

This paper presents several applications of E-Prime, starting with general semantics and then moving out into other parts of the world.

Non-Aristotelian Premises

The so-called Non-Aristotelian Premises (Non-Identity, Non-Allness, and Self-Reflexiveness) have appeared in various books and papers. Evidently Korzybski's appreciation of their key significance evolved during the ten-year period between the publication of *Science and Sanity* (1933) and the Second American Congress on General Semantics (1943). These now-familiar "laws" do not appear grouped together as such in *Science and Sanity* (Note 1), but they did receive explicit treatment in Korzybski's Congress paper as quoted below:

(1) A word is not the fact, feeling, situation, relation, etc.

(2) A word covers not all the characteristics of an object, situation, fact, feeling, etc..

(3) Language is also self-reflexive in the sense that in a language we can speak about language.(7)

Let us now consider these premises from the viewpoint of E-Prime. It would seem that both the first and third need recasting slightly. One possible E-Prime variant for each of those appears below:

(1') No two structures can exhibit absolute sameness in all respects; most particularly, a structure on the symbolic level (such as a "word") has characteristics that differ significantly from those of other structures associated with it on the object level or event level (such as the fact, feeling, situation, relation, etc., labeled by the given "word").

(3') We can use language self-reflexively, in the sense that in a language we can speak about that language, but we must recognize that the resulting symbolic structures will belong to higher orders of abstraction than those we ascribe to the symbolic structures of the initial language.

The statements in (1') and (3') make use of a two-part distinction between levels of abstraction (event level, object level, and symbolic level) and orders of abstraction on given levels. The writer has discussed and employed this analytical technique in several papers (Note 2); more recently Welte has also found this distinction useful in his anthropological research, evidently independent of the writer's efforts. (Note 3)

Perhaps again, as in the initial paper on E-Prime, the writer should admit that the statements in (1') and (3') do not have the terse cogency of the original forms in (1) and (3). But despite their seeming pedestrian quality, they present a necessarily fuller description. The premise as written in (3') also seems to the writer to lead more directly into considerations of the multiordinality of key terms. (Note 4)

Map-Territory Analogy

Now let us turn to the Map-Territory Analogy, a teaching procedure used by Korzybski in explication of the Non-Aristotelian Premises and in illustration of the importance of structural factors. In E-Prime these familiar statements may appear as follows:

> A "map" belongs to a level of abstraction different from that of the "territory" it represents.
>
> A "map" does not contain all the structural characteristics of the "territory" it represents.
>
> A "map" may self-reflexively contain a "map" of higher order that shows the relation between the "territory" represented in some detail to the surrounding "territory."

"Instant General Semantics"

The increasing tempo of life today has contributed to the growing use of "instant" products. Whether coffee, tea, or whatever, the "instant" versions of items usually supply a slightly degraded product that tries to trade convenience for quality.

E-Prime supplies a kind of "Instant General Semantics." Although it clearly provides only a partial version, the contributions E-Prime makes in relieving us from the linguistic miseries of the "is of identity" and subject-predicate language amount to significant contributions.

One does not acquire this particular instant product without some semantic labor. Readers may demonstrate this to themselves by writing their next letter in E-Prime.

Talking about Dogs, etc.

Some time ago, while driving along, the writer and his then-four-year-old daughter noticed a large shaggy dog walking down the street. As we returned home later, the little girl asked, pointing, "Daddy, is that the *same* dog we saw a while ago?" (Note 5) Upon reflection it becomes apparent that one cannot answer that question correctly either by "yes" or "no."

As noted earlier (4), it becomes necessary to use E-Prime as augmented by Korzybski's extensional devices: E_k-Prime. With the richness of that language we can describe the recalled object-level happening, observed at time t_1, as $Dog_1{}^{t_1}$. Then, at time t_2, we can rephrase the earlier question as: "Daddy, do I see $Dog_1{}^{t_2}$ or $Dog_2{}^{t_2}$?" Then Daddy can properly reply, "I think that we see $Dog_1{}^{t_2}$." While granting that this second question may exceed the capabilities of most four-year-olds, how about us forty-year-olds?

One may choose to see this consequence to the dog encounter: If we need E_k-Prime (at least) to speak accurately about shaggy dogs, surely we need this or better to discuss more complicated matters of greater moment.

Discussion

Several people have offered the suggestion that, even with the adoption and use of E-Prime, one may still identify one order or level of abstraction with another.

The term "identification" labels an undesirable and un-speakable semantic reaction. An individual who suffers noticeably from such semantic reactions may require extensive retraining, which will surely entail more than linguistic means alone. The suppression or, indeed, the adoption of a finite set of terms cannot offer an effective method for changing semantic reactions, unless this activity represents just one part of a multifaceted program.

In the writer's opinion, however, E-Prime offers these services:

- E-Prime completely removes the insidiously easily available and culturally acceptable handmaidens of subject-predicate language and is-of-identity forms.

- E-Prime forces the issue by tending to make fallacious constructions more noticeable and hence more obviously needful of revision.

- By introducing the constraint of avoiding *all* forms of an all-too-commonly used linguistic form, a heightened degree of verbal consciousness becomes forced upon the given individual writer. This consciousness can lead to two particularly beneficial developments: (1) greater care in linguistic sensitivity; and (2) consciousness of abstracting on a more general level.

It seemed desirable to emphasize, above, the matter of E-Prime removing a culturally-approved—at least approved in the Aristotelian culture—pacifier. The forms of "to be" have become so placidly a part of the background noise of conventional speech that one has to make an effort in order to perceive them. A peculiarly difficult point to convey to some people consists of the observation that one simply does not *need* the verb "to be" in order to speak, relate, analyze, etc.

The writer has put together a number of papers in E-Prime, dealing with topics somehow related to general semantics. The Appendix shows the results of applying E-Prime to an excerpt from the Declaration of Independence, to demonstrate that E-Prime can readily flourish in such a nontechnical area.

In a discussion of multiordinal terms, Korzybski (6) included the following analysis of a higher-order mechanism:

> I recall vividly an argument I had with a young and very gifted mathematician. Our conversation was about the geometries of Euclid and Lobatchevski, and we were discussing the dropping and introduction of assumptions. I maintained that Lobatchevski introduced an assumption; he maintained that Lobatchevski dropped an assumption. On the surface, it might have appeared that this is a problem of "fact" and not of preference. The famous fifth postulate of Euclid reads, "If a straight line falling on two straight lines makes the interior angles on the same side less than two right angles, the two straight lines, if produced indefinitely, meet on that side on which are the angles less than two right angles." We should note, in passing, that a straight line is assumed to be of "infinite" length, which involves a definite type of structural metaphysics of "space," common to the A and older systems. This postulate of Euclid can be expressed in one of its equivalent forms, as, for instance, "Through a point outside a straight line one, and only one, parallel to it can be drawn." Lobatchevski and others decided to build up a geometry without this postulate, and in this they were successful. Let us consider what Lobatchevski did. For this, we go to a deeper level—otherwise, to a higher order of abstraction—where we discover that what on his level had been the dropping of an assumption becomes on our deeper level or higher order abstraction the introduction of an assumption that through a point outside a straight line there passes more than one parallel line.
>
> Now such a process is structurally inherent in all human knowledge. More than this, it is a unique characteristic of the structure of human

knowledge. We can always do this. If we pass to higher orders of abstractions, situations seemingly "insoluble," "matters of fact," quite often become problems of preference. This problem is of extreme semantic importance, and of indefinitely extended consequences for all science, psychiatry, and education in particular.

Now in the case of E-Prime, one may regard this as the result of a comparatively trivial suppression of one speech form out of the some 490,000 words that make up standard English. The writer submits, however, that by completely avoiding "to be" we introduce an important psycho-logical factor: a linguistic implementation of the non-Aristotelian assumption of non-identity. This particular factor operates most importantly through encouraging the use of functional, structural expressions that tend to facilitate visualizations and hence provide a basis for diminishing identifications. The importance of visualization techniques should not require elaboration here.

REFERENCES

1. D. D. Bourland, Jr., "Cálculo Estructural: Métodos Axiomáticos Aplicados a la Semántica General," *Episteme* (Journal of the Argentine Association for Epistemology), 1951, no. 8.
2. D. D. Bourland, Jr., "Introduction to a Structural Calculus: A Postulational Statement of Alfred Korzybski's Non-Aristotelian Linguistic System," *General Semantics Bulletin*, 1952, nos. 8 and 9.
3. D. D. Bourland, Jr., "Semantic Construction: A Time-Binding Mechanism," *General Semantics Bulletin*, 1965/1966, nos. 32 and 33.
4. D. D. Bourland, Jr., "A Linguistic Note: Writing in E-Prime," *General Semantics Bulletin*, 1965/1966, nos. 32 and 33.
5. D. D. Bourland, Jr., and R. P. McManus, "A General Model for Information Transfer Systems," U.S. Navy Electronics Laboratory Technical Memorandum TM-804, May 21, 1965. Excerpt printed in *General Semantics Bulletin*, 1965/1966, nos. 32 and 33.
6. A. Korzybski, *Science and Sanity: An Introduction to Non-Aristotelian Systems and General Semantics*, 1st ed., 1933; 3rd ed., 1948 (Lakeville, Conn.: International Non-Aristotelian Publishing Company, Institute of General Semantics).
7. A. Korzybski, "General Semantics, Psychiatry, Psychotherapy and Prevention," *Papers from the Second American Congress on General Semantics*, ed. M. Kendig (Chicago: Institute of General Semantics, 1943).
8. C. R. Welte, "Levels of Integration," *General Semantics Bulletin*, 1963/1964, nos. 30 and 31.

NOTES

1. Korzybski covered the material summarized in the Non-Aristotelian Premises, of course, as for example on pages 11, 58f, and Supplement III. But he did not collect these three premises together in *Science and Sanity*.
2. See Bourland references 1, 2, and 3, and Bourland and McManus reference 5.
3. See Welte reference 8.

4. See Korzybski reference 6, pp. 433f.
5. Emphasis supplied, of course.

APPENDIX

Excerpt from the Declaration of Independence in E-Prime

We assert and shall operate on the basis of the following explicit postulates:

1. All citizens have equivalent political rights.
2. All citizens simply by virtue of their existence have certain inalienable rights, including life, liberty, and the pursuit of happiness.
3. Men institute Governments in order to secure the rights given above.
4. Governments derive their powers solely from the consent of the governed.
5. Whenever any form of Government operates inconsistently with the previously listed postulates, the People have the right to alter or abolish it, and to institute a new Government.

etc.

"IS"-LESS AND OTHER GRAMMARS

Robert Ian Scott

Science and Sanity deals with our reactions to language, but how do we apply its insights to what we write? In his preface to the second, the 1941 edition, Korzybski suggested five "extensional devices" to make us more aware of the world's complexity, changes, and connections, and of language's limitations in representing them.(1) These devices make *words* more modestly specific, and thus less misleading:

1. index numbers
2. dates
3. *etc.*
4. quotation marks
5. hyphens

But how do we make the structures of our language less intensional, more extensional, as Korzybski also suggested? We need his devices, and also an *is*-less grammar to show us which sentence patterns to use instead of the intensional *X-is-Y* that he found characteristic both of medieval logic and of schizophrenia.

Korzybski's Extensional Devices

We already use index numbers to make crucial distinctions clear: carbon 14 is *not* carbon 12, a Boeing 747 is *not* a Boeing 737, etc. Index numbers on credit cards, licenses, and insurance policies identify

Robert Ian Scott teaches at the University of Saskatchewan, Saskatoon, Canada. Reprinted with permission from the *General Semantics Bulletin*, nos. 38–40 (1971-73).

us less ambiguously than our names do. We need such numbers because Ralph C. Nelson 14442 labels one individual, and Ralph C. Nelson 26375 quite another one. Some say they resent "being numbers," but generally such numbers increase the possibilities of our lives by unconfusing them, and by reminding others that we are *not* precisely like anyone else, thus making it easier to treat each case individually.

Dates and other qualifiers remind us that in time and with other changes every individual changes, as in:

   1   2   3   4   5

In 1953, my 1930 Ford stopped from 30 m.p.h. in 39 feet . . .

(while now, alas, "my" Ford . . .). The five *qualifiers* state functions—a particular car's ability to stop as a function of its age, speed, etc.—one change seen in terms of others, not all of them mentioned: the stopping distance also depends on the brakes, tires, road, driver, weather, etc. Qualifiers let us discuss such functions (the facts or changes that compose situations) and help us gather the data we need to do so accurately by making the questions, reports, and predictions involved usefully specific.

Beyond Words

Why use *etc.*? It may remind us that what we don't say can prove crucial, as in logical arguments that prove useless, or factually wrong. No description can include everything, so the world keeps on surprising us, but English does include terms that suggest its incompleteness, that may make us more wary—*etc., and all, and such, includes, for example,* the ellipsis—and that may get us to look beyond words to the world, whose complexity makes even the most elaborate language misleadingly simple. Yet languages must simplify; we cannot take the time to mention all the facts that might matter. Languages do so in abstract and arbitrary ways, as C. S. Peirce suggested by classifying signs as Icons, Indices, or Symbols.(2) Icons *resemble* what they signal in structure (as maps and pictures do) or in some sensed quality. Indices *result from* what they mean, as clues and symptoms do. But words and other Symbols don't necessarily resemble or result from what we may take them to mean. We can say almost anything, so we need to question words and their causes and results.

We may find such questioning more apt to happen when we put quotation marks around such trickily ambiguous, multiordinal, and sometimes explosively emotional terms as "love," to remind ourselves and our readers that these words are only words, sounds, or marks we use as labels, that they are possibly misleading, and that we could use other words to label the same event or experience, often with very different results.

The *X-is-Y* calls its subject two names, X and Y, *noun+noun-or-adjective*, a static and often only verbal classifying that may make us forget that nothing exists alone or had any meaning apart from its time, place, causes, and results, the connections by which hyphenated terms may define their subjects. Connect two of the ways we see something, as we do when we speak of Einstein's *mass-energy* equation ($E=mc^2$—how one quantity varies as, and perhaps because, another quantity does), of *stimulus-response* psychologies and other *cause-result* relationships, of *import-export* balances, and we may see situations in more of their connections and complexity as interconnected, self-balancing-yet-always-changing structures. Our growing awareness of ecology may produce more such terms, which may change our view of the world and ourselves, and change our lives—*man–world* relationships, perhaps, and *life–death* balances—opposites seen as coexisting and mutually dependent, and not as mutually exclusive, despite medieval logic.

Index numbers, dates, *etc.*, and quotation marks seem easier to use, and more common, but limit only single terms or phrases; hyphenated terms refer to, require, and change our understanding of whole fields as structures of relationships, and by using such complex-describing compounds, we may describe subjects by what they do, thus avoiding misleading identifications and oversimplifications that lead to inaccurate predictions and other frustrations, including the two-valued orientations and resulting polarizations that make squabbles harder to avoid, and harder to settle. Also, by inventing and trying out hyphenated terms, we can look for unexpected connections, using experiments with language as a way to make discoveries about the world beyond our language.

Choosing Grammars

Without these extensional devices, the *X-is-Y* makes such blindly intensional and general judgments as "She's stupid!" and such unanswerably abstract questions as "What is love?" all too easy. But even with Korzybski's devices, the *X-is-Y* gives us judgments when we need reports and explanations first: "In 1970, Belinda wasn't intelligent about Jack's Volvo 122, etc." still leaves us wondering what happened. We need a more informative sentence-pattern, one that asks and answers more useful questions than just the often only intensional "how do I want to name and classify this subject?"

In his essay "The Chinese Written Character as a Medium for Poetry," written in or before 1908, Ernest Fenollosa claimed that using *is* caused what he called "the tyranny of medieval logic." He suggested that we use active verbs and the sentence-pattern *subject-verb-object instead*.(3) In thus distrusting *is*, Fenollosa anticipated Korzybski. In seeing other types of verbs—the negative, the passive, the copulative or linking verbs (including *is*), and presumably also the various complex verbs—as less direct, less emphatic variations of the active verbs, and hence other sentence-patterns as less basic variations (transformations) of the active verb's *subject-verb-object* pattern, Fenollosa seems to anticipate at least a part of one of the basic assumptions of Noam Chomsky's transformational grammar some fifty years later.

Both Fenollosa and Chomsky seem to assume that we can transform any sentence-pattern into any other, but if so, then which pattern we choose as a basis for a grammar becomes a matter of convenience, because then no pattern can claim to provide the only possible basis for all the rest; we can start a grammar from any sentence-pattern, which makes a multiplicity of grammars possible.

Chomsky's grammar starts from the sentence-pattern *noun-phrase+verb-phrase*, NP+VP for short, which we may see as another way of saying what traditional grammars do, that sentences have a subject plus a predicate containing a finite verb.

Fenollosa starts from a more specific pattern, *subject-verb-object*, SVO for short, which he claims communicates facts more concretely and tersely than the *X-is-Y* can, because the SVO structure resembles that of the *actor-action-acted upon* cause-result relationships that compose the world. We have here a distinction between an intensional grammatical structure (the *X-is-Y*) and an extensional one (the SVO), and two principles to guide our choice of grammars: generally, the more complex the pattern basic to a grammar, (1) the more unambiguously specific and informative the questions and answers that pattern generates, and (2) the less complicated the grammar, for any given size of lexicon, and level of morphemic complexity and of descriptive adequacy.

We might wish that Chomsky had started from some more complexly specific kernel than NP+VP, and that he had made a clear semantic and syntactical distinction between the judging-and-classifying *X-is-Y* and the reporting-what-happens SVO, but apparently he took the NP+VP for granted, as the only possible kernel from which sentences and grammars can start, when in fact we have a choice. The 1957 version of his grammar excludes semantics, and the 1965 version looks for semantic classifications of our world and words within an implicit "deep structure" of simple statements whose nouns, at least, he classifies in series of two-valued choices as animate or not, human or not, which seems to me an oversimplification of the many-valued matrices we may actually use—but here we need experimental tests.

Nowhere, so far as I know, does Chomsky mention Fenollosa or Korzybski or seem concerned that his terms "grammatical" and "mind" may have no clear extensional reference. He defines a successful grammar as one that produces all the grammatical sentences of a language, and no ungrammatical sentences, but since grammatical sentences are in turn defined as those a success grammar produces, his definition seems a merely verbal circle. He apparently hopes to discover the structure of human minds by analyzing the structures of the sentences they produce, as if he thinks that results always resemble their causes, and thinks of the structures of languages as both the Index and the Icon of our minds.

Since he denies the possibility of nonhuman languages but not that other animals have brains, he apparently means something in or additional to brains by "mind." In any case, his use of "kernel" to mean the basic sentence-pattern of a grammar suggests that he assumes that from such simple seeds or kernels whole sentences and grammars grow ("in the mind"). But other kernels than his NP+VP may provide more usefully productive and specific recipes for forming sentences (and longer pieces of speech or writing), and his NP+VP-based analyses of already-formed sentences may not describe whatever actually happens in the brain or mind as we form such sentences. We need to try a variety of grammars.

We can classify grammars by the sentence-patterns they use as kernels and by what they use these kernels for, as in this paradigm of a few of the many grammars possible (see diagram on page 80). The numbers 1–24 identify some but not all of the grammars possible. Since we can arrange the SVO in five other orders (one of them the VSO shown here), the SVOQ (subject-verb-object-qualifier) in 23 other orders, the J,I,SVOQ (interjection-invocation-subject-verb-object-qualifier) in 719 others; since omission generates still more patterns; and since we may find other uses or

BASIC PATTERN (kernel)	CHARACTERISTIC ACTIVITY		
	Analyzing sentences	Predicting which word comes next in sentences	Generating sentences
a sentence =			
subject+predicate	1	2	3
NP+VP	4	5	6
sentence-modifier +(NP+VP)	7	8	9
1234	10	11	12
SVO	13	14	15
SVOQ	16	17	18
J, I, SVOQ	19	20	21
VSO	22	23	24
(etc.)			

activities for grammars, this diagram represents only one corner of a very large and complex set of possible grammars, a set whose boundaries we cannot yet determine. Each grammar has its characteristic scope, activity, and degree of intensionality or extensionality:

> *Grammar 1:* Like Latin grammars, traditional English grammars concentrate on analyzing sentences, on taking them apart in order to name and classify their parts, but since their definitions of these parts (words, phrases, clauses) include ambiguities, so do their analyses, as C. C. Fries has shown.(4)

> *Grammars 4 and 6:* Chomsky calls his 1957 and 1965 grammars "generative," but he also uses them to analyze existing sentences (grammar 4). Like traditional grammar, their scope includes isolated single sentences; in other words, they tend to ignore the expansion of single sentences into whole pieces of speech or writing, and the verbal, social,

and paralinguistic and kinesic contexts and causes and results of the isolated sentences they generate or analyze.

Grammars 7 and 9: Bruce L. Liles' transformational grammar adds a sentence modifier such as an adverb or an interjection before Chomsky's NP+VP, thus producing a greater variety of sentences.(5)

Grammars 2, 5, 8, 11, etc.: Claude Shannon and Warren Weaver's information theory concentrates on predicting what word might come next in any pattern, but does not say which words or patterns to start with, nor which patterns produce grammatical English sentences.(6)

Grammars 10 and 12: C. C. Fries' code for the parts of speech and sentence-patterns suggests that he thought 1234 (*noun+linking verb+adjective+adverb*, as in "Sue is sad now") the basic sentence-pattern of English: we may see it as a more specific variation of the *X-is-Y*, and thus see Fries' grammar as particularly intensional. Fries ignored questions of meaning, including the semantic consequences of such a choice of pattern, and used 1234 to classify words as this or that part of speech (grammar 10). He also ignored how we get from one sentence to the next, as when we expand a single sentence into a whole piece of writing, as did Paul Roberts, whose high school textbook *Patterns of English* shows students how to use various patterns, 1234 included, to generate sentences.(7)

Grammar 15: Fenollosa advocated SVOs as the basis from which to produce prose and poetry; he said the SVO's terser, more concrete sentences represent the world's actor-action-thing acted upon cause-result relationship more vividly, directly, and precisely than does the *X-is-Y*'s merely verbal classifying, which, if true, makes 15 a particularly extensional grammar (and 18 and 21 even more precisely so).

Grammar 18: By adding adverbial qualifiers to Fenollosa's SVO, the SVOQ includes the dates Korzybski recommended, to produce sentences that tell us not only *who? did what? to whom?* (the SVO) but also *when? where? how? why?* We need to ask the first six of these questions to have information to report, and the last question, the *why,* to explain those reports. Permutations of the SVOQ define the degrees of grammaticality of sentences (the more scrambled or interrupted the SVOQ, the fewer native speakers of English who find the sentences grammatical, or even understandable), and word-blocks representing the S, V, O, and Q and the types of words that cluster with them make the distinctions between *permutation, addition,* and *omission* (rearranging, adding, or removing such parts of patterns as the S or V or O or Q: the three basic types of transformation) and *clustering* (rewriting one part of a pattern in a more complicated way) and *substitution* (of one word for another in any part of a pattern) more clearly than Chomsky's grammars do. Also, by expanding upon and repeating SVOQs in complex and compound ways with subordinate and coordinate conjunctions, we can expand single sentences into whole pieces of writing, and can do so extensionally and coherently by using the S, V, O, and Q to ask connected series of usefully specific questions.(8)

Grammar 21: I devised grammar 18, which I call "transformational rhetoric," to produce tersely informative written English; by adding *interjections* (such as *yes, oh, ow*) plus invocations to name the person to whom the speaker addresses the sentence to the SVOQ, we can produce such conversational sentences as "Hey, John, I love Mary now!": J for *interjection,* I for *invocation.*

Grammar 22: James D. McCawley of the University of Chicago proposes a VSO-based grammar for analyzing the deep structures of English sentences. He sees this grammar as transformationally tidier and semantically more accurate than grammar 4, but my experiments with permutations of the SVOQ show that without an extra transformation back to the order SVO, speakers of English find verb-first arrangements of sentences less grammatical and more confusing than any other orders.(9)

Of the others, the possible grammars apparently not yet developed by anyone:

3, 6, and 9 would produce sentences, but 15, 18, and 21 seem more economically specific, generating a greater variety of grammatical sentences (and of useful questions and answers) with fewer operations.

13, 16, and 19 analyze sentences as variations or combinations of SVO, SVOQ, and J, I, SVOQ. Analytic grammars (1, 4, 7, etc., down the lefthand column) tend to rewrite single sentences as many simpler sentences, as in Chomsky's search for a deep structure, the very simple pattern NP+VP, which he seems to hope to find in every sentence of every language. Generative grammars (such as 12, 15, 18) tend to assemble simpler parts and patterns into more complex patterns, including whole pieces of writing (and grammar 24 seems an exceptionally roundabout and cumbersome way to do so).

An E-Prime Grammar

One of Korzybski's students, D. David Bourland, Jr., writes and advocates what he calls E-Prime, English without the verb *to be* in any of its forms, and has begun a paper on its sentence patterns.(10) A grammar of a part of English should prove at least a little simpler and shorter than a grammar of all the language (among other patterns, an E-Prime grammar would exclude passive verbs, many complex verbs, and Fries' 1234 and its variations). A grammar can show us how to choose which patterns, and which words to put into those patterns, one word after another. Why bother? Think of the time needlessly wasted by people trying to write, or writing in confusing ways that mislead or puzzle others, and of the consequences of such misuses of language.

Some Recipes for Is-less Writing

The reliable uses of *X-is-Y* apparently include only the following:

1. Sentences about systems of signs that say one sign or combination of signs *equals* or means the same as or can replace another, as in "1+1=2" and in the rewrite rules of Chomskian grammars, where the arrow in "NP→D+N" means the NP (noun phrase) *can be written as* a D plus an N (a determiner like *the* plus a noun like *dog*), but notice that an ambiguity here may confuse us: we can in fact write or rewrite a noun phrase in many ways, but does the writer of the rule distinguish precisely between his limited set of rules as a never-total map of the language, and the much more complex language itself? Does he mean his arrow to mean (1) *can be rewritten only in this way*, or (2) *may be rewritten in this among many other ways*?

2. Negative statements defining the limitations of language, such as Korzybski's reminder that cow_1 is *not* cow_2, etc.

3. Statements about measurements, such as "It's thirty below!" whose accuracy needs checking, changes in time and place, etc.

4. Other predictions, such as "There's a cat in my desk," where *is* means *you will find*, whose accuracy needs checking and changes in time, etc.

But in all four cases, more specific active verbs such as *equals, differs from, measures, find*, can replace the ambiguous *is*, and we need them to distinguish between its four uses here. In arithmetic, for instance, 1+1=2, but in fact, add two one-pound forces and the result may measure anything from zero to two pounds, depending upon the angles involved and possibly also other factors: statements about self-contained systems of signs (item 1) differ from statements of facts (items 3 or 4).

Linguists often list *is* as one of the ten most-used words, and the most-used verb, in English, but to say "Grass is green" can blind us to the complex and changing cause–result relationships between the light, the air, the grass, and our eyes, which *may* make *some* grass seem what we but *not* everyone calls "green" to *some* observers. To say "I'm sad" may seem a report, but it judges sensations, we can say it without cause, and it may prove a deceptive or a destructive self-fulfilling prophecy: say it often enough, and you may make it true by a process of self-hypnosis.

Instead of the *X-is-Y*, we may use these patterns (and their various elaborations) as recipes not just for sentences, but for whole pieces of writing:

1. SVOQ (or J, I, SVOQ) to ask and answer the questions we need to make reports and inferences, and to produce such variations as 2, 3, 4, and 5.

2. Balanced equation sentences, such as *"The more X, the more* (or *less) Y,"* to sum up how one function varies as another does, thus making some hyphenated term more specific: we can make the *weight-speed-stopping distance* clearer as well as more specific by saying "The greater the weight or speed, the longer the stopping distance" (which a mathematical formula would make still more precise).(11)

3. Predictions link two or more SVOQs in compound or complex ways to say "do *what,* and *what else* might happen?"

4. Recipes list a series of steps, operations to perform, all in the right order, as in "To make gingersnaps, first do 1, then 2, then . . . ," using a series of subjectless VOQ commands until the last step completes the finished product. Like other predictions, recipes help us choose what we want to do, and we judge their usefulness and accuracy by whatever actually happens. Recipes also tell us precisely what to do to achieve a goal, and when and how, and thus whether we can. No other pattern so concentrates on both particular physical acts and their order, making both its references and its structure so directly extensional.

5. *Thesis-proof-conclusion* arguments can make us look beyond words to facts by giving us one or more reasons after an "SVOQ *because* . . . ," or one or more examples after an "SVOQ, *as we can see it* . . . ": both the reasons and the examples invite us to check their accuracy, and thus our willingness to believe the argument. The conclusion answers some version of the question "so what?" and its answer also invites or needs extensional checking.

From such repetitions, variations, and questionings of SVOQs we can start to write. To such *is*-less structures, we can add any or all of Korzybski's extensional devices. We can also replace any one-word S or O in them with more complexly informative clusters of words, including the pattern *X-is-Y* (or Z or . . .), which may encourage us to look at a subject in many different ways, as in these variations of the *X-is-Y*:

> Considered as a politician, Hamlet . . .
>
> As a son, Hamlet . . .
>
> As a worried king's stepson, Hamlet . . .
>
> As a lover for Ophelia, Hamlet . . .   does what to whom?
>
> Used as an excuse for repressive actions, Hamlet . . .
>
> As an example of manic-depressive behavior, Hamlet . . .

We may find many such combinations trivial because predictable, of course, in that they tell us little or nothing we didn't know already. But as Arthur Koestler has shown, unexpected combinations and connections produce discoveries, including jokes, poems, tragedies.(12) Changing from the dogmatically static and final *X-is-Y* to the tentative looking at an X *as* Y, *as* Z, etc., in many different ways, may help us escape the blind ruts of habit by finding such combinations or connections, letting us turn apparent failures into successes: what doesn't work *as* synthetic rubber *might* work *as* snuff *or* glue *or* a fuel for rockets . . . some "mistakes" seem worth making, for what we can learn from them: when at first something doesn't work, try again in a different way or time or circumstances (the changes and differences that Korzybski's extensional devices help us notice).

Korzybski's map-territory metaphor, itself an example of the X-*as*-Y, suggests that we can map any territory in many different ways, and can analyze or produce samples of a language by many different grammars. Traditional grammars analyze sentences by naming the parts they isolate "noun," "verb," etc. Transformational grammars analyze sentences in terms of the changes needed to transform one sentence-pattern to another. But a generative *is*-less grammar can extend our awareness beyond words to the world, by giving us recipes that produce reports and explanations, and questions for finding facts and testing them, and *X-is-Y*'s to suggest fresh approaches, thus helping us to explore the world before we judge it.

NOTES AND REFERENCES

1. Alfred Korzybski, *Science and Sanity: An Introduction to Non-Aristotelian Systems and General Semantics*, 1933, 4th ed. (Lakeville, Conn.: International Non-Aristotelian Library, 1958), xlvii–lii.
2. C. S. Peirce, *Philosophical Writings*, ed. Justus Buchler (New York: Dover, 1955), 102–15.
3. Ernest Fenollosa, "The Chinese Written Character as a Medium for Poetry," in *Instigations*, ed. Ezra Pound (New York: Boni and Liveright, 1920), 357–88;

Noam Chomsky, *Syntactic Structures* (The Hague: Mounton, 1957) and *Aspects of the Theory of Syntax* (Cambridge: M.I.T. Press, 1965); ;Robert Ian Scott, "Two Ways to Determine the Most Useful Kernel for English," *Linguistics* 45 (1968):67–75.
4. C. C. Fries, *The Structure of English* (New York: Harcourt, Brace, 1952).
5. Bruce L. Liles, *An Introductory Transformational Grammar* (Englewood Cliffs, N.J.: Prentice-Hall, 1971).
6. Claude Shannon and Warren Weaver, *The Mathematical Theory of Communication* (Urbana: University of Illinois Press, 1949).
7. Paul Roberts, *Patterns of English* (New York: Harcourt, Brace, 1956).
8. Robert Ian Scott, *The Writer's Self-Starter* (Toronto: Collier-Macmillan, 1972) and "Teaching Elementary English Grammar with Color-Coded Word-Blocks," *Elementary English* 45, 7 (1968): 972–891; see also Wendell Johnson, "You Can't Write Writing," in *The Use and Misuse of Language*, ed. S. I. Hayakawa (Greenwich, Conn.: Fawcett, 1962), 101–11.
9. James D. McCawley, "English as a VSO Language," *Language* 46, 2 (part 1)(1970:286–99; Robert Ian Scott, "A Permutational Test of Grammaticality," *Lingua* 24, 1(1969):11–18; Andreas Koutsoudas, "Gapping, Conjunction Reduction, and Coordinate Deletion," *Foundations of Language* 7, 3(1971):337–86.
10. D. David Bourland, Jr., "A Linguistic Note: Writing in E-Prime," *General Semantics Bulletin* 32–33 (1965-1966):111–14; "The Semantics of a Non-Aristotelian Language," *General Semantics Bulletin* 35 (1968):60–63; Anonymous, "The Un-Isness of Is," *Time*, Canadian ed., May 23, 1969, 40. I want to thank Mr. Bourland also for his detailed comments of March 5, 1973, on an earlier version of this paper.
11. Notice that we can omit any part of the SVOQ: the S in commands, the V in such "balanced equations," the O, the Q, but we understand these omissions in terms of the SVOQ as a whole set or field of relationships that have a topology of their own.
12. Arthur Koestler, *The Act of Creation* (London: Hutchinson, 1964).

SPEAKING IN E-PRIME:
An Experimental Method for
Integrating General Semantics
into Daily Life

E. W. KELLOGG III

I FIRST READ Alfred Korzybski's *Science and Sanity* in 1976, and felt deeply impressed by the manifest validity and comprehensive character of his work on non-Aristotelian thinking.(1) Even so, I at first had very little success in incorporating the insights gained into my daily life. The principles seemed so transparently obvious in hindsight ("the map is not the territory," "the word is not the thing," the repeal of "the law of the excluded middle," etc.), that I made the common beginner's error of assuming that simply reading *about* general semantics would train one in the *use of* general semantics. Although some books proved very helpful to me (in particular Ken Keyes' *How To Develop Your Thinking Ability*, with those delightful and singularly apropos cartoons by Ted Key), it seemed clear that having an intellectual understanding of non-Aristotelian thought does not necessarily allow one to practice it.(2)

I began a self-training program in which I focused on practically applying a single aspect of general semantics on any given day. For example, I might focus on the multiordinality of terms, and make a serious effort to increase my awareness of the orders of abstraction inherent in what I read, said, and heard during my daily activities. On another day I might try to eliminate the either-or, all-or-none orientation by thinking more in terms of possibilities and probabilities. As I gained experience, I found some small, but significant, changes in my "mental machinery" resulting from my self-training efforts, including an increasing number of *spontaneous* instances of non-Aristotelian thinking. Even so, these efforts proved mostly ineffectual, as I continued to habitually think and evaluate in the old Aristotelian way. Clearly, I needed a simple, but comprehensive system of discipline that would force me to incorporate

Reprinted from *Et cetera* 44, no. 2 (1987).

the various principles of general semantics into daily life.

When I had almost given up on finding such a discipline, I discovered D. D. Bourland Jr.'s article "A Linguistic Note: Writing in E-Prime" in a back issue of the *General Semantics Bulletin*.(3) In essence, the term E-Prime refers to an English language derivative that eliminates any use of the verb "to be" (basically "am," "is," "was," "are," "were," "be," and "been"). In this article Bourland argued for the use of E-Prime as a writing discipline that allows one to minimize many "false to facts" linguistic patterns inherent in ordinary English usage. Without going deeply into the advantages of E-Prime at this point, its use automatically eliminates the false to facts "is of identity" (i.e. John is a man) and the "is of predication" (i.e. The leaf is green), two main stumbling blocks to non-Aristotelian thinking. I decided to make E-Prime an integral part of my self-training efforts. If I couldn't consistently *act* in accordance with general semantics principles I could at least *write* in accordance with them!

At first, my writing in E-Prime sounded stilted and contrived, and I had to write first drafts in ordinary English, and then laboriously translate them. I used E-Prime exclusively in my personal writing, and soon gained enough facility that I wrote, albeit awkwardly, first draft versions in it. Fortunately, at this point in my career I had the task of writing my dissertation. The exercise of writing the first draft in E-Prime gave me a practical and personally convincing demonstration of the potential power of E-Prime as a catalyst and clarifier of thought. The use of E-Prime clarified many aspects of my experimental work, and made obvious many inherent assumptions that ordinary English usage had concealed. Although the final version did not make exclusive use of E-Prime (I wrote too awkwardly in it for that), I had gained a great deal of experience in writing in E-Prime, and solid confirmation of its value as a tool in promoting non-Aristotelian thought.

Over the next few years I wrote exclusively in E-Prime in both personal and professional communications. As I gained experience, I found it easier to express myself, until I reached the point where writing in E-Prime felt more natural for me than writing in ordinary English. During the summer of 1978, after I had explained the value of E-Prime to a few acquaintances, one of them asked me why I didn't *speak* in E-Prime if I felt so strongly about its value as a tranformational tool. I realized that I no longer had a satisfactory answer to that question. When I had originally begun writing in E-Prime, I had found it so difficult that I had not even considered the possibility of speaking in it, but in 1978 this situation no longer applied. Writing in E-Prime had already proved itself to me many times over as a valuable training discipline in non-Aristotelian thinking. Would not speaking in E-Prime prove far more valuable?

Haltingly, and with many mistakes and errors, I began the task of learning to speak in E-Prime.

How Does E-Prime Work?

At this point, it seems appropriate to give a fuller explanation of how E-Prime might work. In his book *Language, Thought and Reality*, Benjamin Lee Whorf gives numerous examples of languages and cultures that support his "principle of linguistic relativity."(4) This principle states that the structure of the language you use influences the way you perceive "reality," as well as how you behave with respect to that perceived reality. Although one could describe E-Prime simply as English without any use of the verb "to be," such a definition misses the profound changes in personal orientation resulting from such a change.

In essence, E-Prime consists of a more descriptive and extensionally oriented derivative of English that automatically tends to bring the user back to the level of first-person experience. For example, if you saw a man, reeking of whisky, stagger down the street and then collapse, you might think (in ordinary English) "He is drunk." In E-Prime one would think instead "He acts drunk," or "He looks drunk," both of which statements obviously coming closer to an accurate description of the actual experience, and involving fewer covert assumptions than the English original. After all, one might have encountered an actor (practicing the part of a drunken man), a man who had spilled alcohol on himself undergoing a seizure of some kind, etc., etc. The E-Prime statement still leaves these possibilities open, whereas the "is" statement does not. Although E-Prime usually reduces hidden assumptions, it does not exclude them (for example, you may have seen a woman, or a robot, or an alien, etc. that looked like a man and acted drunk). E-Prime fosters a worldview in which the user perceives situations as changeable rather than static, and where verbal formulations derived from experience indicate possibilities rather than certainties. Subjectively, I have found my creativity greatly enhanced, as many problems that *"are* unsolvable" in ordinary English only *"seem* unsolvable" in E-Prime! This shift in attitude can make a great difference.

Thus, removing the "to be" verb from English results in a language of a more phenomenological character, in that this change automatically causes a reduction of the number of assumptions in even simple sentences. Statements made in E-Prime almost always mirror first person experience far more adequately than the "is" statements they replace. E-Prime also greatly encourages one to use the active voice ("Smith$_1$ did it") rather than the often misleading and information-poor passive voice ("it was done"). Of course, as Bourland pointed out, one can continue the modification of E-Prime even further, adding for example the alterations and non-Aristotelian tools that Korzybski recommended (dating, indexing, etc.), bringing one to E-Prime$_k$. My own version of E-Prime (E-Prime$_p$) aims at a phenomenological ideal, of ever more adequately representing the territory of my experience while ever more clearly communicating with others.

Perhaps I can make the potential advantages of such a phenomenological approach clearer by drawing an analogy with computer languages. Computers operate with a variety of different programming languages, but these differ tremendously in their efficiency and inherent versatility. A beginner usually learns to program using BASIC, a computer language that most resembles English, which makes it easy to learn and so initially the most convenient language to use. But the novice programmer pays a price in using BASIC, in that the computer has to translate BASIC into the "machine language" it uses in processing information, and which actually corresponds to the "computer's experience." This translation takes time and also involves the inherent risk of errors entering the process. One also loses versatility, as BASIC (a language composed of very high order abstractions for the computer) can only include a partial representation of the available operations programmable in machine language itself. Thus an operation programmed in BASIC may take thousands of times longer for a computer to execute than one written in machine language, while an operation available in machine language may prove impossible to program in BASIC. Thus one can draw the general conclusion that the more closely a computer programming language (the map) mirrors machine language (the territory), the greater the potential efficiency and accuracy of that language in communicating directions and information to the computer itself.

Although humans do not appear to process information as computers do, much of the analogy still applies. For humans, "machine language" corresponds to the "silent level" of experience. One might expect therefore that the more closely a language models the

Speaking in E-Prime

structures of experience, the more efficiently and accurately it could work in external communication (with others) and internal information processes (with oneself, thinking). As an example, let's take an ordinary statement in English, such as "The leaf is green," and make a gradient of translations, each perhaps more adequately representing the "silent level" of experience itself.

STATEMENT	LITERAL TRANSLATION
The leaf is green.	the leaf = green
The leaf has a green color.	The leaf has a green color for everyone.
I see a green leaf.	At this moment I see a green-colored leaf.
SILENT LEVEL	(. . . .)

As this example illustrates, an E-Prime version of an "is" statement can increase the adequacy of the statement in conveying a "silent level" experience. Of course native speakers usually understand that one should not literally interpret a statement such as "the leaf is green" as "the leaf = green," and that it usually means something closer to "Look at the green leaf." But why not say so in the first place! Or to take another example:

STATEMENT	LITERAL TRANSLATION
$Smith_1$ is a drunk.	$Smith_1$ = drunk.
$Smith_1$ acts like a drunk.	$Smith_1$ acts like a drunk all the time.
$Smith_1$ often acts like a drunk.	
SILENT LEVEL	(. . . .)

Some Possibilities of the "Silent Level" Experience

1. $Smith_1$ threw up on my rug at my party last night. (Actually he threw up because of eating spoiled fish.)

2. When $Smith_1$ walks he staggers, and he goes around in a state of mental confusion. (Actually, $Smith_1$ has Alzheimer's disease.)

3. Smith$_1$ drank a fifth of whisky at my party last night, acted in a belligerent and obnoxious manner, and then threw up on my oriental carpet. He has acted similarly several times before, keeps liquor in his desk at work, and smelled of whisky every morning last week. (Smith$_1$ really does drink too much!).

Obviously, one can reach a point of diminishing returns by describing experience too closely. Either E-Prime or E-Prime$_k$ strike a nice balance in this regard, as they tend to "keep one honest" and aware of the divergence between described and experienced events (by the use of such words as *seems, appears, acts,* etc.). On the whole, E-Prime statements use the same number of words as their ordinary English counterparts, while providing additional useful information in the who, what, and how categories.

Thus, writing and speaking in E-Prime confer a number of advantages to anyone seriously interested in training themselves in non-Aristotelian thinking. I have found speaking in E-Prime an efficient and effective discipline, as its use forces me to incorporate general semantic principles in an integral way almost every time that I open my mouth! I also frequently translate the speech of others into E-Prime, and this has served me well as a buffer against signal reactions in my own thinking and behavior. I can often smooth out arguments in my vicinity simply by interjecting E-Prime translations of key statements into conversation. For example, if someone says "That is a stupid idea!" I might reply "What don't you like about it?" rather than "It is not!" Principally because of this tactic, I haven't had a real argument with anyone in years, although I have had a number of heated discussions!

Still, what about the disadvantages of E-Prime? Do any exist? Unfortunately, yes, and the prospective student will have to decide on the relative importance of them. First, you lose the helping verb function of "to be" indicating a continuous process. For example the statement "It is raining outside," translates to "It rains outside." One also loses the use of "to be" indicating a future tense, as in "He is coming." In E-Prime one could say "He comes" (dramatic!), or "He will come later." The E-Prime versions may sound awkward to some, but to me it seems more a matter of taste and convention than of any real loss of meaning.

To a large extent, one gives up much of the power of manipulation when writing and speaking in E-Prime. A number of therapeutic disciplines, such as Ericksonian hypnosis, or Neuro-Linguistic Programming, depend on techniques involving ambivalence in language and primitive patterns of magical thinking (i.e. "the word *is* the thing," "the part *is* equal to the whole," etc.) to induce a state of confusion and suggestibility and finally a beneficial change in the patient.(5, 6, 7) Such therapists use "fire to fight fire," reportedly with a great deal of success.(8) Unfortunately, such methods of treatment foster and depend on primitive thinking patterns, which stand in direct opposition to the intent behind E-Prime, or of general semantics for that matter. E-Prime aims at clarification, not obscuration of language; at specificity, rather than ambiguity; at communication, rather than manipulation. Its use might substantially handicap therapists of this kind.

Even outside of therapy, most routinely use language to manipulate others, to provoke a physical or emotional response. In many ways "is" statements have much greater emotional impact than their E-Prime$_k$ equivalents. "You are an idiot!" has a much greater emotional impact than "You act like an idiot sometimes!" "Is of identity" statements have the ability to powerfully stimulate signal reactions, not even giving a chance for the unprepared individual to buffer the blow. Speaking in E-Prime may not seem like much of a disadvantage in this respect under ordinary circumstances, but it can constitute a handicap in using language of the form "You are a #@%&*!" However, spoken language has its emotional impact not only through *what* you say but through *how* you say it. Voice tone, rhythm, and inflection can drastically change the perceived meaning of a sentence. An innocuous "Yes dear," said sarcastically, can provoke an explosive response ("Don't you use that tone of voice to me!"). Spoken language thus has both cortical and thalamic (or perhaps right and left brain) components that can work together congruently or antagonistically. In this sense, E-Prime only modulates and does not control the affective content of speech.

In a more poetic context the E-Prime user loses much of the power of metaphor ("He is a tiger"), although one can compensate for this loss by using similes ("He acts like a tiger!"). As E-Prime aims at honesty and integrity in communication and thought, it may seem obvious that as it progresses toward this goal, the user correspondingly loses the ability to deceive, confuse, and manipulate. Some used car salesmen might find this an insuperable obstacle, but therapists do have possible alternatives. For example, Albert Ellis' Rational Therapy might substitute for more manipulative techniques, as it has aims similar to those of general semantics. In fact, Ellis and others translated some of his major works into E-Prime, which makes them perhaps the only books currently (1987) published in such a format.(9)

Of course, learning to write and speak in E-Prime involves the considerable disadvantage that one has to devote a great deal of time and effort to the task, especially in the early stages. Writing acceptably in E-Prime initially involves additional drafts, and even final versions may sound awkward and stilted in style until you learn the ropes. I've included an E-Prime Primer in a later section, in which I pass on some suggestions that might help an E-Prime student during the transition period. At least when writing you usually have the time to polish your work—a luxury not usually available when speaking E-Prime!

When I first tried speaking in E-Prime I quickly found myself in trouble. Often, three-quarters of the way through a sentence I found myself with no way out but through an "is, was, are, or were." I left a lot of sentences hanging in the air because of this! Other times "to be" contractions (I'm, it's, you're) crept in, usually unnoticed until after I had finished a sentence. And worst of all, occasionally I found myself speaking in "pidgin E-Prime" of the "me Tarzan, you Jane" ilk, where I simply left a form of "to be" out of a sentence and hoped for the best. Initially I talked much less than usual, and had to carefully consider and mentally rehearse each sentence before I said anything. I have no doubt I sounded rather odd during my early months of speaking in E-Prime, but strangely enough almost no one ever remarked on this. Actually, I did receive one comment on my speech about a year after I had begun speaking in E-Prime. At a conference, a perceptive woman wondered about my nationality. She apparently had a very good ear for accents, but could not place mine, and wanted to know the country I had originally come from!

A Proposed Program for Learning to Write and Speak in E-Prime

As a first step, concentrate on using E-Prime in unimportant notes or letters you write, and in your personal diary. At first you may go through several drafts before you reach an acceptable version, but persevere. After you have practiced writing in E-Prime for a week or so and feel comfortable with it to some extent, I *highly* recommend that you either write a biographical sketch of yourself (a page or two) in E-Prime, or better yet translate an already existing version (like your résumé) into E-Prime. This exercise may demonstrate some of the inherent advantages of E-Prime to you as nothing else can.

After you have gained some real facility in writing in E-Prime, begin to use it for more serious work. Although it seems a good idea to have a goal of 100 percent E-Prime in a final draft, expect to have a few "to be" sentences in the text in cases where the E-Prime version sounds overly awkward, etc. Count any reduction in the incidence of "to be" in your written work as an achievement in the right direction. With continued effort your expertise in writing in E-Prime will increase to the point where few, if any, readers will detect any abnormality of writing style: more than likely you will receive compliments as to the clarity and improved quality of your finished work.

When you write easily, and feel satisfied with the way that you communicate in E-Prime, you will probably already have begun to occasionally speak in it. At some point, if you really want to reap the full benefits of the discipline, you will have to make a serious commitment to speaking in E-Prime *exclusively*, because *speaking* in E-Prime forces one to learn how to *think* in E-Prime. Just as with learning a foreign language, a time comes when you begin to think in the language rather than just translate sentences into it, so with learning to speak in E-Prime. Unfortunately this process usually requires total immersion in the foreign language and culture, and a serious commitment on the student's part. As we do not live in an E-Prime culture, this makes your own personal commitment to speak in E-Prime doubly important.

A Primer for Writing and Speaking in E-Prime (Practical Hints)

Simply put, E-Prime proper allows you the use of the entire vocabulary of the English language with the following exceptions: *be, is, am, are, was, were, been, being* (as a verb), and the "to be" verb contractions of *m's, 's,* and *'re*. To begin, you need only focus on the simple(?!) task of not using any of these words.

E-Prime$_k$ adds to the basic E-Prime structure by employing the extensional devices Korzybski recommended (indexes, dates, etc., quotes, hyphens) which encourage awareness of abstracting, while restricting language usage (for example avoiding "allness" statements) to forms that encourage a non-elementalistic, and non-absolutistic point of view.(10) See Korzybski(1, pp. xlviii–1) and Keyes(2) for further information.

Finally we have my own preferred form of E-Prime (E-Prime$_p$), which operates from a phenomenological point of view.(11) This form includes the modifications already mentioned for E-Prime$_k$, plus any others that allow the language that one uses to more adequately represent the territory of the "silent level" of one's actual experience. E-Prime$_p$ aims at a practical, yet transparent and presuppositionless language that reduces the discrepancies between the "map" and "territory" of experience to a bare minimum. This describes my goal in the continuing transformation of my personal language, and though not presently attainable, like the North Star, it has proved itself a useful navigational aid.

You may use these general substitutes for forms of "to be"—seem(s), appear(s), feel(s), act(s), look(s), etc. However, try not to overdo these terms.

Suggestion #1: If you find it difficult to compose a sentence in E-Prime, refer to the basic "silent level" experience and describe the actual event. Examples:

STATEMENT	POSSIBLE E-PRIME TRANSLATION
The World of Null-A is a great book!	I really enjoyed reading the book *The World of Null-A!*
I am fine.	I feel fine.
This food is good.	This food tastes good.

Suggestion #2: Take an "is" statement at a high level of abstraction/assumption and bring it down to earth. Remove the assumptions and work with what you have left.

STATEMENT	POSSIBLE E-PRIME TRANSLATION
Joan is smart.	Joan makes $500,000 a year.
Cleve is smart.	Cleve scored 160 on an I.Q. test.
Linda is helpful.	Linda helped me.

Suggestion #3: Replace the "is" with an action verb.

STATEMENT	POSSIBLE E-PRIME TRANSLATION
David is a doctor.	David practices medicine.
Risa is a teacher.	Risa teaches epistemics.
He is a car mechanic.	He repairs cars.

Speaking in E-Prime

Suggestion #4: Say what you mean.

STATEMENT	POSSIBLE E-PRIME TRANSLATION
Is Leia there?	Can I speak with Leia?
What is your name?	What do you call yourself?
How are you?	How do you feel?

Suggestion #5: Change the sentence from the passive to the active voice.

STATEMENT	POSSIBLE E-PRIME TRANSLATION
It was done.	Olof did it.
The experiment was conducted . . .	Mike conducted the experiment . . .
Jack was blessed.	The Pope blessed Jack.

In speaking E-Prime in a non-E-Prime world, I sometimes resort to "pidgin E-Prime" in order to avoid statements that, although they make better logical sense than their English equivalents, sound awkward. For example, if someone asks me "Who are you?" instead of saying "I call myself Ed," I simply say "Ed." Of course, I assume the questioner really meant to ask "How do you label yourself?" and not "With what verbal concepts do you identify yourself as an existential being?" Other languages (for example French and Spanish) do in fact ask questions about one's name in a logical manner (Comment vous appelez vous?, Como se llama usted?). No matter how improved E-Prime versions of idiomatic English phrases seem from a general semantics point of view, they may still sound a little peculiar and out of the ordinary to the unprepared listener. However, in general E-Prime statements meet with as much social acceptance as, and in fact seem more readily understandable than, the "is" statements they replace.

While first learning to speak in E-Prime, you may have to mentally rehearse each sentence before you say it. For a while people might find your conversation a trifle limited, but they probably will not notice. Most people seem to like to hear themselves talk most of all, and they will appreciate your reticence! Nodding the head, looking intelligently interested and occasionally mouthing words and phrases such as "yes," or "perhaps," "I agree," "indeed," etc., etc., proves adequate in all but the rarest of conversations, where someone actually wants to talk *with* rather than *at* you! In such a case, if you take on an attitude of deep thought, even half finished phrases and pidgin E-Prime may command respect! As mentioned earlier with respect to arguments, I have also found it valuable to practice translating the statements of others into E-Prime during conversations, and then echoing the E-Prime statement back to the original speaker. Unfortunately, the opposite also occurs, and I have often found my E-Prime statement repeated back to me (or obviously interpreted) as the "to be" counterpart. However, repeated applications of the E-Prime version will usually drive the point across.

When you begin speaking in E-Prime you may often find yourself half-way through a sentence before you find to your dismay that you have nowhere to go but "is." I suggest in such cases you either stop, and rephrase the sentence into E-Prime, or if you have already finished the sentence, redo the sentence orally or mentally. As a final step to polishing your use of E-Prime, you might enlist a spouse or a close friend to monitor your speech. Offer them a dollar for each time they catch you using a form of "to be" in conversation, when you don't immediately correct yourself. Even though I have "mastered" spoken E-Prime I still routinely find various forms of "to be" (particularly the dreaded contractions I'm, he's, she's it's and you're) creeping into my speech. This should not surprise anyone—I live in an "is-rich" linguistic environment that has an impact on me through the spoken and written word. E-Prime cushions this impact, and can at least eventually lead to relative freedom from it in the privacy of one's own thoughts and speech.

Conclusion

To the public, the general semantics movement has offered many books that clearly and convincingly argue the case for the theoretical advantages and enhanced effectiveness of non-Aristotelian thinking as compared to the habitual "normal" thinking of Western culture. If general semantics has a major defect it occurs not at a theoretical but at a practical level. Even some people who have a longstanding commitment to general semantics freely admit to having minimal success in *comprehensively* practicing it in daily life. Over fifty years ago in *Science and Sanity* Korzybski clearly envisioned general semantics as a discipline that not only would do more than simply facilitate "clear thinking," but would profoundly affect the "whole man" in many aspects of daily life. Thus, although the aims of general semantics appear clear, general semantics needs more effective methods for attaining these aims.

In my experience, writing and speaking in E-Prime has proven itself an effective discipline for integrating non-Aristotelian thinking and behavior patterns even into so-called habitual or even "unconscious" levels. I not only write and speak in E-Prime, I think and even dream in it. Although E-Prime does not train one in *all* aspects of non-Aristotelian evaluation, it does a thorough job of training in some aspects, and facilitates the learning of many others. To my knowledge, objective studies of the actual benefits of writing and speaking in E-Prime do not exist at this time (1987). Subjectively, I have found it to have significantly enhanced my creativity and problem-solving ability, as well as my interpersonal communication skills. K. L. Ruskin made similar findings, when she used both written and spoken E-Prime$_k$ to advantage in a work situation involving the development of a complex computer system.(12) In my opinion, learning to write and speak in E-Prime can constitute the heart of an effective system of self-training in general semantics, and deserves serious consideration from anyone committed to the integration of non-Aristotelian processing into their habitual thought and behavior.

NOTES AND REFERENCES

1. Alfred Korzybski, *Science and Sanity* (4th ed., Lakeville, Conn.: International Non-Aristotelian Library and Publishing Company, 1958).
2. Kenneth S. Keyes, Jr., *How to Develop Your Thinking Ability* (New York: McGraw Hill, 1950 and 1979). Reprinted as *Taming Your Mind* (Coos Bay, Ore.: Love Line Books, 1975).
3. D. David Bourland, Jr., "A Linguistic Note: Writing in E-Prime," *General Semantics Bulletin* 32–33 (1965/1966):111–14.
4. Benjamin Lee Whorf, *Language, Thought, and Reality,* (Cambridge: M.I.T. Press, 1956). See also C. Weggelaar, "The Whorf Hypothesis: The Case of Dutch and English," *Et cetera* 39 (1982):332–43.
5. Richard Bandler and John Grinder, *Patterns of the Hypnotic Techniques of Milton H. Erickson, M.D., Volume 1* (Cupertino, Calif.: Meta Publications, 1975).
6. Richard Bandler and John Grinder, *The Structure of Magic: A Book about Language and Therapy, Volume I* (Palo Alto, Calif.: Science and Behavior Books, 1975).
7. Marcel Mauss, trans. by Robert Brain, *A General Theory of Magic,* (New York: Norton, 1972).
8. Sidney Rosen, ed., *My Voice Will Go With You: The Teaching Tales of Milton H. Erickson,* (New York: Norton, 1982).
9. Albert Ellis and Robert A. Harper, *A New Guide to Rational Living* (North Holly-

wood, Calif.: Wilshire, 1975), and Albert Ellis, *Anger: How to Live With and Without It* (Secaucus, N.J.: Citadel Press, 1977).
10. Alan Walker Read, "Language Revision by Deletion of Absolutisms," *Et cetera* 42 (1985):7–12.
11. For an introduction to phenomenology see Edmund Husserl's *Cartesian Meditations: An Introduction to Phenomenology,* trans. by Dorion Cairns (The Hague: Martinus Nijhoff, 1973) or Maurice Natanson's *Edmund Husserl: Philosopher of Infinite Tasks* (Evanston, Ill.: Northwestern University Press, 1973).
12. K. L. R. Bourland, "Coping with Semantic Problems in System Development," in *Coping with Increased Complexity: Implications of General Semantics and General Systems Theory,* ed. by D.E. Washburn and D.R. Smith (New York: Gordon and Breach Science Publishers, 1975). (This author also publishes under the name K. L. Ruskin.)
13. Those interested in seeing some examples of E-Prime in action in my scientific papers might look up the following:
    a. E. W. Kellogg III, M. C. Yost, and A. P. Krueger, "Superoxide Involvement in The Bactericidal Effects of Negative Air Ions on *Staphlococcus albus,*" *Nature* 281 (1979):400–401.
    b. E. W. Kellogg III, "Air Ions: Their Possible Biological Significance and Effects," *Journal of Bioelectricity* 3 (1984):119–36.
    c. E. W. Kellogg III and M. C. Yost, "The Effects of Long-Term Air Ion and D.C. Electric Field Exposures on Survival Characteristics in Female NAMRU Mice," *Journal of Gerontology* 41(1986):147–53.

D. David Bourland, Jr.

TO BE OR NOT TO BE: E-Prime as a Tool for Critical Thinking

E-Prime!—The Fundamentals

AMBROSE BIERCE, in his famous *Devil's Dictionary*, defined logic as "The art of thinking and reasoning in strict accordance with the limitations and incapacities of the human misunderstanding." As we become conscious of our misunderstandings, we improve the quality of our thinking, and most particularly our thinking about thinking, which Richard Paul defines as "critical thinking." In this chapter I will describe an offshoot of Korzybski's system (26, 27) known as E-Prime: English without any form of the verb "to be." The name comes from the equation $E'=E-e$, where E represents the words of the English language, and e represents the inflected forms of "to be."

We have heard of the unfortunate effects produced on English literature by the infamous "Person from Porlock." A similarly unknown "Person from Tolland (Connecticut)" produced a more beneficial effect on me when, in 1949, I held a Fellowship for study with Alfred Korzybski at the Institute of General Semantics in Lime Rock, Connecticut. This Person, whose name I can no longer retrieve, wrote to the Institute suggesting that, in view of the problems Korzybski had discussed in connection with the "*is* of Identity" and the "*is* of Predication," perhaps we should just abandon *all* uses of the verb "to be." While no one else at the Institute seemed particularly interested in this suggestion, it struck me as having considerable merit, provided one could really do it.

An earlier version of this paper appeared in *Et cetera* 46, no. 3 (Fall 1989).

The Institute staff at that time had perhaps reached its apex, consisting of Korzybski, M. Kendig, Charlotte Schuchardt (later Mrs. Allen Walker Read), Ralph Hamilton, Lynn Gates, David Levine, and myself. Guthrie Janssen had just finished editing *Selections from Science and Sanity* (28) and still lived in the immediate area. The letter from Tolland did not excite anyone else in this collection of critical thinkers, but it gnawed at me. The time fit me just right: I had a paper in preparation for the Third Congress on General Semantics. I decided to revise it once again to see if I could say, and indeed say better, what I wanted to convey without using any form of "to be." In the process of this revision, I acquired an intermittent, but severe, headache that lasted for about a week. The final paper had a peculiar clarity, despite the fact that one "was" crept in. It eventually appeared as reference (3).

Between 1949 and 1964 I used E-Prime in several papers, but did not discuss this matter lest I become regarded as some kind of nut. Finally some close friends convinced me that a wider audience might feel interested in E-Prime. Encouraged particularly by my friend Charles Chandler of Princeton, New Jersey, I prepared a brief report that appeared as reference (4). Subsequently two other studies discussed applications to the non-Aristotelian premises and to political documents.(5, 7)

In early 1969 the New York Society for General Semantics invited me to give a talk on E-Prime. This I did, trying to do so *in* E-Prime. By and large I succeeded (some people listened precisely for this—then and now they consist of a sharp, feisty bunch). Subsequently, Kellogg (23) accomplished this and recommends it highly. His excellent *Et cetera* paper contains many helpful suggestions.

Interest in E-Prime reached a peak in 1969. After mention of this oddity in a footnote of a paper by Allen Walker Read, *Time* magazine sent an interviewer to me to discuss E-Prime. A friendly article appeared in the issue of May 23, 1969. Unfortunately, in the process of writing this friendly piece, *Time* attributed to me two quotations of statements I never made: one incredibly awkward, and the other such a gross transgression of E-Prime that it actually made publication at the bottom of a piece in *The New Yorker* magazine. Thanks, *Time!*

Introducing E-Prime

Let us turn now to what we can expect to happen to our writing and talking when we in fact do so in E-Prime.

Depending on exactly how one defines "word," most scholars regard the English language as embracing some one to two million "words," or lexical items. (Note 1.) In E-Prime one simply does without twenty or so of those lexical items, specifically the "to be" family: be, is, am, are, was, were, been, being; plus contractions—'m, 's, 're; plus various archaic and dialectal forms—e.g., war, wert, beest, amn't, ain't.

While statistically E-Prime only makes trivial changes relative to the English lexicon, it does affect the syntax. Even this effect, however, does not seem as severe as it might appear. This unexpected lack of severity proceeds from the well-known "richness" of the English language, which provides a wealth of linking verbs (seem, appear, verbs related to the senses), apposition, etc., that can take over most of our habitual applications of "to be." On the other hand, E-Prime does admittedly entail the necessity of expressing the progressive aspect by using ". . . continues to . . . ," and it makes use of the passive voice difficult or even impossible. (Note 2.)

In marked contrast with the areas of the lexicon and syntax, E-Prime delivers major and unexpected consequences to English semantics.

The E-Prime revision of English, although trivial in some respects, has deep underlying epistemological antecedents and consequences. Critical thinkers have struggled with the semantic consequences of the verb "to be" for hundreds of years. These distinguished persons include Thomas Hobbes (18), Augustus de Morgan (30), Bertrand Russell (34), Alfred North Whitehead (38), George Santayana (35), and Alfred Korzybski (27).

Their concern, and ours as critical thinkers, centers upon two semantic usages of "to be," Identity and Predication, which have these general structures:

a. Noun Phrase$_1$ + TO BE + Noun Phrase$_2$ (Identity)
b. Noun Phrase$_1$ + TO BE + Adjective Phrase$_1$ (Predication)

where *TO BE* represents an appropriately inflected form of the verb "to be."

Critical thinkers have argued against using statements having the structure of (a) because they immediately produce high-order abstractions that lead the user to premature judgments. Consider the following example:

c. John is a farmer.

The immediate consequence of such an identification at the very least brings about unjustified abbreviation, which can severely interfere with communication. For example, consider the follow-

ing three sentences about "John":
  d. John farms three acres.
  e. John owns and operates a 2,000-acre farm.
  f. John receives $20,000 a year from the government for not growing anything on his farm.

We could even carry this illustration into a different dimension:
  g. John, after living in the city all his life, has just bought a farm.
  h. John grew up on a farm and has farmed there for sixty-one years.

Despite the fact that (d) through (h) make extremely different statements about "John," most English-speaking people feel comfortable making the jump from any one of (d) through (h) to (c). Critical thinkers trained in general semantics hold that (c) does not represent a valid higher-order abstraction that could come from such observations as (d) through (h), but rather a possibly incorrect and certainly inadequate abbreviation of the larger picture.

Of course, because of the uniqueness of structures on the event level and the process character of "reality," no structure can have precise identity with another—or even with itself at two different times, for that matter. Hence we can categorically deny the validity of any Identity relation. And, accordingly, any linguistic structure that conveys or assumes an Identity relation does not correspond well with "reality." As Korzybski would put it, "The map does not fit the territory."

A decade before Korzybski, George Santayana described those matters somewhat poetically as follows:

> The little word *is* has its tragedies: it names and identifies different things with the greatest innocence; and yet no two are ever identical, and if therein lies the charm of wedding them and calling them one, therein too lies the danger. Whenever I use the word *is*, except in sheer tautology, I deeply misuse it; and when I discover my error, the world seems to fall asunder, and the members of my family no longer know one another. (35, p. 123)

Let us now consider Predication, as illustrated in the following statements:
  i. The earth is flat.
  j. The earth is round (spherical).
  k. The earth is somewhat pear-shaped.

The verb "to be" carries with it a huge intellectual momentum of completeness, finality, and time independence. Still, each of the statements (i) through (k) does describe the earth adequately for some *restricted* purposes. This dual condition of adequacy-inadequacy seems characteristic of the Predication usage of "to be" and provides both its charm and its danger.

Early presentations of Korzybski's methodology evidently did not clearly explain the notion of the "*is* of Predication" despite its importance. Classical logicians have long called statements that have an "*is* of Predication" as the main relational term "subject-predicate" statements. As Bertrand Russell put it:

> The belief or unconscious conviction that all propositions are of some subject-predicate form—in other words, that every fact consists in some thing having some quality—has rendered most philosophers incapable of giving any account of the world of science and daily life. (34, p. 24)

Korzybski stated the importance of this matter in the following way:

> The subject-predicate form, the "is" of identity, and the elementalism of the Aristotelian system are perhaps the main semantic factors in need of revision, as they are found to be the foundation of the insufficiency of this system and represent the mechanism of semantic disturbances, making general adjustment and sanity impossible. (27, p. 371)

We may note in passing that the statements of both Russell and Korzybski contain one or more uses of the "*is* of Identity." (See Note 3.)

We can agree, I trust, that the Identity and Predication uses of "to be" do not reflect factual circumstances in the world as we experience it.

> Everything in the "real world" changes: sometimes so rapidly that we may not notice the changes directly (as in the case of a table that appears solid), sometimes so slowly that we can (as in the case of a river).
>
> Every person, as well as every "thing," undergoes such changes.
>
> One particular verb in English—"to be"—carries with it archaic associations and implications of permanence and static existence that we do not find in the "real world."

We have devoted much of the preceding material to a discussion of the epistemological reasons for avoiding the semantic usages of the "to be" of Identity and Predication. Other usages of that verb exist, of course, including the following:

l. Auxiliary. (John is reading. Ivan is plotting. The rose is wilting.)
m. Existence. (I am. Descartes was. You *may* be, but then again . . .)
n. Location. (John is here. That is neither here nor there.)

Both editions of the *Oxford English Dictionary* list twenty-four distinct usages for "be," providing more detail on the categories of uses slightly different from those long discussed by Korzybski and other students of general semantics. The OED provides historical information on these four "branches" of usages: I. "Absolutely" (existence); II. "With adverb or prepositional phrase" (includes location); III. "With adjective, substantive, or adjective phrase" (includes both Predication and Identity); and IV. "With participles and infinitives" (auxiliary).

For many years, as noted above, several titans of critical thinking have inveighed against the Identity and Predication usages, *while continuing to use them*. Piecemeal attempts to avoid the undesirable usages of "to be" simply have not worked. E-Prime provides a simple discipline that *does* work. Even Korzybski and some of his most prominent students regularly fell into what we might call the "Is Trap." I shall give three examples of the "Is Trap" in action:

> *Korzybski.* Prior to the advent of E-Prime, Korzybski had more to say about the inherent dangers of the "to be" of Identity and Predication than any other critical thinker. And yet he himself fell into the "Is Trap" to the extent of using those two constructions in some 37 percent of his sentences in *Science and Sanity*.
>
> *Bois.* For a number of years the late J. Samuel Bois served as the chief lecturer for the Institute of General Semantics at its annual seminars. Many, including this writer, consider his book *The Art of Awareness* (2) an excellent introduction to general semantics. And yet Bois used the "to be" of Identity and Predication in about 42 percent of his sentences in that text.
>
> *Read.* In a discussion of these matters, the noted lexicographer Allen Walker Read agreed that one should "call attention . . . to the undesirable '*is* of identity' and '*is* of predication' " (as in reference 33), but still rejected the most positive technique for doing more than just "call attention." Read sought to justify his rejection on the basis of a set of allegations that do not apply to E-Prime (e.g., the latter does *not* make it impossible to express the progressive aspect, the passive voice, metaphor, adjectives, and appositives). He continues to use the "*is* of identity" and the "*is* of predication."

Those three linguistically sensitive critical thinkers seemingly could not avoid the undesirable uses of "to be," while allowing themselves the luxury of the other uses. At least, so they wrote—and spoke.

The Impact of E-Prime on Writing and Speaking

In this part of the chapter I will present four of the major consequences of using E-Prime in written and spoken utterances.

1. *Vanishing Questions.* One simply cannot ask a number of questions—some would say pseudo-questions—that have preoccupied many people. What *is* man? What *is* woman? *Is* it art? What *is* my destiny? Who *am* I? Such questions, by virtue of their semantic structure, set the stage for identifications and confusions in orders of abstraction. They tend to lead to discourse in which the likelihood of useful information generation or exchange declines precipitously. One might better ask questions on a lower order of abstraction such as these: What characterizes man or woman uniquely? In what way can I relate to this art form, if any? What can I do *now* to improve my future possibilities? May I have another drink?

2. *Vanishing Internal Instructions.* Various schools of psychotherapy have recognized the importance of the silent assumptions that we hold about the world and ourselves. Other schools, especially the "rational therapy" developed and practiced by Dr. Albert Ellis, also recognize the importance of what we tell ourselves, vocally and subvocally. "Self-suggested nonsense," Dr. Ellis calls this in its undesirable forms. Most of us have encountered people whose life patterns have decayed as they kept repeating to themselves such comments as these: "I *am* a failure, consequently . . ." "I *am* a success, therefore . . ." "She *is* a Catholic, so . . ." "He *is* a Jew, hence . . ." "I *am* a teacher, so what I *am* doing must *be* teaching . . ." "Since I *am* the head of this household . . ."

3. *Abbreviations.* Forms of "to be" encourage and indeed facilitate the making of abbreviated statements that may turn out to convey little or no information, although we often behave as if they do. For example, we often see such empty comments as: "It *is* clear that . . ." or "Well, business *is* business . . ." or "The problem *is* just a matter of semantics . . ." Let us discuss that last assertion. While of course most human problems involve important (and usually unexplored because unperceived) semantic issues, these issues do not evaporate just because someone has labeled them thusly. Some people use "It's just semantics" as an analysis stopper. One might productively respond to such a comment by pointing out, "Certainly; at least in part. Now let's try to clarify some of those semantic problems."

Confusion due to improperly abbreviating with "to be" even occurs in primary schools. All too frequently we still hear teachers insisting that children drill in arithmetic by saying "One plus one *is* two; one plus two *is* three; etc." The perfectly correct mathematical expression "equals" certainly need have no more inherent mystery for the young than "plus." The unnecessary use of *is* in this context may have partial responsibility for the difficulties some children experience with fractions. They can readily see the differences between 1/3 and 2/6, say. The first fraction may *equal* the second, but obviously some trouble could arise for those taught to translate "=" as "is."

4. *Return of the Role Players.* As mentioned above, E-Prime makes use of the passive voice somewhat difficult. One may have to resort to constructions with the somewhat scruffy auxiliary verb "to get" as in "The work got done." Rather than being a drawback, this consists of one of the greatest contributions of E-Prime. This facet of E-Prime forces users to bring the role players into explicit prominence or to indicate their ignorance of them. For example, many writers of technical and scientific papers forget that "objectivity" resides in the *persons* conducting the various experiments, etc., rather than in the passive forms used in reporting the results. I know of two instances in which scientists applied E-Prime to their complete report because this technique actually forced them to make explicit some important early details. One instance involved the failure of a sensor on a satellite, and the other concerned the fact that contractor personnel did not switch on a certain antenna. In both instances early versions of the reports in question said something like, "The data were not available." Subsequent digging for the role players brought useful information to light.

"Say That in E-Prime"

E-Prime has come into a certain amount of criticism because some, in the first blush of enthusiasm, have seemed to claim too much for the practice of writing and speaking without using any form of "to be." The use of E-Prime does not guarantee, in itself, that the resulting material or utterance will sparkle with vitality and validity. Using E-Prime *does* have the effect of encouraging the explicit recognition that somebody made the given assertion. It also tends to lower the order of abstraction, which may produce clearer, easier-to-understand material.

But make no mistake: one can reflect his bigotry in E-Prime; one can make invalid (or worse, partially valid) statements in E-Prime; and one can make cynical, self-serving statements in E-Prime.

Before giving examples of what one might call "E-Prime Gone Wrong," let us consider an aspect of the matter of "meaning" that becomes involved here.

At parlor-trick time, occasionally one encounters a person who challenges the E-Primer to "Say that in E-Prime." I try to resist such games because, in point of fact, one *cannot* take a statement or longer body of material and, recasting it in E-Prime, say "the *same* thing." Sure, you can launder the "to be's" out of the original material. The E-Prime version will probably sound less pompous, perhaps sound more pedestrian, but to some extent the original "meaning" will have suffered some perturbation.

Let us now discuss the results of laundering material in a variety of contests, beginning with the *"is* of Predication."

A "Classical Example": The kind of meaning perturbation just described applies even to the overworked, standard example of problems associated with:
   o. The rose is red.

Korzybski liked to point out in his seminars that statement (o) "falsifies everything we know about the world and the human nervous system," since it allocates the "redness" only to the rose and leaves out of consideration the key role played by the human nervous system. Korzybski suggested that we might more appropriately say:
   p. I see the rose as red.
   q. The rose looks red to me.
   r. The rose looks gray to me and some other color-blind people.

One might even encounter:
   s. As a consequence of the interaction, indeed the transaction, between the light reflected by the rose and the processes of my nervous system, various nonverbal perceptions that I generate may stimulate an abstraction on the symbolic level such as "red" or "gray" or something else.

I admit that statement (s) has associated with it a very low probability—probably restricted to those the late Harry Holtzman referred to as "the newly semantic."

My main point consists of this: None of the statements (p) through (s) "means" the *same* as statement (o). Korzybski and other teachers of general semantics have long hoped that, at about this point, their students would clap hand to brow and say, "Gloriosky, Zero, if trivially simple statements like (o) can generate complexity like this upon analysis, maybe I should stop using that old *'is* of Predication.'"

Other Examples: I will present three examples of "laundering": an anecdote, a short instance, and a longer one. Please note that all examples come from the "real world." Some linguists go overboard contriving their own examples to illustrate dubious points.

1. *Anecdote.* Some thirty years ago some of my associates in an operations research firm had spent a lot of time writing and polishing and rewriting and repolishing a report that they could not seem to bring to a satisfactory completion. Then C. H. Morgan volunteered to rewrite the report in E-Prime. After he had done so, it became obvious why the report had seemed unsatisfactory: The usual linguistic forms had obscured the shallowness of the analysis and the inadequacies in the discussion of results. This made it comparatively simple for Morgan and others to proceed to produce a sounder report.

2. *Short Example.* I have had trouble locating satisfactory sources of really vile material to "launder." I would not touch religious writing for this purpose, for such would unnecessarily affront some folks, no matter what the source of the religious writing. The writings of sexists—both male and female—also seem more like trivial stereotyping than efforts to communicate, except to the claque. I also had to reject as examples the writings of the hospitalized "insane" at this time, since that kind of material merits extensive treatment in its own right, probably in collaboration with one or more psychiatrists.

Germany's Third Reich offers a quotation that seems vile enough for anybody. In his diary for February 5, 1939, Joseph Goebbels stated,

   t.   The Jew is a waste product.

(From the translation by Taylor, 37.) Notice the externalization of the insult. To launder statement (t) somewhat, we could produce:

   u.   The Nazis regard the Jew as a waste product.

While statement (u) still seems contemptible, notice the slight improvements due to the introduction of the role players. Furthermore, while we could reasonably, even pyrotechnically disagree with statement (t), statement (u) seems quite valid. Wrong-headed at its foundation, distressing perhaps, but correct. What people formerly called "true."

3. *Longer Example.* In looking for a "real world" example of arch-cynicism, given the constraints discussed in example 2 above, I finally turned to that everyday whipping boy Machiavelli. I somewhat arbitrarily selected the opening material of Chapter 18 of *The*

Prince for study. Table 1 contains a quotation of the material studied, for comparison with Table 2. The latter gives an E-Prime laundered version. I find the version contained in Table 2 more readily understandable than that of Table 1, but with plenty of cynicism intact.

The preceding three examples illustrate adequately that, operating within the bounds of E-Prime, one can still produce material that could seem shallow, bigoted, or cynical to others. On the other hand, in my opinion E-Prime does not constitute a threat that advertisers or others could use as a clever way to get mendacious, self-serving messages across to a gullible public. If anything, the increased clarity arising from the use of E-Prime would tend to expose such chicanery rather rapidly.

Aphorisms: A friend suggested to me that aphorisms usually bristle with forms of "to be," and hence they might provide an interesting grist for E-Prime laundering. Consulting reference (1), I found that some 60 percent of its aphorisms employed one or more uses of the *"is* of Identity" or *"is* of Predication." Table 3 contains the results of laundering ten aphorisms from reference (1). I hold no particular brief for the E-Prime versions of the aphorisms. One *can* do it; but afterwards, what do you have? If the reader would like to try his or her hand at this sort of thing, I will give two interesting cases below. In addition, you can check on how much you can improve on my versions in Table 3.

    v. The credulity of love is the most fundamental source of authority. (Freud)

    w. Whatever you say a thing is, well, it is not; for the word is not the thing. (Korzybski)

I would have laundered the aphorism given in (v), except that I simply do not understand what Freud wanted to say. If you do, and can launder it, please keep the information to yourself.

The Korzybskian aphorism merits some discussion. Korzybski liked to spring this one even on people comparatively untrained in his system, for the shock value. Of course, this sort of ponderous playfulness goes over better in some circles than others. One can sort out the issues alluded to in (w) with the aid of a Structural Differential, but I fear that such clarification did not always happen. I offer (x) as a "laundered" version of (w):

    x. One must differentiate carefully between structures on the Object Level ("perceived reality") and related structures on the Symbolic Level.

This concludes my inquiry into E-Prime Gone Bad. Enough.

TABLE 1

ORIGINAL VERSION
EXCERPT FROM CHAPTER 18 OF *THE PRINCE*
"CONCERNING THE WAY IN WHICH PRINCES
SHOULD KEEP FAITH"

Everyone admits how praiseworthy it is in a prince to keep faith, and to live with integrity and not with craft. Nevertheless our experience has been that those princes who have done great things have held good faith of little account, and have known how to circumvent the intellect of men by craft, and in the end have overcome those who have relied on their word. You must know that there are two ways of contesting, the one by the law, the other by force; the first method is proper to men, the second to beasts; but because the first is frequently not sufficient, it is necessary to have recourse to the second. Therefore, it is necessary for a prince to understand how to avail himself of the beast and the man. This has been figuratively taught to princes by ancient writers, who describe how Achilles and many other princes of old were given to the Centaur Chiron to nurse, who brought them up in his discipline; which means solely that, as they had for a teacher who was half beast and half man, so it is necessary for a prince to know how to make use of both natures, and that one without the other is not durable. A prince, therefore, being compelled knowingly to adopt the beast, ought to choose the fox and the lion; because the lion cannot defend himself against snares, and the fox cannot defend himself against wolves. Therefore, it is necessary to be a fox to discover the snares and a lion to terrify the wolves. Those who rely simply on the lion do not understand what they are about. Therefore a wise lord cannot, nor ought he to, keep faith when such observance may be turned against him, and when the reasons that caused him to pledge it exist no longer. If men were entirely good this precept would not hold, but because they are bad, and will not keep faith with you, you too are not bound to observe it with them. Nor will there ever be wanting to a prince legitimate reasons to excuse this nonobservance. Of this endless modern examples could be given, showing how many treaties and engagements have been made void and of no effect through the faithlessness of princes; and he who has known best how to employ the fox has succeeded best.

TABLE 2

E-PRIME VERSION
LAUNDERED EXCERPT FROM CHAPTER 18 OF *THE PRINCE*
"CONCERNING THE WAY IN WHICH
PRINCES SHOULD KEEP FAITH"

Every one admits that praiseworthy princes should keep faith, and live with integrity and not with craft. Nevertheless, in our experience those princes who have done great things have held good faith of little account, and have known how to circumvent the intellect of men by craft, and in the end have overcome those who have relied on their word. You must know that there exist two ways of contesting, the one by the law, the other by force; one may properly use the first method for men, the second for beasts; but because the first frequently does not suffice, one must necessarily have recourse to the second from time to time. Therefore a prince must understand how to avail himself both of the beast and of the man. Ancient writers have taught this point figuratively to princes. They describe how the Centaur Chiron, given Achilles and many other princes of old to train, brought them up in his discipline; which means solely that, as they had a half-man, half-beast for a teacher, he had the capability of teaching the princes how to make use of both natures, for neither one without the other will suffice. If a prince becomes compelled knowingly to adopt the beast, he ought to choose the fox and the lion; because the lion cannot defend himself against snares, and the fox cannot defend himself against wolves. Therefore one must act like a fox to discover the snares, and like a lion to terrify the wolves. Those who rely solely on the lion do not understand the true nature of their enterprise. Therefore a wise lord cannot, nor ought he to, keep faith when others could turn such observance against him, and when the reasons that caused him to pledge it exist no longer. If men behaved properly this precept would not hold, but because they normally behave badly and they will not keep faith with you, you too should not feel bound to observe it with them. Nor will a prince ever lack legitimate reasons to excuse this nonobservance. One could give endless modern examples of this, showing how princes have abrogated many treaties and engagements through their faithlessness; and he who has known best how to employ the fox succeeded best.

TABLE 3

STUDY OF APHORISMS*

1. a. The difference between journalism and literature is that journalism is unreadable and literature is not read. (Wilde)
   b. We can define the difference between journalism and literature in this way: we regard journalism as unreadable, while we simply do not read literature.
2. a. Whatever is not nailed down is mine. Whatever I can pry loose is not nailed down. (Collis P. Huntington)
   b. Anything not nailed down belongs to me. Whatever I can pry loose has become no longer nailed down.
3. a. The best qualification of a prophet is to have a good memory. (Halifax)
   b. In order to become a prophet one must have a good memory.
4. a. The handwriting on the wall may be a forgery. (Hodgson)
   b. Perhaps a forger produced the handwriting on the wall.
5. a. There is properly no history, only biography. (Emerson)
   b. History does not exist, only interlocking biographies.
6. a. To be engaged in opposing wrong affords but a slender guarantee for being right. (Gladstone)
   b. The simple fact that you oppose wrong does not prove the correctness of your position.
7. a. For a man to achieve all that is demanded of him, he must regard himself as greater than he is. (Goethe)
   b. For a man to achieve all that people demand of him, he must have an exaggerated picture of himself.
8. a. Diplomacy is to do and say the nastiest thing in the nicest way. (Goldberg)
   b. Diplomacy makes us do and say the nastiest thing in the nicest way.
9. a. A practical man is a man who practices the errors of his forefathers. (Disraeli)
   b. A practical man practices the errors of his forefathers.
10. a. The hardest thing is writing a recommendation for someone you know. (Kim Hubbard)
    b. The better you know someone, the harder becomes the task of writing a recommendation for him.

*Source: Reference (1). In each instance, (a) gives the original form of the aphorism, and (b) provides an E-Prime analogy.

E-Prime Versus Science and Art

Although one might have trouble believing it, I have heard E-Prime criticized on the basis that (1) it could have dire effects on the practice of science, or even (2) it could stunt literature, poetry, etc.

More precisely, a confused critic allegedly asked, "How could you do science with E-Prime? You couldn't say what something *is*." Of course, for the best refutation of that position, one merely needs to cite more or less extensive reports that have already appeared in E-Prime. They range from articles and dissertations in astrophysics (36), to biology (22, 24, 25), to psychology (31), even to linguistics (6). The latter, incidentally, I include despite my observation that on some faculties they have trouble deciding whether to consider linguistics a "soft science" or a "hard humanity."

And yet . . . and yet the critic's question also reflects the confusion felt by many concerning the nature of scientific endeavor. I believe that most students of the sciences nowadays take the position that, as soon as one departs from the sheer taxonometric phase of a science, one tends increasingly to see a focus on investigations of the variation of some variables with others, leading iteratively to the development of theories that contain key points for experimental verification.

Let us look in a somewhat detailed way at the research process, which lies at the heart of any scientific effort. It might surprise you to know that some people involved in scientific or technical activities believe that, basically, the research process amounts to little more than that shown in Figure 1. The fallacy embedded in Figure 1 consists of the assumption that one can take useful data without having a theory to indicate what data to collect. I have seen this in the case of oceanography, wherein some laboratories have spent considerable money on the collection of vast amounts of largely meaningless data. They had embarked prematurely on an extensive data-gathering series of programs.

Figure 2 illustrates the stages and feedback loops

```
FIGURE 1

GATHER DATA
    ↓
ANALYZE DATA
    ↓
REPORT RESULTS

Naive approach to
the research process
```

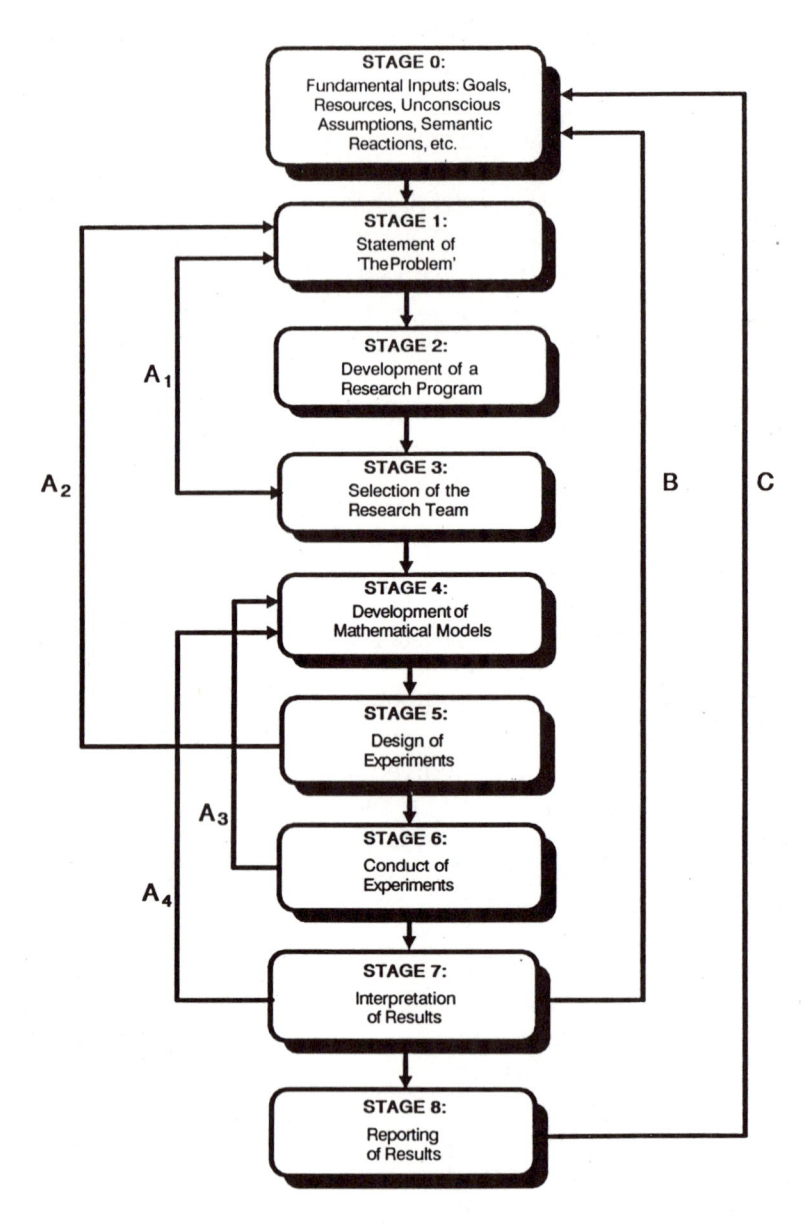

Figure 2: Nine Significant Stages in a Typical Research Process (0-8)

that I regard as most important in the research process (8). The potentially cyclic paths in Figure 2 labeled A1 to A4 represent feedback paths important when conducting some given research project. The path labeled B shows the relevance of one project to subsequent ones performed by the same individual or group, while path C represents the more formal process whereby one affects other research workers (and conversely).

Now about art—remember that the E-Prime revision began as an epistemological consequence of Korzybski's appreciation of the everyday consequences of science. His focus zeroed in on how those scientific and psychiatric insights could assist us in attaining an increasingly "sane" approach to the problems we all encounter in our lives, hence the title of his major work, *Science and Sanity*. E-Prime . . . English without the verb "to be". . . listen carefully. . . . Can anyone hear in the preceding sentence any suggestion that we "should" rewrite Shakespeare, the Holy Bible, the Declaration of Independence, etc., in E-Prime? I have certainly never made such a suggestion, although I did provide as an illustration a beginning of the Declaration rewritten in E-Prime.

And yet . . . and yet, who knows? Perhaps E-Prime *does* have a serious contribution to make in novels, poetry, etc. Let us recognize that E-Prime does not amount to a debased, hand-tied-behind-the-back version of English. It not-so-simply removes a smear on the windshield of language. Perhaps the improved clarity will help those who seek to contribute to the literary arts. I believe those with the ability, ambition, and background should give this model a spin, kick its tires, etc. I leave this fascinating challenge to those who can conjugate the artistic possibilities of E-Prime. I would like to help them but, as Harry Holtzman put it, at this point I do not have that many good months left.

Politics and Language

In the years immediately following World War I, Alfred Korzybski observed the stark differences between the consequences of engineering and scientific activity and the fruits of political activity. He pointed out that, when engineers build a bridge, it normally functions as designed. But when politicians "build" a treaty or a government, it usually collapses amid great human suffering.

Korzybski's analysis led him to conclude that the fundamental factor responsible for that discrepancy in performance consists of the structure of the languages used by both those who design bridges and those who design governments. The engineers and scientists use a language (mathematics) that has a structure similar to that of the bridges, hence the language produces predictability. However, the politicians normally employ a language of archaic structure that uses static terminology in describing dynamic human socioeconomic issues. As Korzybski pointed out, to the extent that a treaty, constitution, etc., incorporates this kind of static-dynamic discrepancy, one may expect undesirable and unstable consequences.

To put this somewhat differently, Korzybski asserted in his books that dynamic social institutions, if based upon static premises, must ultimately collapse. And if we inquire into this matter semantically, we find that the use of the verb "to be" constitutes the main source of static premises and assertions in ordinary English.

Recognizing the insidious role that "to be" theoretically may perform in sociopolitical contexts, I analyzed several important, basic political documents. The purpose consisted of determining to what extent the language in the documents exhibited a static character, as indicated by their reliance on the *"is* of Identity" and *"is* of Predication."

I chose the following political documents for study:

TABLE 4

POLITICAL DOCUMENT STUDY

Document	Sentences in Sample	Percentage of Sentences with One or More Uses of Identification or Predication
Constitution of the U.S.A.		
a. Main Body*	99 [†]	20.2
b. Complete	166 [†]	21.6
The Communist Manifesto	444 [†]	26.2
The Blue Book	207	48.8
The Prince	175	53.6
Politics	188	60.1

* Exclusive of amendments.
[†] Complete document, not a sample.

Table 4 shows the results of the analysis of sentences in these documents. Some distortion in the results may exist, since the documents by Machiavelli and Aristotle appear in English translations. However, the original languages in both cases belong to the Indo-European family, so the distortion probably does not amount to too much. Marx and Engels allegedly wrote the *Communist Manifesto* in several "original" languages, including English. Engels supposedly edited the English version that I analyzed.

In my assessment, the results given in Table 4, ranked in accordance with the increasing appearance of the uses of Identity and Predication, also correlate precisely with the great flexibility and power of our Constitution, with the sterility of Mr. Welch's nightmare, and with the rigid dogmatism of Aristotle. I submit that these results give quantitative substantiation for Korzybski's thesis.

Concluding Remarks

Apart from any epistemological considerations, E-Prime can assist the user in attaining a kind of vigorous clarity that increasing numbers of people have found worthwhile. Of course I know of only some of those who have found E-Prime useful in their writing and speaking. E-Prime has found application in two doctoral dissertations—one in astrophysics (by Dr. D. A. Schwartz in 1968) (36), and one in psychology (by Dr. R. H. Moore in 1977) (31), one licenciatura thesis in linguistics (mine in 1974) (6), a master's thesis in Biblical studies (by Bryon C. Cannon in 1987) (10), and a multivolume research report by the U.S. Naval Air Systems Center (Project IMP in 1971).

Of course, it pleased me greatly to learn that the noted psychotherapist Dr. Albert Ellis thought enough of the benefits of E-Prime that he has rewritten five of his books in this manner (12–16).

Scientific papers by Dr. E. W. Kellogg III that show "E-Prime in action" have appeared in *Nature* (25), *The Journal of Bioelectricity* (22), and *The Journal of Gerontology* (24). Further applications have appeared in various places by C. A. Hilgartner, M.D. (17), K. L. Ruskin, M.D. (9), Dr. Ruth Ralph (32), Elaine C. Johnson (20), Paul Dennithorne Johnston (21), Charles H. Morgan, and T. J. Hefferon. (See Note 4.)

The diversity of applications described above testifies to the generality and utility of E-Prime.

I offer E-Prime to those interested in critical thinking as an easily teachable technique that has immediate benefits. In writing and talking it provides a method for materially reducing "the human misunderstanding." As the current ad for Nike Athletic Shoes puts it, "Just do it."

NOTES

1. This conventional position ignores the names of the integers after some arbitrary cut-off point. Otherwise, we would have to say trivially that most modern languages contain at least a denumerably infinite number of words.
2. The comparatively minor syntactic consequences of E-Prime reflect the same linguistic functions operating that account for the fact that some natural languages lack a verb that corresponds exactly to "to be," including Russian, Hungarian, and Mandarin at least. It seems interesting to note that the speakers of those languages alone account for about 20 percent of the world's population.
3. The lack of an adequate treatment of the *"is* of Predication" has led to some unfortunate confusion. The *"is* of Predication" statement has the basic structure given in statement (b) (page 103). In the early days of the transformational approach to syntax, Chomsky (8) gave the following rewrite rule for a sentence (S):
    (N1) S→NP+VP
    where *NP* represents *noun phrase* and *VP* represents *verb phrase*. In pre-Bloomfieldian "traditional" grammars, linguists called the NP of (N1) the "subject," and the VP of (N1) the "predicate" (e.g., Jesperson, reference 19, p. 97). The slight difference in terminology and the great difference in significance between the philosophical *subject-predicate* and the linguistic *subject+predicate* provided the raw material for problems. For more on this matter see reference 29, p. 121.
4. I wish to express my appreciation for the editorial suggestions offered by Russell Joyner and Dr. E. W. Kellogg III.

REFERENCES

1. W. H. Auden and Louis Kronenberger. *The Viking Book of Aphorisms: A Personal Selection.* New York: Viking, 1962 (reissued in 1981).
2. J. Samuel Bois. *The Art of Awareness.* Dubuque, Iowa: Wm. C. Brown, 1966.
3. D. David Bourland, Jr. "Introduction to a Structural Calculus: A Postulational Statement of Alfred Korzybski's non-Aristotelian Linguistic System." *General Semantics Bulletin,* 1952, nos. 8 and 9.
4. D. David Bourland, Jr. "A Linguistic Note: Writing in E-Prime." *General Semantics Bulletin,* 1965, nos. 32 and 33.
5. D. David Bourland, Jr. "The Semantics of a Non-Aristotelian Language." *General Semantics Bulletin,* 1968, no. 35.
6. D. David Bourland, Jr. A Non-Aristotelian Paradigm for Linguistics. Licenciatura thesis, Universidad de Costa Rica, San José, Costa Rica, 1973.
7. D. David Bourland, Jr. "The Language of E-Prime," in *Coping with Increasing Complexity,* ed. by D. E. Washburn and D. R. Smith. New York: Gordin & Breach, 1974.
8. D. David Bourland, Jr. "Semantic Factors in the Research Process," in *Research Designs in General Semantics,* ed. by Kenneth G. Johnson. New York: Gordon & Breach.
9. K. L. R. Bourland (now K. L. Ruskin). "Coping with Semantic Problems in Systems Development," in *Coping with Increasing Complexity,* ed. by D. E. Washburn and D. R. Smith. New York: Gordon & Breach, 1974.
10. Bryon C. Cannon. *An E-Prime Approach to the Holy Bible.* M.S. diss., Fort Hays State University, Fort Hays, Kansas, 1987.
11. Noam Chomsky. *Syntactic Structures.* The Hague: Mouton, 1957.
12. Albert Ellis. *How to Live with a Neurotic.* 2d ed. North Hollywood: Wilshire Book Co., 1975.
13. Albert Ellis. *Sex and the Liberated Man.* Secaucus, N.J.: Lyle Stuart, 1976. 2d ed.

of *Sex and the Single Man*.
14. Albert Ellis. *Anger: How to Live with and without It*. 2d ed. Secaucus, N.J.: Citadel Press, 1977.
15. Albert Ellis and Robert A. Harper. *A New Guide to Rational Living*. 2d ed. North Hollywood: Wilshire Book Co., 1975.
16. Albert Ellis and William J. Knaus. *Overcoming Procrastination*. 2d ed. New York: Signet Books, 1977.
17. C. A. Hilgartner. "Chain Indexing in Experimental Design" *General Semantics Bulletin*, 1968, no. 35.
18. Thomas Hobbes. *Leviathan*. 1651. Reprint. New York: Liberal Arts Press, 1958.
19. Otto Jesperson *Essentials of English Grammar*. London: Allen & Unwin, 1933.
20. Elaine C. Johnson. "Discovering E-Prime," *Et cetera* 45 (1988), no. 2.
21. Paul Dennithorne Johnston. "Escape from a Frozen Universe: Discovering General Semantics." *Et cetera* 46 (1989), no. 2.
22. E. W. Kellogg III. "Air Ions: Their Possible Biological Significance and Effects," *Journal of Bioelectricity* 3 (1984):119–36.
23. E. W. Kellogg III. "Speaking in E-Prime," *Et cetera* 44 (1987), no. 2.
24. E. W. Kellogg III and M. C. Yost. "The Effects of Long-Term Air Ion and D.C. Electric Field Exposures on Survival Characteristics in Female NAMRU Mice," *Journal of Gerontology* 41 (1986):147–53.
25. E. W. Kellogg III, M. C. Yost, and A. P. Kruger. "Superoxide Involvement in the Bactericidal Effects of Negative Air Ions on *Staphlococcus albus*," *Nature* 281(1986):400–401.
26. Alfred Korzybski. *Manhood of Humanity*. New York: Dutton, 1921. 2d ed., 1950, distributed by the Institute of General Semantics.
27. Alfred Korzybski. *Science and Sanity*. Lakeville, Conn.: International Non-Aristotelian Publishing Co., 1933. 4th ed., 1958.
28. Alfred Korzybski. *Selections from Science and Sanity*. Lakeville, Conn.: International Non-Aristotelian Publishing Co., 1948. 8th ed., 1976.
29. Laura L. Lee. "The Relevance of General Semantics to the Development of Sentence Structure in Children's Language," in *Communication: General Semantics Perspectives*, ed. by Lee Thayer. New York: Spartan, 1970.
30. Augustus de Morgan. *Formal Logic*. 1847. Reprint. London: Open Court, 1926.
31. Robert H. Moore. *Alienation in College Students: A Rational and Semantic Analysis*. Ph.D. diss., Walden University, Tallahassee, Florida, 1977.
32. Ruth Ralph. "Getting Rid of the *To Be* Crutch," in *Classroom Exercises in General Semantics*, ed. by Mary Morain. San Francisco: International Society for General Semantics, 1980.
33. Allen Walker Read. Personal communication. 1976.
34. Bertrand Russell. *Our Knowledge of the External World*. Chicago: University of Chicago Press, 1914.
35. George Santayana. *Scepticism and Animal Faith*. New York: Scribner.
36. Daniel A. Schwartz. *The Spatial Distribution of the Diffuse Component of Cosmic X-Rays*. Ph.D. diss., University of California, San Diego, 1968.
37. Fred Taylor. *The Goebbels Diaries (1939–1941)*. New York: Putnam, 1983.
38. Alfred North Whitehead. *The Principle of Relativity with Applications to Physical Science*. Cambridge: Cambridge University Press, 1922.

Part Three

FURTHER APPLICATIONS OF E-PRIME

Can one use E-Prime for creative writing?

PAUL DENNITHORNE JOHNSTON **LABELS**

A LUMP BREAKS the water off the starboard bow. Bramble's bald cranium appears, then his gaunt face. He shakes his skull-like head, hawks, spits, snorts, swims to the dinghy, grabs the rail, and hauls himself aboard in a cascade of water, long arms and legs flailing. Pinky struggles to balance the wildly careening craft. Dripping, Bramble plops down in the stern with a sigh. His white eyebrows arch, then congeal in a grim line. He brushes water from leathery cheeks and forehead, pulls a sodden handkerchief from his khaki shorts, and blows his long sharp nose.

Pinky, his plump red face creased with anguish, slides across to the center of the midship thwart. His white midriff bulges over blue sweatpants. With the back of his hand, he wipes salt spray from his weedy black mustache. "I didn't think she'd jibe."

"Everybody jibes once in a while, young man."

"Your head . . . "

"Should've seen it coming. This hangnail here distracted me."

"Think you have a concussion?"

Bramble runs a palm over his shining pate. "One lump or two?" he says, and smiles. "You want to hoist the sail?"

Pinky squints up the mast. His thick shoulders droop. "I cut the halyard after the boom hit you. I panicked."

"You bikers know how to row?"

"Come on, Uncle. You've known me all my life."

Pinky slots an oar into the port oarlock, lifts the other oar over Bramble's head, and lowers it into the starboard oarlock. Frowning into the setting sun, he rows carefully toward shore.

Bramble straightens. "Angie saw the whole thing."

©1991 by Paul Dennithorne Johnston. All rights reserved.

"I'll never learn to sail," says Pinky, suddenly pulling hard on the squeaking oars.

Standing in the cottage doorway, Angie watches their approach, hands on high square hips. She lumbers out onto the porch, her sun-dried face wrinkled with worry, as Pinky and Bramble halt at the steps. With a big callused hand, she shoves gray hair away from her eyes. She ducks under the eaves, walks down three creaking steps, straightens to her full height.

"Sit."

Bramble lowers his buttocks onto the top porch step and Angie examines his head. Water collects on the weathered gray wood near Bramble's bare feet.

"I'll call Doc Halabut."

Bramble snorts. "You'd call your Doc Halabut at the drop of a hat."

"Your bump looks like a fried egg sitting on a cantaloupe."

"I really blew it," says Pinky, grimacing. "Bramble said to watch the leach."

"Don't blame yourself, Nephew. I could've looked," says Bramble, rising. He turns to Angie. "I won't see any doctor, Sis. Understand?"

"Get out of those wet clothes this minute, Bramble. I'll run you a hot bath. I got wood to chop."

Yellow robe draped over his lanky frame, Bramble sits in the porch swing, sipping bourbon and water, watching stars appear over the bay. In a while, they eat supper of broiled scrod, white sauce, parsley potatoes, and baby peas. No one speaks, except to ask for essentials. Angie and Pinky watch "Star Trek." Bramble goes to bed.

In the morning, Angie washes dishes as Bramble eats a ham and egg breakfast. "I insist on calling Doc Halabut."

Bramble spreads Angie's strawberry jam on rye toast. "Pour me some what-you-call-it, Sis."

"I put your sandwich in your briefcase. Don't buy doughnuts."

Angie sets a saucer on the draining board, wipes her hands on her apron. Her straight gray hair splays across her back as she turns to lift a red enameled coffeepot off the blue flame. She stands behind Bramble's right shoulder, one hand on hip, the coffeepot in the other.

"Don't argue with me, Bramble."

"Pinky up yet? Said he had a nine-thirty, some guys from Silicon Valley."

"Staring at his computer since six. Might as well talk to the dead."

Bramble jumps up. "Got to go. Tell Pinky I'll see him at supper.

Did you feed Bruiser? Where'd I put my thingamy?"

"I just poured your coffee."

"Goes on your head."

"Your *hat*." Angie glares at Bramble, then picks a gray tweed deerstalker from a battered wood chair.

"Thanks."

Bramble squashes the deerstalker onto his head, grabs his briefcase, and lopes out, whistling. Angie fills the kitchen doorway, hands on hips, red-striped dish towel over her left shoulder. "I'll phone Doc Halabut now."

"Your nickel."

Bramble starts the Woody and reverses out of the clapboard garage. He races the engine while he looks at a sail on the horizon, glances up at the lighthouse, then down at a broken nail on his left thumb.

Bruiser utters a long tortured howl as the station wagon moves away. He runs after it, until his chain snaps taut and yanks him off his short legs. He lunges repeatedly against his tether until Bramble's car disappears behind a dune. Flopping down on the dry grass, he chews on his right forepaw.

Bramble drives along the coast road to the village. He buys a *New York Times* and a jelly doughnut. At San Carlos Avenue, he heads east through a mile of eucalyptus. He parks in faculty lot D and strides to his office in a two-story stucco and redwood cantilever-roofed building clinging to a hill over the lake. He sits at his desk, stares at a translucent patch on the white doughnut bag as he bites at his broken nail, then opens his paper and glares at the headlines.

A little later, Bramble shoulders himself into the computer lab, half a jelly doughnut in his mouth, powdered sugar on one cheek, as he manipulates the doorknob with his left hand, his stained *Kiss This Eccentric* coffee mug in his right. Six students stare at PCs in silent concentration. Bramble sits before a vacant 386 clone, types with one hand, holding the coffee cup to his mouth, his cheeks bathed in steam.

Bramble looks up. Serina stands hunch-shouldered at his elbow. When their eyes meet, she flinches. He lowers his gaze.

"Morning, Serina."

"Good morning, Professor. Um. . . ."

Serina's head turtles further down between her shoulders. She smiles for a split second, then her lips tighten. Her narrow shoulders sag. Her breasts rise, then fall as she exhales heavily. She looks past Bramble. Her gold-pink hair catches dappled sunlight. She lifts a thin wrist and squints at a spring-wound watch with a large analog dial numbered in black on white. She wrinkles a freckled nose, sucks in her cheeks.

"It crashed again," she says in a near whisper.

Bramble remains in his task chair as he scoots it across to Serina's PC. He studies the monitor a moment, grunts.

"Use the . . . this damn thing?"

"The mouse went dead."

"What if you reboot and try from the keyboard?"

Serina presses control, alt, and delete keys simultaneously. The screen blanks, then rows of text and numbers scroll down. A memory-check message appears, accompanied by a series of clicks. The drives beep, the tape drive buzzes, the C prompt appears.

"Didn't see the mouse stuff," mutters Bramble. "Look at the autoexec file."

Serina types, leans forward, squints. "I forgot a colon in the mouse path," she says. "I never do anything right."

Bramble moves a large hand toward Serina's shoulder, then withdraws it. "You do OK," he says gruffly, and rolls his chair away.

At 12:10, Bramble strides into his office, sits at his desk, pulls out the right-hand leaf, and places a paper towel on it. He takes a plastic zip bag from his briefcase, removes a tuna sandwich, and puts it on the towel. He opens a double-depth drawer in his desk and lifts out a bottle of stout and an English half-pint pewter mug, takes a small Swiss army knife from the pocket of his tartan waistcoat, opens the bottle-opener blade with his right thumbnail, pops the top off the stout and pours the black liquid into the mug. He looks at the white head of foam as it settles in the mug, sighs, raises the drink in a silent toast, sips the bitter liquid, and holds it on his tongue.

"Bless the Irish in us," he mutters, takes a large swallow and sets down the mug beside the sandwich.

That evening, as Bramble turns into the dirt drive, he sees Doc Halabut sitting in the porch swing. Bramble parks in the garage, shuts the pine doors, and drops the two-by-four latch into place. Bruiser hurtles toward Bramble, yelping and slobbering, rears back on his hind legs when his chain runs out. Bramble steps back to avoid whipping paws, squats and scratches the old basset's torn floppy ears, then lopes up the narrow boardwalk and drops into his rocker. Bruiser lies in the sand, watching Bramble with sad baggy eyes.

"Evening, Doc. Social call?"

"Bump on the head, Bramble?"

"Told Angie I don't need a quack."

"Guess it didn't affect your personality, Bramble."

Bramble grins.

"OK, Doc. Do your worst. You'll find nothing wrong."

"Headaches? Blurred vision? Dizziness?"

"No."

Doc Halabut hauls himself out of the swing. The porch deck squeaks. With a wheeze, he picks up his leather bag. "Indoors?"

In the parlor, Doc Halabut examines Bramble with flashlight, stethoscope, rubber mallet.

"I have all my parts in good working order," says Bramble.

"Perhaps," mutters Doc Halabut, rocking back on his heels. "Speech OK?"

"Fine."

"Not what I hear."

"Any slurs, I'll give you fifty bucks."

Doc Halabut holds up his stethoscope. "What do you call this?"

"Think I've gone senile? I call it your damn stethoscope, Doc."

"This?"

"Tongue depressor. Put your crap back in your thingamy and go home."

"Where?"

"That black leather thing you quacks carry around like some damn religious fetish."

"This?"

"Uh-huh."

"More of a relic than a fetish, eh? I want to know what name you give it."

"You keep your medicine and your hypodermic and your incense burner in there."

"Angie said you couldn't remember the names of things."

"Damn lie."

"Tell me the name of my black leather fetish, Bramble."

"I stored it in memory, Doc. I just can't retrieve it right now."

"We call this the doctor's proverbial black bag."

"I knew that, a bag or satchel."

"What do you do when one of your computers has a memory problem, Bramble?"

"I run a diagnostic . . . hey, wait a minute!"

"I can't find a thing wrong, Bramble, but I feel concerned about your inability to name things. Did it happen before you got hit on the head?"

"Perhaps my height does it. The thoughts can't get up here."

"You have high thoughts? Ha. I'll schedule you for some tests at Pinewood General."

Bramble sighs. "Got to admit, it feels weird. I know a thing's shape, feel, taste, what it does. I can define it by function—the machine-that-tells-the-time in your pocket, for example. I know everything I ever did about your black bag, or a disk drive, or a rudder. Just sometimes I can't put a name on it. We should have labels glued on things."

"We do. You just can't see them."

"Had a nightmare last night. I could see the electrons zooming around in everything. The table looked transparent, and I could see all the molecules that held it together. The same with the floor and the walls and everything in the room. Then the boundaries that made one object distinct from another disappeared. I couldn't tell where the table left off and the lamp began. I could only see this all-enveloping amorphous suffocating blur. I woke up in a cold sweat."

"Really?" Doc bends to pick up his bag. His breath rasps.

"Had supper, Doc? Angie bought some nice pork chops at O'Flaherty's. Homemade apple sauce. New potatoes. Fresh asparagus. Apricot pie."

Doc Halabut lowers himself into an overstuffed chair. He sighs, closes his eyes, and puffs out his cheeks. "Apricot pie? I don't know why some lucky guy didn't marry Angie long ago."

"*You* hooked up with a medical student."

"Damn fine doctor she turned into, God rest her soul. Couldn't cook worth a hoot."

When Bramble wakes, he doesn't recognize the place. He lies in white stuff. Around him hangs gray stuff. One eye open, he watches it. Light plays here and there. Some light belongs to the top of his head, some belongs to his belly. The light has a feeling, a sort of buzzing, low or high pitched, depending where he looks.

Bramble sits up suddenly.

"Christ!" he yells. "My nightmare's come to life!" The stuff surrounding Bramble crystallizes: cotton sheet, brass bedpost, bentwood chair, threadbare oval rug on black waxed floorboards, chintz curtains billowing in the breeze. Bramble sniffs, grimaces.

"Before you connect the dots. Jesus. Nowhere-land. Dead man's eyes."

Bramble drags himself out of bed, hauls on a brown woolen robe. He shaves, showers, brushes his teeth, dresses in white socks, gray checked slacks, black loafers, olive green shirt, red paisley bow tie, gold waistcoat, brown herringbone tweed jacket with suede elbow patches and leather buttons.

"Dedicated follower of fashion," says Pinky as Bramble enters the kitchen.

Bramble pours coffee. Pinky hacks pancakes with his fork, his cheeks bulging. Bramble opens the oven, flips six pancakes onto a plate, sits, and pours on maple syrup. "Seen Angie?"

"I heard her."

"I do, now. Seems like the more she chops firewood, the more she loves it."

Pinky peels an orange. "You can't recall the names of things?"

"Says who?"

"Angie does. And I noticed it at supper. You said *thingamy* a lot. You got a malfunction in your labeling device."

"Why have names? Why not just point? Never mind. Dumb question."

Pinky lays orange slices on a pancake, slaps another pancake on top. "I fed Bruiser. He gets more neurotic every day. I had an idea, Bramble. Suppose you reconceptualize. Take this sugar bowl, for example. Suppose you call it X?"

"OK, pass me X. Good pancakes, Pinky."

"Think of each name as a conceptual box or pigeonhole. Half the box holds meaning and the other half holds the letters or numbers that constitute its label."

"Sure, pass the M for my coffee."

"See, it works!"

"What if I give it an M and you give it an R?"

"Take the next step, and add a third compartment to your box. Put a social-consensus constant in there. Instead of saying *X equals rye toast*, you say *Thing-on-my-plate equals X equals rye toast*."

Bramble blows on his coffee. "What can I do in the face of such genius?"

Pinky frowns. "One day they'll look back at the twentieth century and ask how we survived, using such primitive software."

"And you don't mean DOS."

"I have all these weird verbal relationships inside my head. If I put that kind of garbage in a program, it would crash. Don't worry about how society assigns labels, Bramble. It seems pretty arbitrary, except for onomatopoeia. As you say, just point, and if that doesn't work, shout."

Bramble sips coffee. "X . . . coffee. Coffee . . . X.Hummm. . . ."

"Remember your programming," says Pinky. " This *equals* X. X *equals* cup of coffee."

"Why not just say *I call this a hardboiled egg*?"

"You could, but you can't remember the names of things."

"This equals BS."

"You equal a stubborn old coot."

"A bald one, at that."

Pinky puts on a black leather jacket. He combs jet black hair, puts on a helmet emblazoned with fluorescent-orange electron symbols.

"Got a minute this afternoon, Bramble?"

"Will they let you out of your cage?"

"Wrote a program last night. I'll bring it over."

Pinky waves, goes out, gets on his Harley and roars away.

Pinky barges into the computer lab and pounds across the room, then stops abruptly, inhales. In the wavering sunlight from a lakeside window, Bramble and Serina sit at a PC. Bramble, the keyboard in his lap, uses the down-arrow key to scroll through a PAL program.

"Stop," exclaims Serina. "There. What if you put another Down Image? Wouldn't it move you on to the editing form?"

Motionless, Pinky gazes at Serina. He shakes his head, drops his helmet at a vacant workstation, pulls up a black-and-chrome task chair.

"Nephew and former student, Pinky," says Bramble, typing, eyes on the monitor. "Serina, doctoral candidate."

Pinky grins. "Still making your victims write your Fully Integrated Accounting and Inventory System Modified to a Unique Business Situation?"

Bramble glares. "Mundane, perhaps, but . . . "

". . . but if you buy it off the shelf you won't learn a thing."

Serina frowns. "The student always knows more than the teacher," she says in a near whisper. "Especially the teacher's nephew."

Pinky's face falls. Serina pushes back her chair, stands, picks up a blue motorcycle helmet.

Pinky's eyes widen. "That seven-fifty outside. . . ."

"Somebody has to own it."

"Original paint. Nice."

Pinky takes a floppy disk from a zip pocket, hands it to Bramble who rolls along to the next workstation and slips it into a disk drive. Serina gathers her gold-red hair and slips on her helmet. Pinky sits, pulls the keyboard close, begins typing.

"I wrote this last night." He turns to Serina. "I hit my uncle on the head with the boom when I jibed our dinghy and now he forgets the names of things. I feel guilty, I guess." He swivels back to the screen. "So I wrote this program. Probably won't do any good, but I had to do something. I got to thinking of a name as an entity completely separate from the object it represents, so I made the continuum you see here. It shows the distance between the thing and the label that people attach to it. B-One represents the object itself—a book, for example. B-Two represents the idea *book*. B-Three represents the label *book*. Notice the gaps in between. B-Four could represent a book about a book, and B-Five could represent me talking about this book about a book."

Serina pulls over a chair and sits close to Pinky. "You can touch it, name it, eat it. You always have some kind of gap," she says slowly.

Pinky smiles. "I wanted abstract ideas, too. *Justice, common sense*, things like that. But where do I put them? You could write in a formula, then type out a sentence and the program would compute the abstraction gap for each word, and also a mean for the whole sentence. You'd have to give each word a rating."

Bramble grunts. "I could rate nouns in a scale of one to ten, but damned if I could rate some of the crap politicians use."

"You'd need an open-ended scale," says Serina with a laugh. She removes her helmet, shakes her head to free her hair.

Pinky grins. "The name of a thing—a chair, for example—corresponds to machine language because it lies close to what it represents. And high ideas like *justice* or *honor* seem more like a high-level language, farther removed from what goes on, with all sorts of compilers and interpreters in between."

"You'd have to put in action words," says Serina in her whisper voice. "Run, talk, spit, investigate, except a word like *investigate* would go higher up the scale."

"Where'd you get your Harley?" asks Pinky. He types. The screen clears. Serina smiles.

"I've had three."

"Haven't seen it around."

"I come from upstate."

"You know Sylvester's out on Main Highway?"

"Heard of him."

"I won't let anybody else touch my bike."

"I do my own work. I put in new rings last month but I share an apartment now, no place to do anything."

"You could use our garage. Bramble wouldn't mind, would you?"

Bramble snorts. "Oh, I still exist, do I?" He smiles at Serina. "Any good with four wheels?"

The sound of heavy footfalls comes from the corridor. Bramble looks at his watch, gets to his feet. "Will you lock up, Serina?" He puts a hand in his pocket and brings out a flat brass object. "Here, take the what-you . . . the key."

Bramble glances back as he goes out. Pinky and Serina sit close, talking in low voices. In the village, Bramble walks into the Golden Abalone, stands at the bar, and asks Larry for a pint of draft Guinness. He carries his stout to a window seat, sits, watches a fishing boat enter the harbor and tie up at Jason's Wharf. Across the water, the setting sun and its path of sparkles disappear. In shadow now, the lighthouse has lost its pink hue. Bramble wiggles the hangnail on his left thumb. He takes out his Swiss army knife, opens the scissor blade, trims the damaged nail. He drops the cutting into a heavy dimpled glass ashtray. He sips his stout and smiles.

A NON-ARISTOTELIAN PARADIGM FOR LINGUISTICS

D. David Bourland, Jr.

I. INTRODUCTION

A. General

This paper presents a new approach for the field of linguistics, based upon the non-Aristotelian formulations of Alfred Korzybski (1933). More precisely, after presenting the characteristics of two of the currently most important linguistic paradigms, and discussing their shortcomings, this paper presents a paradigm more in keeping with the non-Aristotelian nature of the world as currently known.

An interesting property of linguistic schools consists of the tendency to appropriate an excessively general term for their self-description. In the case of the descriptive school as it developed in the United States, which stemmed basically from the program set down by Bloomfield (1933), someone applied the name "structuralism" to it. Since every language not only has "a structure, " but indeed within a specific language one may speak or write using a language having semantic structure more or less appropriate in comparison with the events, situations, etc., described, this name seems excessively general, if not misleading. In a similar way, Noam Chomsky introduced a powerful new paradigm (1957, 1962, 1965), but it acquired the excessively general name "generative-transformational." Of course, he could hardly bestow his own name on his efforts, but we can perceive his works as both (1) presenting a more powerful paradigm for linguistics, as contained in the cited publications, and (2) going overboard from a philosophical point of view, as illustrated by the assertions made in Chomsky (1966). It seems inevitable that adherents to any paradigm, perhaps including the one developed in this paper, will seek to carry it beyond the bounds where it offers useful insights, but this process merely facilitates the birth of the succeeding paradigm.

Licenciatura thesis submitted to the Universidad de Costa Rica, 1973.

B. The Matter of Paradigms

In his outstanding historiography of science, Thomas S. Kuhn (1962) described the details of the life cycle of "generations" of scientific efforts. He defined as basic *paradigms* those overreaching contributions that shared two characteristics: "Their achievement was sufficiently unprecedented to attract an enduring group of adherents away from competing modes of scientific activity. Simultaneously, it was sufficiently open-ended to leave all sorts of problems for the redefined group of practitioners to resolve" (page 10). In Kuhn's view, the scientific process consists of exploring the ramifications of a paradigm ("normal science"), until eventually so many observations become apparent that the basic paradigm cannot account for, that the way becomes paved for a "revolution, "which generates a new paradigm. The field of physics offers perhaps the clearest-cut case of paradigm–revolution–new paradigm, as described extensively by Kuhn, but the basic mechanism of course applies to all sciences including linguistics.

C. Linguistics Paradigms

The last forty years have seen the rise of two major paradigms in the field of linguistics in the United States. The first, whose charter Bloomfield presented in his *Language* (1933), had its roots in the mechanistic empiricism of early twentieth-century science. One might say that Bloomfield, Sapir, and the others who made significant contributions to the Empirical Linguistics that we will call the *Bloomfieldian* paradigm took linguistics from its anthropologic and philologic origins and made the field a science. However, regarding "meaning" as a mentalist manifestation and hence decidedly unscientific, they essentially turned their backs on this messy matter. (See the position described in Bloomfield [1933, p. 142f].) This paradigm organized the facts of language in terms of phonology (starting with the *phoneme* as a fundamental construct) and morphology (with the *morpheme* as the basic construct), and then moved on to syntax. Despite occasional allusions to semantics, linguists devoted little energy in this direction.

Various of his followers elaborated the general outline presented by Bloomfield. Outstanding among them we should mention the work called (by Gleason (1965, p. 82) the "first important attempt to give a comprehensive description of English within the framework" of Bloomfieldian linguistics, *An Outline of English Structure* by G. L. Trager and H. L. Smith, Jr. (1951). Gleason calls this work "in many ways the culmination of the linguistic developments since Bloomfield." Evidently one of the most successful efforts to apply immediate constituent analysis consisted of Eugene A. Nida's *A Synopsis of English Syntax* (1960).

The Bloomfieldian paradigm assumes that man behaves (including linguistically) only under control of stimuli; hence, if one knew all the operative stimuli, one could predict a man's behavior (including his linguistic behavior) with certainty. Bloomfield (1933, p. 33) attributes the "variability of human conduct" to "the fact that the human body is a very complex system." As some have expressed the basic assumption of this paradigm, it assumes that "Man is a machine."

Seemingly diametrically opposed to the Bloomfieldian paradigm, but from the more general viewpoint adopted in this thesis sharing certain important fundamental assumptions, one may find the self-styled Rationalist Linguistics, or what we will call the *Chomskian* paradigm. As mentioned previously, one must distinguish carefully between the here-unquestioned contributions to linguistic analysis and the subsequently adopted philosophical postures. These portions (of technique and philosophy) seem much more separable than has often happened in the history of science. However, in the writer's opinion this results from the fact that, in linguistics, such techniques as immediate constituent analysis of sentences and generative transformational analysis of sentences correspond to the experimental techniques or analytical devices employed by other sciences. More precisely, those and analogous techniques for linguistic analysis correspond to such matters as titration in chemistry, the microscope in macrobiology, the telescope in astronomy, the mass-spectrograph in physics, and the slide rule, the digital computer, and the typewriter relative to all the fields mentioned plus others.

D. Assumptions of the Chomskian Paradigm

In his book *Cartesian Linguistics*, Chomsky (1966) took his philosophic lead from Descartes and the Port-Royal school of grammar and logic of the middle and late 1600s. He began his presentation of the philosophical principles that underlie his paradigm by discussing what Descartes, Cordemoy, La Mettrie, Schlegel, Humboldt, and others have had to say concerning the "creative use of language" by humans as showing a marked difference in kind from the extremely limited employment of symbols by animals. The Cartesian view held that, "In its normal use, human language is free from stimulus control and does not serve a merely communicative function, but is rather an instrument for the free expression of thought and for appropriate response to new situations" (Chomsky [1966, p. 13]). Whereas, on the other hand, "Animal 'language' remains completely within the bounds of mechanical explanation as this was conceived by Descartes and Cordemoy" (Chomsky [1966, p. 11]). One may summarize this *first* fundamental assumption of Cartesian-Chomskian linguistics as: "Man is a rational animal," which consists of a parallel form to Descartes' famous statement: "Cogito, ergo sum."

Next, the Cartesian-Chomskian paradigm assumes (as the *second* fundamental assumption) a "fundamental distinction between body and mind" (Chomsky [1966, p. 32]). Chomsky relates this distinction to the dichotomy of the *deep structure* of a sentence (the underlying mental "reality") in contrast to the *surface structure* of the same given sentence ("the superficial organization of units which determines the phonetic interpretation and which relates to the physical form of the actual utterance"). One may conclude from this assumption "that deep and surface structures need not be identical" (Chomsky [1966, p. 33]).

The *third* assumption asserts that:

> The principal form of thought (but not the only one—[as discussed below]) is the judgment, in which something is affirmed of something else. Its linguistic expression is the proposition, the two terms of which are the "*sujet*, qui est ce dont on affirme" and the "*attribut*, qui est ce qu'on affirme." The subject and attribute may be *simple*, as in *la terre est ronde*, or *complex* ("composé") as in *un habile Magistrat est un homme utile á la République* or *Dieu invisible a créé le monde visible* (Chomsky [1966, p. 33]).

To state the above succinctly, this assumption holds that the basic form of thought consists of the subject-predicate proposition.

The *fourth* assumption accounts for the complex propositions, said to underlie all human thought. These other forms of thought result from the combination of "simple propositions" by using special particles: *not, or, and, if, implies* (Chomsky [1966, p. 41]). The *fifth* and final major assumption of the Cartesian-Chomskian linguistic paradigm states that:

> General features of grammatical structure are common to all languages and reflect certain fundamental properties of the mind (Chomsky [1966, p. 59]).

This assumption lies behind the search for "linguistic universals" and constitutes a significant departure from the Bloomfieldian paradigm, which tends to emphasize the divergent characteristics of different languages—primarily through focusing almost entirely upon what the Cartesian-Chomskian paradigm calls surface phenomena.

The five assumptions given above, which underly the Cartesian-Chomskian paradigm, proceeded from the best understanding of the physical world, the human nervous system, and "logical" processes available in the late 1600s. The next chapters present the details of a linguistic paradigm more in keeping with certain advances made during the past three hundred years.

II. INADEQUACIES IN THE ASSUMPTIONS OF THE CHOMSKIAN PARADIGM

A. General

The process of developing the formal assumptions of a non-Aristotelian paradigm for linguistics requires a somewhat detailed discussion of certain inadequate assumptions of the Chomskian paradigm, because this latter consists of the leading guide for linguistic studies today. The followers of the Chomskian paradigm have already provided adequately detailed criticisms of the Bloomfieldian paradigm, including most prominently Chomsky himself (1957, 1962, 1965, 1966). Despite the fact that the details of the Bloomfieldian and Chomskian linguistic paradigms differ profoundly, they share an important fundamental characteristic as discussed in Chapter 4.

B. Aristotelian and Non-Aristotelian Orientations

Beyond question, no philosopher has had anywhere near as great an influence on Western orientations, and hence civilization, as the great Aristotle, who lived and wrote some 2300 years ago. As Wendell Johnson (1946) put it,

> What Aristotle did was to observe the behavior, and especially the language, of the people of his day and of his world. He was a remarkably astute observer. Then he formulated in words, words that have proved

to be all but indelible, the as-if-ness, so to speak, of the behavior and the language of his people. What he said, in effect, was this: "They act as if, they talk as if, all that they feel and believe and live by might be reduced to three fundamental premises or rules. First, they seem always to talk and to act as if a thing is what it is. It is possible to put it in this general form: A is A. That is to say, man is man, truth is truth, etc. This we may call the premise or the law of identity.

"In the second place, they speak and they behave as if they assumed that anything must either be a particular thing or it must not be that particular thing. We may give this notion the general form: Anything is either A or non-A. That is, anything is either a man or it is not a man, anything is either true or it is not true, etc. We may call this the premise or *law of the excluded middle*. It represents the fact, as I observe it, that men are oriented in an either-orish, or two-valued way.

"Thirdly, they talk and they conduct themselves generally as if they took it for granted that something cannot both be a particular thing and also not be that particular thing. This we may state in the general form: Something cannot be both A and non-A. That is, something cannot be both a man and not a man, something cannot be true and not true, etc. We may refer to this as the premise or *law of non-contradiction*.

"These, then, the laws of identity, of the excluded middle, and of non-contradiction—these appear to be the basic laws of thought for these people. It will be noticed that each implies the others: If A is A, then everything must be either A or non-A, and, of course, nothing can be both A and non-A. It may be said that the law of identity is basic to the other two; but at least, if it is accepted—and it appears to be—the other two laws are necessary also, are required by the law of identity. These three laws, then, taken together, constitute the basic mold in which men shape their feelings and their thoughts and all their living reactions."

In large measure they still do. These laws are, in the final analysis, what we speak of when we speak of *common* sense. That is to say, they are, and they have long been, commonly accepted. Most of us, however, are as unconscious of Aristotle's laws, as such, as he formulated them and as they have been expounded by teachers of logic ever since, as were the ancient men whose actual conduct and language the laws were intended to describe. But once stated, they sound as "right" to us as doubtless they did to the ancient Greeks . . . (p. 7–8).

It is appropriate that we take due pains not to leave the impression that Aristotle is to be regarded as having been a malicious or stupid person. Beyond question he was neither. His contribution to human progress was stupendous. The difference between an Aristotelian and a more primitive society is vast indeed. As a matter of fact, insofar as the consequences of Aristotle's generalizations have been unfortunate, they have been due chiefly to the shortcomings not of Aristotle himself, but of his followers. After all, when Aristotle formulated his laws he made it possible for men to become not only more highly conscious, but also more effectively critical, of their behavior and their language. But men made the tragic error of mistaking the laws of Aristotle for laws of *nature*, to be consciously employed but not revised. They accepted them as Truth in an absolute, that-is-that, A-is-A, sense. Consequently, if they were Truth, modifications or contraries of them were non-Truth. Thus, they were perpetuated, and they were used wittingly and unwittingly to build a system of doctrine and an elaborate social structure . . . (p. 9).

Modern science since the late 1800s has provided extensive data to demonstrate validity of the process character of "reality." Some structures, such as a desk, change so slowly that one rarely perceives the incessant submicroscopic activity. Other structures, such as apples and rivers, change rapidly enough for this activity to become apparent to the unaided eye. The process character of "reality" destroys the basic validity of the Aristotelian *law of identity*. Nevertheless, the *notion* of identity, conveyed in our surface linguistic structures by the verb *to be*, remains with us today. Although implicit in the other two premises and widely accepted subsequently, Aristotle himself evidently did not regard the premise of identity as basic to his logical system (see Ferrater [1971, p. 903]). Furthermore, the identification of one event with another plays a basic role in many neuroses and psychoses (see, for example, Campbell [1943], Kelley [1951], Korzybski [1933, 1941, 1946], and Mergener [1943]). These instances usually involve behaving toward one person (in the present, say) as if that person "is" either someone else or the same person at an earlier time. Korzybski (1951) gave the following succinct illustration of degrees of identification:

> One may have a nightmare that he "is" a Stalin. That may be innocent enough. One may have daydreams of being a Stalin. That is more serious. One may proclaim consciously, "I am Stalin, " and believe in it, and begin to shoot people who disagree with him; usually such a person is locked up in a hospital, and he usually is a hopeless case (p. 173f).

Returning now to the so-called Aristotelian laws of thought, we see the Aristotelian *law of the excluded middle* reflected in the either-or, black-white orientation that has become so largely rejected today among the intelligentsia—evidently as a result of Korzybski (1933) and his very widely read student, Hayakawa (1941). One must recognize that the excessively restrictive "either-or orientation" appears in many guises. The following terms dichotomously reflect this orientation: good-bad, right-wrong, worthwhile-worthless, legal-illegal, useful-useless, valid-invalid, true-false, mature-immature, sane-insane, success-failure, etc. The important point in this connection of course has to do with the lack of recognition of any "between-ness" by those who use (and really believe) such polar terms. By his rejection of the Aristotelian premises as inadequate for the complexities of life during our times, Korzybski (1933) consciously ushered in a non-Aristotelian epoch.

Lest one object to the above comments on the grounds that a two-valued ("true" or "false") system must lie at the foundations of any "logical" system, it seems necessary to point out that, similar to the law of identity, a two-valued system characterizes *Aristotelian* logic, not *all* logic. Jan Lukasiewicz (1918) formally introduced the notion of a three-valued logic. He subsequently developed this formulation (1920, 1921), and finally Lukasiewicz generalized these procedures to a many-valued logic (1922, 1930). And further, lest one dismiss Lukasiewicz as an impractical dreamer, his work in parenthesis-free notation (1931) became applied in the middle 1960s in the design of digital computers (called "Polish logic" in the computer industry).

C. Korzybski's Formulation of Time-Binding

In his discussion of the philosophical foundations of the Chomskian paradigm for linguistics, Chomsky (1966, p. 3ff) took great pains to distinguish carefully between the mechanistic, stimulus-response view of mankind offered by the neo-Bloomfieldians, and to account for the "creative aspect of language use."

This paper adopts the definition of man formulated by Korzybski (1921), and presented by him as follows:

> If we analyse the classes of life, we readily find that there are three cardinal classes which are radically distinct in function. A short analysis will disclose to us that, though minerals have various activities, they are not "living." The plants have a very definite and well known function—the transformation of solar energy into organic chemical energy. They are a class of life which appropriates one kind of energy, converts it into another kind and stores it up; in that sense they are a kind of storage battery for the solar energy; and so I define *the plants as the chemistry-binding* class of life.
>
> The animals use the highly dynamic products of the *chemistry-binding* class—the plants—as food, and those products—the results of plant-transformation—undergo in animals a further transformation into yet higher forms; and the animals are correspondingly a more dynamic class of life; their energy is kinetic; they have a remarkable freedom and power which the plants do not possess—I mean the freedom and faculty to move about in *space*; and so I define *animals as* the space-binding class of life.

> And now what shall we say of *human* beings? What is to be our definition of Man? Like the animals, human beings do indeed possess the *space-binding* capacity but, over and above that, human beings possess a most remarkable capacity which is entirely peculiar to them—I mean the capacity to summarise, digest and appropriate the labors and experiences of the past; I mean the capacity to use the fruits of past labors and experiences as intellectual or spiritual capital for developments in the present; I mean the capacity to employ as instruments of increasing power the accumulated achievements of the all-precious lives of the past generations spent in trial and error, trial and success; I mean the capacity of human beings to conduct their lives in the ever increasing light of inherited wisdom; I mean the capacity in virtue of which man is at once the heritor of the by-gone ages and the trustee of posterity. And because humanity is just this magnificent natural agency by which the past lives in the present and the present for the future, I define *humanity*, in the universal tongue of mathematics and mechanics, to be the *time-binding class of life* (p. 58f).

Korzybski further dealt with the matter of animals and their "progress" as follows:

> It may be contended by some that animals have been making "progress" or some may say that animals also "bind-time." This use of words would again become mere verbalism, a mere talking about words—mere speculation having nothing to do with *facts* or with correct thinking, in which there is no intermixing of dimensions. . . . If people are pleased to talk about the "progress" of animals, they can hardly fail to see clearly that it differs both in function and in type or dimension from what is rightly meant by human progress; human time-binding capacity lies in an entirely different dimension from that of animals. So, if any persons wish to talk of animal "progress" or animal "time-binding," they should invent a suitable word for it to save them from the blunder of confusing types or mixing dimensions (p. 63).

Subsequently, Korzybski (1933) described the man-animal differences in terms of a differential ability to make higher-order abstractions:

> In our field, where we have to formulate sharp differences between the nervous responses of "man" and "animal," we say that animals stop abstracting or linking of signals on some level, while humans do not. The latter abstract in indefinitely higher orders—at least potentially.
> Here we encounter a fundamental and sharp far-reaching difference between the nervous functioning of "animal" and "man." This abstracting in indefinitely higher orders no doubt conditions the mechanism of what we call human "mentality." If we stop this abstracting anywhere, and rest content with it, we copy animals in our nervous processes, involving animalistic semantic reactions. As will be shown later, this is

the actual case with practically all of us, owing to our Aristotelian education and theories. This "copying animals" in our nervous responses is, perhaps, a natural tendency at an extremely low level of development; but as soon as we understand the physiological mechanism, we can correct our education, with corresponding human semantic results. Naturally, such "copying animals" by humans must be a process of arrested development or regression. It must be pathological for man, no matter how severe or how mild the affliction may be. Various absolutists, and the "mentally" ill in general, show this semantic mechanism clearly (p. 332).

The time-binding definition of humanity consists of the non-Aristotelian counterpart to the first assumption of the Cartesian-Chomskian paradigm, which holds in effect that "Man is a rational animal."

D. The Principle of Non-Elementalism

Korzybski (1933, p. 1) described as a general semantic mechanism the tendency in the Aristotelian orientation to split verbally that which one cannot separate in actuality. For example, one can never observe organisms apart from some environment; the recognition of this fact eventually led to the macro-biological notion of an "organism-as-a-whole-in-an-environment." One may separate "emotions" and "intellect" verbally, but in actuality one can never have either entirely independent of the other. One may verbally separate "space" and "time," but only within the limitations of Newtonian physics; the more comprehensive Einsteinian theory requires their merger as "space-time." And, most importantly for present purposes, one may separate "body" and "mind" verbally, but in the real world one can never encounter the one (pertaining to a living human) without the other. The need for this more comprehensive orientation of course lies at the foundation of psychosomatic medicine.

Korzybski (1933, p. 289) focused attention on the frequent appearance of the hyphen in many non-elementalistic expressions. It seems interesting to note that the style followed by the journal of the Linguistic Society of America, *Language*, calls for the complete elimination of the hyphen unless the next element begins with a capital letter.

When one removes such a "delusional" verbal split as the separation of "body" and "mind" from the lexicon of valid expressions, one has dismantled the second assumption of the Chomskian paradigm: that one can validly separate "mind" and "body."

E. Propositions and Mathematical Logic

In order to present the reasons why we must reject the next two assumptions made by Chomsky, it seems necessary to provide some background material on the nature of "propositions."

In their classic *Gründzuge der Theoretischen Logik,* Hilbert and Ackerman (1928) gave the following summary of the history of mathematical logic as translated in the 1950 edition in English:

> The first clear idea of a mathematical logic was formulated by Leibnitz. The first results were obtained by A. de Morgan (1806-1876) and G. Boole (1815-1864). The entire later development goes back to Boole (p. 1).

We will have occasion to return to those sources, Augustus de Morgan and George Boole, but first let us present some background material on the general nature of a "proposition, " first in logic and then as it has evolved in mathematical logic.

Reichenbach (1947) described the classical version of this notion quite clearly, as follows:

> Consider the proposition "Aristotle was a Greek." It is an atomic proposition since it includes no propositional operations. . . . If we regard its inner structure, however, we see that the proposition consists of two parts. Grammatically speaking it contains a *subject*, the word "Aristotle," which refers to a man, and a *predicate,* the word "Greek," which refers to a property of that man. These two parts are not of a similar logical nature but represent the general distinction between a *thing* and a *property.* The proposition tells us that the thing has this property; in order to do so it contains the phrase "was a," which indicates that the thing-property relation holds between the objects denoted by the words "Aristotle" and "Greek" (p. 80).

Notice that Reichenbach makes the point that a proposition (more specifically an *atomic* proposition) consists of a *thing* asserted to have a *property,* combined or related by a form of "to be." Nowadays we would call the name for a *thing* a noun phrase (NP), and the name for a property, in general, an adjective phrase (AP). Hence we see that the structure of an atomic proposition consists of:

1. NP+BE+AP

where "BE" represents an appropriate form of the verb "to be."

The following excerpt from Boole (1847) shows the background of Reichenbach's treatment:

> A Proposition is a sentence which either affirms or denies, as, All men are mortal, No creature is independent.

A Proposition has necessarily two terms, as *men, mortal*; the former of which, or the one spoken of, is called the subject; the latter, or that which is affirmed or denied of the subject, the predicate. These are connected together by the copula is, or is not, or by some other modification of the substantive verb.

The substantive verb is the only verb recognized in Logic; all others are resolvable by means of the verb *to be* and a particle or adjective, e.g., "The Romans conquered"; the word conquered is both copula and predicate, being equivalent to "were (copula) victorious" (predicate) (p. 64).

Boole's notion of a "substantive verb" received further treatment in the following (Boole [1854]):

> Class III. *Signs by which relation is expressed, and by which we form propositions.*
>
> Though all verbs may with propriety be referred to this class, it is sufficient for the purposes of Logic to consider it as including only the substantive verb *is* or *are*, since every other verb may be resolved into this element, and one of the signs included under Class I ("Appellative or descriptive signs, expressing either the name of a thing, or some quality or circumstance belonging to it" [p. 27]). For as those signs are used to express the active or passive relation of the subject of the verb, considered with reference either to past, to present, or to future time. Thus the Proposition, "Caesar conquered the Gauls," may be resolved into "Caesar is he who conquered the Gauls." The ground of this analysis I conceive to be the following:—Unless we understand what is meant by having conquered the Gauls, i.e. by the expression "One who conquered the Gauls," we cannot understand the sentence in question. It is therefore truly an element of that sentence; another element is "Caesar," and there is yet another required, the copula is, to show the connexion of these two. I do not, however, affirm that there is no other mode than the above of contemplating the relation expressed by the proposition, "Caesar conquered the Gauls"; but only that the analysis here given is a correct one for the particular point of view which has been taken, and that it suffices for the purposes of logical deduction. It may be remarked that the passive and future participles of the Greek language imply the existence of the principle which has been asserted, viz.: that the sign *is* or *or* may be regarded as an element of every personal verb (p. 35).

The close association of the verb "to be" with the notion of a "proposition" does not consist of an aspect of mathematical logic only, although it has come under perhaps its closest scrutiny in this discipline. For an example from a more classical treatment essentially contemporary with that of Boole, consider the following from John Stuart Mill (1872):

A Non-Aristotelian Paradigm for Linguistics 147

> A proposition ... is a portion of discourse in which a predicate is affirmed or denied of a subject. A predicate and a subject are all that is necessarily required to make up a proposition: but as we cannot conclude from merely seeing two names put together, that they are a predicate and a subject, that is, that one of them is intended to be affirmed or denied of the other, it is necessary that there should be some mode or form of indicating that such is the intention; some sign to distinguish a predication from any other form of discourse. This is sometimes done by a slight alteration of one of the words, called an *inflection*; as when we say, Fire burns; the change of the second word from *burn* to *burns* showing that we mean to affirm the predicate burn of the subject fire. But this function is more commonly fulfilled by the word is, when an affirmation is intended, is not when a negation; or some other part of the verb *to be* (p. 49–50).

After Boole, one of the most significant contributions to the field of mathematical logic consisted of the *Principia Mathematica* of Whitehead and Russell (1913). By this time logicians had begun to recognize some of the shortcomings of the subject-predicate proposition. One can easily detect the shift away from this form in the following excerpt:

> Atomic propositions may be defined negatively as propositions containing no parts that are propositions, and not containing the notions "all" or "some." Thus "this is red," "this is easier than that," are atomic propositions.
>
> Atomic propositions may also be defined positively—and this is the better course—as propositions of the following sorts:
> $R_1(x)$ meaning "x has the predicate R_1";
> $R_2(x, y)$ or xR_2y, meaning "x has the relation R_2 (in intension) to y";
> $R_3(x, y, z)$, meaning "x, y, z have the triadic relation R_3 (in intension)";
> $R_4(x, y, z, w)$, meaning "x, y, z, w have the tetradic relation R_4 (in intension)";
> and so on *ad infinitum*, or at any rate as long as possible. Logic does not know whether there are in fact n-adic relations (in intension); this is an empirical question. We know as an empirical fact that there are at least dyadic relations (in intension), because without them series would be impossible. But logic is not interested in this fact; it is concerned solely with the *hypothesis* of there being propositions of such-and-such a form. In certain cases, this hypothesis is itself of the form in question, or contains a part which is of the form in question; in these cases, the fact that the hypothesis can be framed proves that it is true. But even when a hypothesis occurs in logic, the fact that it can be framed does not itself belong to logic. (p. xv)

Subsequently both Whitehead and Russell took great exception to the subject-predicate proposition, as will appear below. It seems necessary to add, however, that, a generation after *Principia Mathematica* appeared, some mathematical logicians had begun to avoid this construction entirely. Quine (1940), for example, used class membership to define atomic propositions. While still tied to a two-valued logic, he has dispensed with the subject-predicate proposition. His whole system involves the primitive terms (1) class membership ($\in$), (2) joint denial ($\downarrow$), and (3) quantification (indicated by parentheses).

One must distinguish carefully between (1) the grammatical structure "subject+predicate, " in which the term "predicate" refers to the verb and associated complements, etc., and (2) the "subject-predicate" structure, which consists of an item in the logical attic now avoided by most people. Most particularly, we must reject efforts by modern linguists to use the now-outmoded "atomic proposition" as the basis for a linguistic paradigm. Such a rejection amounts to a rejection of the third and fourth assumptions of the Chomskian paradigm (the basic form of thought consists of the subject-predicate proposition, and others consist of combinations of subject-predicate propositions).

F. The Matter of "Universals"

Whereas the Bloomfieldian paradigm emphasized the differences between languages, the Chomskian paradigm focusses upon precisely the reverse—the many factors that, on deeper levels of analysis, languages share. Unfortunately, those who adopted the Chomskian paradigm have chosen to speak of these matters in an excessively all-encompassing way.

At the very most one might search for linguistic "globals," but to speak of linguistic "universals" involves unnecessarily vast assumptions concerning the nature of nonterrestrial symbolic activities that, at the very least, seem premature. One cannot simply excuse this choice of terminology on the grounds that it consists of an arbitrary symbol used technically, because in order to communicate the basic elements of a paradigm one must try to convey the appropriate semantic reactions to a wide audience. One does not have the same leeway in such a pursuit as one has while in the midst of devising an abstract system such as a grammar. Consequently, the fifth assumption of the Chomskian paradigm seems to need some slight refocusing, although it does not suffer from the fundamental defects present in the other four. Chomsky's fifth assumption holds that "general features of grammatical structure are common to all languages and reflect certain fundamental properties of the mind." As we see it, the problem consists of determining the nature of the individual grammars before commenting upon "all languages."

III. REJECTION OF THE VERB "TO BE"

A. General

Before proceeding with the development of a non-Aristotelian paradigm for linguistics, it seems necessary to address a rather basic issue involved in the language of discourse and hence in syntactical efforts to formalize everyday language. This consists of the role played in the past by the verb "to be," in English, and analogous symbols in other languages. Although some languages do not have verbs directly analogous to the "to be" of English (e.g., Tagalog, Hungarian, and some Chinese languages), this verb has entered into many basic formulations of earlier linguistic efforts in undesirable ways. This chapter presents several criticisms of this verb and offers a way out of the dilemma posed by this verb: ubiquitous but also iniquitous.

B. Background

Section E of Chapter II summarized the way in which important contributors to logic—first classical logic, then mathematical logic—evolved away from the inadequate subject-predicate structure. Nevertheless, since this archaic structure has become embedded in our ordinary everyday language, people continue to use it in the fashion described in (1). Section B invited attention to the related Aristotelian construction of identification, which, in our everyday language has the structure:

2. $NP_1 + BE + NP_2$

At first most people when confronted with the rejection of the validity of such forms as (2) tend to react somewhat as follows: What *is* wrong with using "to be"? Why should one not say, for example,

3. John is a farmer.

The answer, fundamentally, has to do with an invalid identification of orders of abstractions, and this point will receive extensive treatment subsequently. The immediate *consequence* of such identifications at the very least consists of an excessive degree of abbreviation, which tends to interfere with communication. For example, surely the following three sentences give greatly divergent information regarding "John":

4. John farms three acres.

5. John owns and works a 2,000-acre farm.

6. John receives $20,000 a year from the government for not growing anything on his farm.

Indeed, we can carry this illustration into a different dimension. Consider these sentences:

7. John, after living in the city all his life, has just bought a farm.

8. John grew up on a farm and has farmed there for 45 years. Despite the fact that (4) through (8) make extremely different statements about John, most people feel comfortable in making the jump from any one of (4) through (8) to: "John is a farmer." The non-Aristotelian orientation holds that (3) does not represent a valid higher order abstraction that could come from such statements as (4) through (8), but rather an invalid abbreviation.

The fundamental problem with (1) and (2) has to do with the excessively tight way "to be" couples two terms or phrases.

C. Philosophical Considerations

The earliest critic of the verb "to be" known to the writer consists of Thomas Hobbes, who wrote in his *Leviathan* (1651, p. 368) that he did not regard this verb as a necessary part of language. He expressed his position as follows:

> And as wee use the Verbe Is, so do the Latines use their Verbe *Est*, and the Greeks their ’Εστι through all its Declinations. Whether all other Nations of the world have in their severall languages a word that answereth to it, or not, I cannot tell; but I am sure they have not need of it: For the placing of two names in order may serve to signifie their Consequence, if it were the custome, (for Custome is it, that gives words their force,) as well as the words Is, Bee, or Are, and the like.
>
> And if it were so, that there were a Language without any Verb answerable to Est, or Is, or Bee; yet the men that used it would bee not a jot the lesse capable of Inferring, Concluding, and of all kind of Reasoning, than were the Greeks, and Latines.

Writing in the Augustan Age, Hobbes naturally assumed that reasoning, among other meritorious human activities, had reached its apex with the Greeks and "Latines." It seems interesting to observe how, from the very beginning of criticism of "to be," those who have pointed out various problems connected with this verb have continued to use it. After drawing attention to this verb, such usage seems most jarring.

Augustus de Morgan (1847), writing just before the Boolean revolution of logic, expressed the excessively all-encompassing aspect of the verb "to be" in the following way:

> The complete attempt to deal with the term *is* would go to the form and matter of every thing in *existence*, at least, if not to the possible form and matter of all that does not exist, but might. As far as it could be done, it would give the grand Cyclopaedia, and its yearly supplement would be the history of the human race for the time (p. 56).

He presented the central role of "to be" in classical philosophy in this way:

> The most difficult inquiry which anyone can propose to himself is to find out what anything *is*: in all probability we do not know what we are talking about when we ask such a question. The philosophers of the middle ages were much concerned with the is, or essence, of things: they argued to their own minds, with great justice, that if they could only find out what a thing is, they should find out all about it: they tried, and failed. Their successors, taking warning by their example, have inverted the proposition; and having satisfied themselves that the only way of finding what a thing is, lies in finding what we can about it; that modes of relation and connexion are all we can know of the essence of anything; in short that the proverb "tell me who you are with, and I will tell you what you are," applies as much to the nature of things as to the characters of men (p. 196).

In effect, de Morgan encouraged the use of a *relational* approach to description and definition, which constitutes the basis of any scientific discipline. For example, in physics one does not merely discuss what gravity "is," but rather one constructs mathematical models that relate gravitational force to mass and distance (Newtonian paradigm), or to space-time curvature (Einsteinian paradigm).

De Morgan also criticized a usage of the verb "to be" that continues to plague beginning students of arithmetic:

> The full definitions of the successive numbers are seen in:
>
> 1 (1+1) {(1+1)+1} [{(1+1)+1}+1], &c.

> That three and one are four is *definition:* it is our pleasure to give the name *four* to 3+1. But that 3+1 is 2+2 is neither definition nor pure identity. It is not even true that "two and two" *is* four; that
>
> [{(1+1)+1}+1] *is* (1+1) + (1+1).
>
> It is true, no doubt, that "two and two" is four, in amount, value, &c. but not in form, construction, definition, &c. (p. 197).

To this day one hears children taught to say "3/6 *is* 1/2, " which may account for some of the difficulties many children have with fractions.

Some years after de Morgan, George Santayana (1923) perceived the role that "to be" plays in the matter of verbal identification, but he did not investigate the effects that such identification can have in our orientations. He stated that:

> The little word *is* has its tragedies; it names and identifies different things with the greatest innocence; and yet no two are ever identical, and if therein lies the charm of wedding them and calling them one, therein too lies the danger. Whenever I use the word is, except in sheer tautology, I deeply misuse it; and when I discover my error, the world seems to fall asunder, and the members of my family no longer know one another (p. 123).

Turning now to the problems with "to be" recognized by Whitehead and Russell, these authors (1913) had had their attention attracted to a variety of linguistic processes in their joint efforts to resolve various paradoxes that had plagued earlier efforts to bring a higher degree of order into mathematical logic. In later studies both authors individually commented on the inadequacy of earlier efforts based upon propositions solely composed of a quality (a predicate) ascribed to some thing (a subject). Bertrand Russell (1914) stated the severity of the issue in this way:

> The belief or unconscious conviction that all propositions are of some subject-predicate form—in other words, that every fact consists in some thing having some quality—has rendered most philosophers incapable of giving any account of the world of science and daily life (p. 24).

In an analogous way, Whitehead (1929) inveighed against the subject-predicate form as a fundamental error, and related this matter to our everyday language:

> The alternative philosophic position must commence with denouncing the whole idea of "subject qualified by predicate" as a trap set for philosophers by the syntax of language (p. 89).

D. General Semantics Considerations

The clearest and strongest indictment of the verb "to be" has come from Korzybski (1933). He stated that:

> The little word "to be" appears as a very peculiar word and is, perhaps, responsible for many human difficulties. . . . Although very little has been done in *structural* analysis of languages in general, and of those of primitive peoples in particular, we know that in the Indo-European languages the verb "to be," among others, is used as an *auxiliary* verb and also for the purpose of positing false to facts identity. . . . Identity may be defined as "absolute sameness in all respects" which, in a world of ever-changing processes and a human world of indefinitely many orders of abstractions, appears as a *structural* impossibility. Identity appears, then, as a primitive "over-emotional" generalization of similarity, equality, equivalence, equipollence, etc., and, in no case, does it appear in fact as "absolute sameness in all respects". . . . If we use the "is" at all, and it is extremely difficult to avoid entirely this auxiliary verb when using languages which, to a large extent, depend on it, we must be particularly careful not to use "is" as an identity term (p. 400).

In connection with Korzybski's remarks about the need for detailed study of non-Indo-European languages, the reader should recall that Bloomfield's *Language* (1933) came out that very same year and established the leading linguistic paradigm for the United States for the next twenty-five years.

Korzybski also had much to contribute relative to the matter of subject-predicate language. Korzybski (1933, p. 306) emphasized that this speech form, with "a structure dissimilar to that of the known world," hampers proper evaluations by interfering with our semantic reactions. In Korzybski (1948) he made this clearer by asserting that subject-predicate statements such as

9. Roses are red.

violate "everything we know about the outside world and the human nervous system." This comment reflects an understanding of the fact that "roses" at most can reflect light waves of various given frequencies, and then as a result of a response by a human nervous system, a feeling of "redness" may result as a transactional matter. Of course, if the given person suffers from Daltonism, the allegedly "red" roses would appear grey. The basic fallacy of the "is" of predication has to do with its expressing a "partial identity" (Korzybski [1933, p. 202]), which leads to a confusion in orders of abstraction, since the quality becomes fallaciously projected onto the object, situation, person, etc., in a denial of the projectional and transactional processes involved. The term "transactional" refers to the demonstrated fact that our perceptions result from an interchange between our human nervous system and objects in the real world outside our skins. Adelbert Ames, Jr., pioneered in developing the experiments which have led to transactional psychology (see Kilpatrick [1961]). Dewey and Bentley (1949) presented the philosophical consequences of these experiments in their *Knowing and the Known*. In summary, Korzybski (1933, p. 371) set up the following priorities:

> The subject-predicate form, the "is" of identity, and the elementalism of the Aristotelian system are perhaps the main semantic factors in need of revision, as they are found to be the foundation of the insufficiency of this system and represent the mechanism of semantic disturbances, making general adjustment and sanity impossible.

Nevertheless, as must have become clear from the quotations, Korzybski himself continued to use the "is" of identity and "is" of predication.

The preceding material has summarized the problems that arise in human communication and orientation as a result of the identity and predication usages of the verb "to be." However, as we all know, the verb "to be" has a variety of other usages in English, including functioning as an auxiliary verb and in constructions expressing existence, location, time, and so on. I. A. Richards, in a piece on literary criticism cited by Korzybski (1948), has allegedly distinguished between some twenty-three different usages. Evidently no one has ever attacked usages other than identity and predication on epistemological grounds.

As indicated previously, even those who raised their voices to caution us against the unreflecting use of "to be" in identity and predication constructions (definitely including Korzybski and most of his students) seemed unable to avoid doing so, while continuing to use "to be" as an auxiliary, etc. This situation suggested to the writer that perhaps only by avoiding this unusual verb altogether could one eradicate the highly undesirable constructions. As an experiment, the writer revised a technical paper that appeared as Bourland (1952) so as to remove all forms of "to be" (except in direct quotations from other authors, of course). Subsequent papers, such as Bourland (1963), Bourland and McManus (1965), and Bourland, Morgan, and Ruskin (1970), further demonstrated the practicality of writing without any recourse to "to be." For ease of reference, Bourland (1965) suggested the term "E-Prime" as a name for this proper subset of English on the basis of the semantic equation

10. $E' = E - e$

where E represents the some 500,000 to one million words of English, and e represents the inflected forms of "to be": *is, are, am, was, were, been, being, be;* the dialectical *ain't* and *am't;* the rarely encountered archaic forms: *war, wast, wert, ben, art, beest,* and *bist;* and sandhi forms: *'m, 's,* and *'re.*

Upon reflection it appeared that others would find E-Prime useful, and this led to the explicit treatment of E-Prime in three papers. Bourland (1965) explored some of the main consequences of writing without using any form of "to be." Bourland (1968) applied E-Prime to the underlying formulations of general semantics: the so-called Non-Aristotelian Premises and the Map-Territory Analogy based upon them. Bourland (1974), presented orally in 1970, provided among other things quantitative support for Korzybski's contentions (1921, 1933) concerning the undesirability of attempting to base dynamic social institutions on static premises.

A number of papers, by the writer and others, have demonstrated the feasibility of E-Prime as a procedure that tends to enhance significantly the clarity of written and oral presentations. Furthermore, E-Prime seems to provide the only practical way to avoid undesirable constructions involving forms of "to be."

This chapter has presented the reasons for the extreme care taken here to avoid any use of this epistemologically undesirable symbol, the verb "to be." One should not interpret the preceding material as an effort to "legislate" the verb "to be" out of existence in the ordinary language of discourse, since languages do not operate that way. However, the subset of English called E-Prime can potentially play a useful role in serious discussions of important matters—in effect as a metalanguage.

IV. ARISTOTELIAN AND NON-ARISTOTELIAN PARADIGMS FOR LINGUISTICS

A. General

While the Bloomfieldian and Chomskian paradigms exhibit obvious surface differences, they both have strong roots in an underlying Aristotelian orientation: the former directly and the latter via an excursion through the elementalistic philosophy of Descartes. Both paradigms share a fundamental reliance upon the mechanisms of identification, two-valued orientations, and marked elementalism basic to the semantic outlook of our Aristotelian heritage. The Chomskian paradigm clearly exhibits those characteristics as illustrated by (1) explicit reliance upon the subject-predicate form for the "principal form of thought, " (2) drawing a sharp two-valued contrast between performance and competence (Chomsky [1965, p. 10f]), and (3) the assumed body-mind dichotomy, reflected in the surface structure–deep structure dichotomy. This latter goes back to Lancelot *et al.* (1660). The Bloomfieldian paradigm suffers from the same basic limitations. While he did not state his epistemological assumptions with the clarity that Chomsky did, Bloomfield (1933) demonstrated his adherence, however unconscious, to Aristotelian principles by: (1) writing with a heavy fraction (a sample indicates rather more than 50 percent) of his sentences involving an identity or predication use of "to be, " (2) considering, evidently as an adequately exhaustive catalog of possible accounts of human behavior, the dichotomous "mentalistic" and "mechanistic" theories (1933, p. 32f), and (3) in common with others who followed his paradigm, elementalistically seeking to conduct linguistic analyses while ignoring or evading as much as possible the meanings of the utterances.

Adherents of both the Bloomfieldian and Chomskian paradigms tacitly assume, furthermore, that meanings reside in words, rather than in humans. For example, we see this in such comments as:

> Our fundamental assumption of linguistics implies that each linguistic form has a constant and specific meaning (Bloomfield [1933, p. 145]).

This chapter presents a body of assumptions that avoid the shortcomings noted above, treating issues that stem from the nature of humanity, language, and linguistics from a non-Aristotelian point of view.

B. The Nature of Humanity

As suggested in Chapter II, a non-Aristotelian approach to linguistics must begin by assuming the time-binding characteristics of man: through symbolic means, humans alone of all living creatures have the ability to function nontrivially in time (Korzybski [1921]). Each generation has the potential (despite self-imposed obstacles that frequently prevent it) of beginning where the preceding one left off, in each field or area of interest to humans. This consists of the *first* and most basic assumption of this paradigm. The creative abilities of humans, who can develop higher orders of abstraction without bound, stand in sharp contrast to the symbolically limited "space-binding class of life [animals]" (Korzybski [1921, 1933]). Associations between two events (such as the ringing of a bell and the subsequent availability of food), when eventually made by animals, have a very low degree of conditionality. In contrast, humans have the potential of reacting with a high degree of conditionality. Hence, as Korzybski (1933) put it:

> Under normal conditions, an animal, to survive, must respond not only to normal stimuli, which bring immediate harm or benefit, but also to different physical and chemical stimuli, in themselves neutral, such as waves of sound or light, etc., which are *signals* for animals and *symbols* for man (p. 333).

The theory developed in Chapter V will provide formal definitions for the notions *signal* and *symbol*.

From a psycho-physiological point of view, the source of the human capability for time-binding resides in the incomparably richer structure of the primarily cortical region in humans than in any other form of life (Herrick [1930]).

C. The Nature of Utterances

Practically all current linguistic studies, with the outstanding exception of Pike (1967), tend to focus upon the sentence—particularly after the Chomskian revolution (in the sense of Kuhn [1962]). This seems both unfortunate and unnecessary, for a variety of reasons. In the first place, people do not speak in sentences very often. Quite apart from transformational rules that may optionally delete a noun phrase, or a verb phrase, or whatever, the stammers, corrections, etc., of actual speech (as distinguished from carefully edited writing) only occasionally amount to "sentences." We find this reflected in the works of some authors, most notably Shakespeare, where one often encounters what school teachers would regard as only speech particles.

A second criticism of the *sentence* focus concerns the need to raise one's sights, from a linguistic point of view, to encompass more than this abstract form of speech: the paragraph, the chapter, the book—these, too, have importance in human affairs, and even more importance than the sentence alone.

For the reasons just presented, in this paper I will use the term "utterance" as basic, and will inquire into its characteristics. This analysis employs the term "utterance" to designate any oral or written speech act, however extensive.

From a non-Aristotelian point of view we must assume that *some human created every utterance*. Consequently it becomes important either to know or have a potential means of finding out who authored any given utterance. This stands in marked contrast to the position taken by those who follow the Bloomfieldian and Chomskian (henceforth various *Aristotelian*) paradigms of linguistics. They elementalistically split utterances from the humans who made them and seek to analyze utterances "on their own merits" without seeming to recognize the artificiality of such an enterprise, with rare exception. The work of John R. Ross seems to evolve away from this type of shortcoming, but the author has only had available secondary sources on Ross's efforts (see Bach and Harms [1968, p. 155f]).

Secondly, we need to recognize explicitly that the author of each utterance had an *intent* (whether conscious or not) in creating it. Such intent may encompass one or more of the following kinds of intentions: convey information, pass time, exhibit friendliness, stimulate appropriate behavior, change attitudes, etc. Consequently, in evaluating any utterance we need to have at least a general notion of the author's intent. This consists of a linguistic analogy for the instructive principle of asking "cui bono?" (who will benefit) in understanding a crime, a new law, etc.

Next we must consider the *environment* of the utterance. The first key factor that we must recognize consists of the *target*, immediate or potential, of the utterance. Occasionally, when people speak to themselves for various reasons, the same individual functions as both the originator and the target of the utterance. Other facets of the environment of the utterance include the space-time considerations: date of origin, possibly other dates (such as date at which the utterance becomes effective, the date at which it becomes ineffective, etc.), the nonverbal and verbal (including the *cultural*) contexts.

Furthermore, each utterance involves a variety of structural factors: we ascribe to the utterance a *semantic structure*, a *syntactic structure*, and a measure of the degree of correspondence between the structure of the utterance and other related structures. Here and subsequently we adopt Korzybski's definition of "structure": a network of relations.

The latter point requires some discussion. It basically consists of a recognition of the point repeatedly made by Korzybski concerning a central aspect of language often overlooked and occasionally ignored on purpose. Let us assume that the *intent* of the person creating an utterance involved (at least as a part, not necessarily the *complete* intent) conveying some information about the "real world." Then we would have a legitimate interest in the degree to which the structure of his utterance corresponds to the structure of the described circumstance, or how well his verbal "map" corresponds to the "territory. " Notice that this observation goes quite beyond the two-valued Aristotelian "true" and "false" to degrees of correspondence. Korzybski (1933) put this matter as follows:

> As words *are not* the objects which they represent, *structure, and structure alone* becomes the only link which connects our verbal processes with the empirical data (p. 59).

Aristotelian paradigms of linguistics, focusing almost entirely on the phonological and syntactical aspects of utterances, wound up with a sterile position that seems to separate utterances from the humanity that created them in an extremely elementalistic way. From the Bloomfieldian paradigm we hear, for example, from Gleason (1965, p. 112):

> Grammar is concerned with only one feature of sentences—their conformity to the system of language. As a grammarian, one can only ask whether or not they are properly constructed in terms of that system. Whether sentences are truthful, appropriate, polite, meaningful, or anything else is no concern to the grammarian as grammarian.

An adherent of the Chomskian paradigm, McCawley (1968, p. 138), put it this way:

> It is of no relevance to linguistics whether a person has correctly perceived and identified the things he talks about; thus one need not know whether there are such things as guardian angels and heaven in order to assign a semantic representation to the sentence: "My guardian angel is helping me to get to heaven. "

Both of the quotations just given indicate that their authors, most likely in common with their colleagues who subscribe to Aristotelian linguistic paradigms, tend to identify (in other words, to confuse) the admittedly narrow concerns of syntactic structure with the whole of language study. As we all know, humans have a tremendous interest in "whether sentences are truthful, appropriate, polite, meaningful, or anything else. " Accordingly, an adequate linguistics paradigm must surely contain provisions to account for such matters. Incidentally, an approach to utterances that does not provide a means to flag factual statements for lacking in structural correspondence to events, happenings, etc., in the "real world" tacitly undertakes to treat seriously (generatively, transformationally, etc.), among other problems, the language of the hospitalized insane. See Zipf (1949, p. 288ff) for an extensive discussion of these problems from both theoretical and empirical points of view.

In passing, it seems desirable to mention that the basic matter of "similarity of structures" contains, as one of its more important consequences, Korzybski's theory of multiordinality, which we will apply to linguistic problems in Chapter VI. This theory recognizes the multiordinality of most important terms "which may have different uses or meanings when applied to different orders of abstraction, " as developed by Korzybski (1933, p. 433ff). This matter will receive detailed treatment in Chapter VI.

D. The Nature of Linguistic Theories

Students of the Indo-European languages have long had available an outstanding example of the phonological and syntactical aspects of linguistics: the grammar of Sanskrit written by Pāṇini in approximately 300 B.C. In praise of this grammar, "one of the greatest monuments of human intelligence, " Bloomfield (1933, p. 11) stated that "No other language, to this day, has been so perfectly described." However, not until the recent ferment brought on by Noam Chomsky have linguists made conscious efforts to develop grammars with both *explanatory* and *descriptive* adequacy, which the generative transformational approach has made manageable.

In recognizing the interrelated notions of grammar, language, and linguistic theory, Chomsky (1965) brought these matters together as follows:

> A grammar can be regarded as a theory of language. . . . A linguistic theory must contain a definition of "grammar, " that is, a specification of the class of potential grammars. We may, correspondingly, say that *a linguistic theory is descriptively adequate* if it makes a descriptively adequate grammar available for each natural language (p. 24).

This paradigm assumes that the central aim of linguistics consists of developing a meta-theory of language of sufficient generality to take into account all known human languages. The internal structure of such a meta-theory will probably have the characteristics of a *system-function* as formulated by Korzybski. This notion builds upon the "doctrinal function" of Keyser (1922) and generalizes the "system function" of Sheffer (1921). Korzybski (1933) described these important functions in the following way:

> A most important extension of the notion of "function" and "propositional function" has been further accomplished by Cassius J. Keyser, who, in 1913, in his discussion of the multiple interpretations of postulate systems, introduced the notion of the "doctrinal function." Since, the doctrinal function has been discussed at length by Keyser in his *Mathematical Philosophy* and his other writings, by Carmichael [1923], and others. Let us recall that a propositional function is defined as an ∞-valued statement, containing one or more variables, such that when single values are assigned to these variables the expression becomes a one-valued proposition. A manifold of interrelated propositional functions, usually called postulates, with all the consequences following from them, usually called theorems, has been termed by Keyser a *doctrinal function*. A doctrinal function, thus, has no specific content, as it deals with variables, but establishes *definite relations* between these variables. In principle, we can assign many single values to the variable terms and so generate many doctrines from *one* doctrinal function. In an ∞-valued non-Aristotelian system which eliminates identity and is based on structure, doctrinal functions become of an extraordinary importance.
>
> In an ∞-valued world of absolute individuals on objective levels, our statements can always be formulated in a way that makes obvious the use of ∞-valued terms (variables) and so the postulates can always be expressed by propositional function. As postulates establish relations or multi-dimensional order, a set of postulates which defines a doctrinal function gives, also *uniquely*, the *linguistic structure*. As a rule, the builders of doctrines do not start with sets of postulates which would explicitly involve variables, but they build their doctrine around some specific content or one special respective value for the variables, and so the *structure* of a doctrine, outside of some mathematical disciplines, has never been explicitly given. If we trace a given *doctrine with specific content* to its doctrinal function without content, but variable terms, then, only, do we obtain a set of postulates which gives us the *linguistic structure*. Briefly, to find the structure of a doctrine, we must formulate the doctrinal function of which the given doctrine is only a special interpretation. In non-mathematical disciplines, where doctrines are not traced down to a set of postulates, we have no means of knowing their structure, or whether *two different* doctrines originated from *one* doctrinal function, or from *two*. In other words, we have no simple means of ascertaining whether the two different doctrines have similar or different structure. Under aristotelianism, these differentiations were impossible, and so the problems of linguistic structure, propositional and doctrinal functions, etc., were neglected, except in the recent work of

mathematicians. The entirely general semantic influence of these structural conditions becomes obvious when we realize that, no matter whether or not our doctrines are traced down to their doctrinal functions, our semantic processes and all "thinking" follow *automatically* and, by necessity, the conscious or unconscious postulates, assumptions, etc., which are given (or made conscious) *exclusively* by the doctrinal function.

The terms "proposition, " "function, " "propositional function, " "doctrinal function, " etc., are multiordinal, allowing many orders, and, in a given analysis, the different orders should be denoted by subscripts to allow a differentiation between them. When we deal with more complex doctrines, we find that in structures they represent higher order doctrines, or a higher whole, the constitutents of which represent lower order doctrines. Similarly, with doctrinal functions, if we take any *system*, an analysis will discover that it is a whole of related doctrinal functions. As this situation is the most frequent, and as "thinking, " in general, represents a process of relating into higher order relational entities which are later *treated as complex wholes*, it is useful to have a term which would symbolize doctrinal functions of higher order, which are made up of doctrinal functions of lower orders. We could preserve the terminology of "higher" and "lower" order; but as these conditions are always found in all *systems*, it seems more expedient to call the higher body of interrelated doctrinal functions, which ultimately produce a system—a *system-function*. At present, the term "system function" has been already coined by Doctor H. M. Sheffer [1921]; but, to my knowledge, Sheffer uses his "system function" as an equivalent for the "doctrinal function" of Keyser. For the reasons given above, it seems advisable to limit the term "doctrinal function" to the use as introduced by Keyser, and to enlarge the meaning of Sheffer's term "system function" to the use suggested in the present work, this natural and wider meaning to be indicated by the insertion of a hyphen (p. 144-45).

We can only speculate, at present, upon the characteristics of a linguistics system-function. Most likely, this will require the development of (1) language-specific doctrinal functions of a generative transformational nature that will contain the semantic, syntactic, and phonological details for given languages; (2) then, perhaps, a series of layers of higher-order doctrinal functions can provide the necessary rules (probably transformational only at such higher levels) for groups and families of languages; (3) on the highest level, we envision a linguistics system function—those rules, etc., that specify the highest interrelations and specifications that lead to the various language groups.

If generally adopted, this focus of research for the future would turn linguistic energies toward developing explicitly formulated higher order theories that could demonstrate the factual unity of languages (on a sufficiently high level). Since the semantic-syntactic aspects of languages seem by far more straightforward and simpler than phonology, it would appear appropriate to begin such an effort with an emphasis on these problems. (See Chapter VI for the reasons for joining "semantics" with "syntax. ")

E. Relations between Components

The two Aristotelian paradigms of linguistics discussed in this paper both recognize the need for three components of a grammar: semantic, syntactic, and phonological. The model offered by Chomsky (1965) assumes the primacy of the syntactical component, with both the semantic and phonological components providing "purely interpretive functions" (Chomsky [1965, p. 16]).

I reject the position for these reasons: (1) it has no empirical confirmation; (2) it violates most people's intuition (this makes the primacy of syntax shaky even within the tenets of the Chomskian paradigm, which regards personal intuition as an important criterion in most areas); (3) it entails an elementalistic assumption relative to the possibility of dealing independently with semantic and syntactic considerations. The utterance-generating system as outlined in Section C of this chapter requires a recognition of a variety of interacting dimensions. Figure 1 on page 164 illustrates how those key dimensions seem to fit together with such factors as phonology and graphology. The interrelation of "semantics" and "syntax" receives detailed treatment in Chapter VI.

V. A NON-ARISTOTELIAN THEORY OF SIGNS

A. General

This chapter contains the basic outline of a non-Aristotelian approach to a theory of signs. We include it in the present investigation as a foundation for the linguistic analysis contained in the following chapter. Otherwise the positions taken in Chapter VI might appear to amount to nothing more than ad hoc criticism.

The basic purpose here consists of attempting to demonstrate explicitly the embedding of the linguistic paradigm in a more general theory of signs.

FIGURE 1:
Key Factors in the Linguistic Process

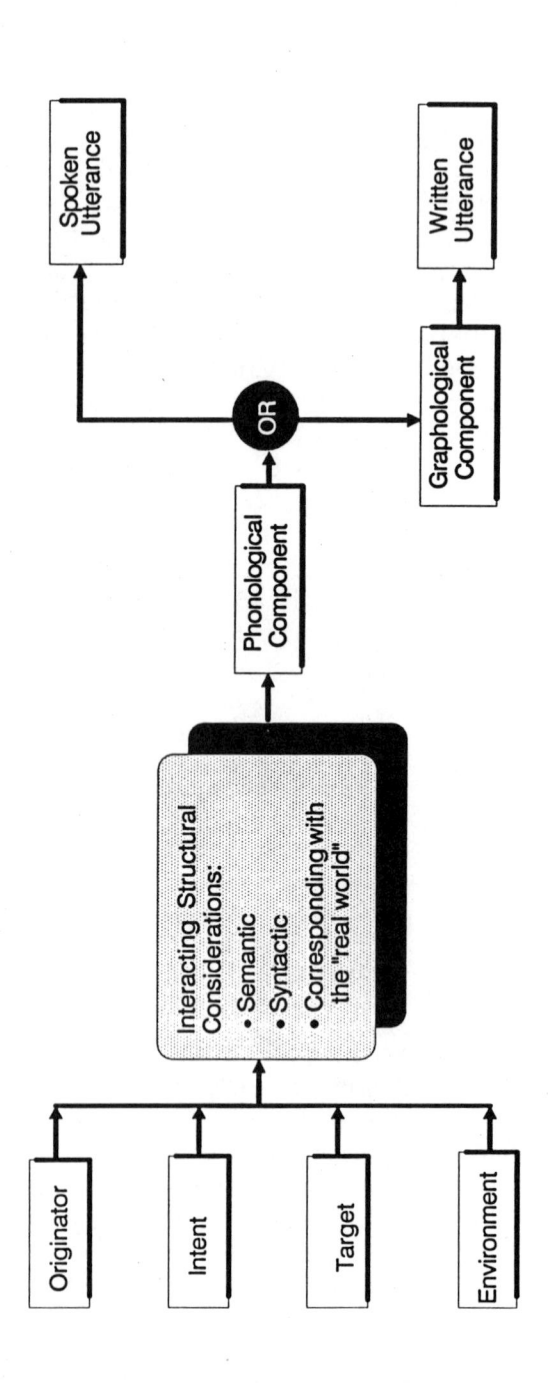

B. Background

In Chapters II and IV we mentioned the two-valued approach to most matters, or emphasis on dichotomies, as one characteristic of the Aristotelian orientation. Interestingly enough, studies of *signs* have often taken the approach of emphasizing one form of trichotomy or another. The work of Charles Sanders Peirce, extending over quite a time period, and the famous *The Meaning of Meaning* by Ogden and Richards (1923) both show this tendency.

Peirce (1903) gave the following definition of *signs*:

> All dynamical action, or action of brute force, physical or psychical, either takes place between two subjects... or at any rate in a resultant of such actions between pairs. But by "semiosis" I mean, on the contrary, an action, or influence, which is, or involves, a cooperation of *three* subjects, such as a sign, its object, and its interpretant, this tri-relative influence not being in any way resolvable into action between pairs. Σημείωσις in Greek of the Roman period, as early as Cicero's time, if I remember rightly, meant the action of almost any kind of sign; and my definition confers on anything that so acts the title of a "sign" (p. 332).

The *sign* trichotomy for Ogden and Richards consisted of symbol, thought, and referent (1923, p. 11 ff). In their system, the symbol does not represent the referent directly:

> Between the symbol and the referent there is no relevant relation other than the indirect one, which consists in its being used by someone to stand for a referent. Symbol and Referent, that is to say, are not connected directly... but only indirectly round the two sides of a triangle (p. 11–12).

In their Chapter V, Ogden and Richards presented a consciously and explicitly Aristotelian theory of signs.

More recently, Charles W. Morris developed a theory of signs explicitly within the behaviorist paradigm, as presented in his *Signs, Language, and Behavior* (1946). Morris defined a "sign" in the following behavioristic way:

> If anything, A is a preparatory-stimulus which in the absence of stimulus-objects initiating response-sequences of a certain behavior-family causes a disposition in some organism to respond under certain conditions by response-sequences of this behavior family, then A is a sign (p. 10).

He further expressed his orientation as follows:

> The issue is not between "mentalism" and "behaviorism," but is solely

a methodological problem: are such terms as "idea," "thought," "mind" more or less precise than such terms as "organism," "stimulus," "response-sequence," and "disposition to response"? In choosing the latter terms we but express the belief that they are the more suitable for scientific advance (p. 28).

I agree that the basic issue involved here consists of a methodological one: both sets of terms suffer from various degrees of elementalism. Use of the first set ("mentalistic" terms) clearly involves tacit assumptions as to the possibility of dealing with such notions as "ideas" and "thoughts," independently of "emotions," and other aspects of a given individual. Use of the second set ("behavioristic" terms) involves tacit assumptions concerning the possibility of isolating an "organism" from its environment other than the "stimulus" and such matters. The latter may work well with rats in laboratories, but the link between such findings and the complexities of human activities and potentialities has received scant proof (see Chomsky's extensive discussion of these matters [1959]). Arthur Koestler (1962) has referred to the standard behavioristic procedure of reasoning from laboratory rats to human behavior as a "ratomorphic fallacy."

Korzybski (1933) regarded behaviorism as a very "naive discipline," and stated that:

> The Behaviourists mean well, methodologically, without realizing fully what scientific methodology is. They completely condemn "introspection," yet they continually use it. Consciousness of abstraction solves the problem of pro- or anti-behaviouristic attitudes, because, when we are fully conscious of abstracting, we should never confuse description with inference, neurologically processes of different order.
>
> Any discipline, to be a science, must start with the lowest abstractions available; which means descriptions of some objective, *un-speakable* level. In *human* psychology,"introspection" is the only *possible descriptive level*, all other methods being inferential (pp. 359–60).

C. The Billboard Analogy

Before beginning to deal with signs as comparatively abstract notions, let us begin with a simple, concrete example. Consider a simple billboard, which advertises some product, such as "Orange Crush." This consists of one kind of sign, beyond doubt. It we study this specific sign seriously, we readily see that:

1. Some workmen made the sign, on behalf of a company which makes and sells a certain product.

2. The intent behind the construction of this sign consisted of a desire to encourage the purchase of the product.

3. The target of the sign consisted of every passing person with the financial means of buying a soft drink.

In addition to those matters, the billboard has a variety of environmental characteristics:

4. The workmen constructed it at some given time; before that it did not exist. Eventually it will either rot or become replaced by another sign.

5. The effectiveness of the sign will depend in part on its physical location relative to other signs and relative to other structures in its vicinity.

And finally, let us consider the multidimensional, structural characteristics associated with the billboard. The sign must convey a message (or statement) in writing or pictures of some appropriate kind, otherwise it would not fall into the category of "signs." Let us assume that the hypothetical sign of this analogy contains only the statement "Orange Crush Tastes Good!" Then we may study these three structural characteristics of the sign:

6. It has a *semantic structure*, which consists of explicitly stated relations. In this case the relations concern the nature of "Orange Crush" from the viewpoint of the sense of taste.

7. It has a *syntactic structure*, which consists of explicit and implicit relations between the units on the next lower level of components of the sign. This implies a hierarchy of levels of units that may enter into the composition of a sign.

8. If one has sufficient interest in the matter, one may investigate the *degree of correspondence* between the semantic structure of the sign and the structure of that part of the "real world" (if any) that the sign describes. This particular instance calls for the simple experiment of obtaining a taste evaluation of Orange Crush. Subsequently the individual can decide for himself the degree to which the semantic structure of the sign corresponds to the structure of the unspeakable characteristics of the outside world: in this trivial case, the taste of Orange Crush.

The eight characteristics presented above constitute the dimensions of signs assumed in this theory. This analogy provides the basis for an intuitive understanding of this theory, presented below in more detail.

D. The Definition of a Sign

Any mark of whatever kind, or any object in the "real world" of whatever kind, has the *potential* of serving as a sign. Generalizing upon the definition used by Zipf (1949, p. 253f), we say that the mark, or object, becomes a sign only when used conditionally for something else by *some organism(s)*. The "something else" then consists of the "meaning" of the sign in that specific context. Experiments and their analyses by Pavlov (with dogs), Yerkes (with apes), von Frisch (with bees), etc., have provided data on the comparatively low level of conditionality possible for animals and insects, in comparison with the unlimited conditionality of humans.

To illustrate the definition given above more concretely (once again, following Zipf), if a carpenter mislays his *hammer* and instead uses a *stone* to drive a *nail*, then the *stone* serves as a sign for the *hammer* in that situation. The *conditionality* of our definition refers to the ability of the carpenter, given his background and present need, to perform the abstractive feat of recognizing that the *rock* could serve as, function as, represent, etc., the *hammer*. When the sign itself has a more abstract quality, as in the case of a "word," it must eventually amount to a use in place of some poorly understood process in the human nervous system.

E. The Types of Signs

We can distinguish clearly between the following types of signs: signals, symbols, quasi-symbols, and symbolisms. They involve increasing degrees of conditionality, as will become evident.

1. *Signals* consist of indications that involve the lowest level of conditionality, as in the mechanistic reaction of a unit of an automated system, or the unconditioned reaction of an animal in the (artificial) context of a behavioristic experiment.

2. *Symbols* consist of representations that may stand for (a) events outside our skin or inside our skin as studied in physics, chemistry, physiology, etc., (b) semantic reactions (psychological events) inside our skins regarded as "sane," or (c) plans for events that may become manifested outside our skins.

3. *Quasi-symbols* consist of the results of semantic disturbances

of a pathological nature as studied in psychiatry.

4. *Symbolisms* consist of abstract aspects of some activity that one may choose to interpret as representing some other activity (or that, in fact, represents some other activity) as in the symbolism employed in some artistic efforts, certain religious activities, and various aspects of other ceremonial affairs. Symbolisms may range in complexity from the several interpretive levels of a complex drama, such as Beckett's *Waiting for Godot*, to a single grapheme as sometimes used in political contexts.

F. Characteristics of Signs

The physical manifestations of a sign depend on its type. In the simplest case, that of signals, the sign becomes activated through or indicated by the presence or absence or change of state of energy to power the given signal. Symbols and quasi-symbols become manifested through verbal utterances, spoken or written. Symbolisms require, for their manifestation, activities or descriptions of activities that ostensibly or actually may seem to have no necessary function as symbolisms.

Signs may have various degrees of complexity. We reject a simplistic division of signs into "simple" and "complex," for signs may range in sophistication from the simple message of a stop light to a pulse of energy of the order of nano-seconds (10^{-9} seconds) in length in a large-scale digital computer; they may vary in the case of symbols from a simple billboard urging people to drink "Orange Crush" to an elegant exposition of a theory in physics; and they may range in symbolism from a coarse gesture of impatience to the overall impact of a drama that operates on a variety of levels simultaneously. We can thus perceive the potentiality of many degrees of complexity.

G. Dimensions of Signs

As suggested above (in Section C), we must pay careful attention to the dimensions of signs, of whatever type. Signs in general, and utterances in particular, have the eight dimensions previously discussed. Specifically, the complete specification of a sign requires information concerning the following matters:

1. Originator
2. Intention of originator

3. Target
4. Times associated with the sign
5. Context: physical, cultural, relative to other signs
6. Semantic structure
7. Syntactic structure
8. Degree of correspondence between the semantic structure and whatever (if anything) this structure describes

Further discussion seems necessary in connection with the three structural dimensions (6–8 above).

Although some may dismiss this point as "merely" a matter of style, one may find a variety of interesting problems by investigating the interactions between dimensions 6 and 7—interactions between semantic structure and syntactic structure. For example, statements interlarded with such surface forms as the "is" of identity and predication usually (and sometimes by design) convey the underlying semantic structure very poorly. Many important characteristics tend to drop out due to the excessive amount of abbreviation provided by such constructions.

For one example, let us consider the following statement, occasionally offered even by linguists:

11.a. The whole thing boils down to this: either man *is* a machine, or he *is* not (emphasis supplied).

This assertion contains two serious problems. The first stems from a two-valued orientation, according to which *one* of the following assertions, and *only* one of them, has confirmable validity (called, within a two-valued Aristotelian orientation, "true"):

11.b. Man *is* a machine.

11.c. Man *is not* a machine.

This seems suspicious, on the face of it: the two-valued orientation rarely survives a careful examination of the complex circumstances some try to force into Procrustean twin beds. Before we can properly interpret 11 in any of its forms, we must first cope with the *is* problem. Consider 11.b. As it stands, it seeks to identify a class name for a living organism with the class name for a type of non-living organism: a patently absurd situation from the point of view of this paradigm. Even version 11.d does not improve upon this situation:

A Non-Aristotelian Paradigm for Linguistics

11.d. John (man$_i$) *is* a machine.

That case tries to identify a living creature with a class name, obviously involving a confusion of orders of abstraction so grossly that (in terms of the present theory) one would surely have to assign *this* utterance to the class of quasi-symbols, an object of interest only in clinical cases. One might encounter objection to this treatment of 11.b on the grounds that that sentence "really" means something like one or more of the following:

12.a. Man acts like a machine (by necessity).

12.b. Man behaves like a machine.

12.c. If we only knew enough we could predict all aspects of human behavior.

12.d. We can predict most aspects of human behavior.

12.e. Some men act like machines in certain circumstances.

12.f. Some aspects of human behavior seem more predictable than others.

Now the statements in 12 provide the basis for a potentially fruitful discussion or analysis. In the writer's opinion, careful consideration will in most instances bring one to the viewpoint that 12.e and 12.f apply to the following: namely, that while some men act like "machines" in some circumstances, nevertheless we can firmly state only that some aspects of human behavior seem more predictable than others.

Now let us consider 11.c, according to which "Man *is not* a machine." Using language with the same syntactic structure as unfortunately employed in 11.c, we might add that:

13.a. Man *is not* a chair.

13.b. Man *is not* a flower.

13.c. Man *is not* a rock.

and so on to the limit of one's patience. On a more formal level, we see that 11.c basically states that:

14.a. Denial: (Man *is* a machine.)

We have shown above that the assertion in parentheses falls into the category of quasi-symbols. Accordingly 14.a amounts to little more than:

14.b. Denial: (A unicorn ate my framis last night.)

14.c. Denial: (John can trisect an angle with a straight edge and compass.)

14.d. Denial: (I have solved the general case of a fifth degree algebraic equation.)

14.e. Denial: (She trapped an elephant in that match box.)

The statements denied in 14.a through 14.e do not correspond to any structure, or describe any actual happening, in the "real world." One would describe their denials all as "tautologies" in Aristotelian logic (14.e does not strictly consist of a tautology). Although valid, these denials do not convey any useful information, for the most charitable interpretation we can put on them amounts to a recognition that the denial of a statement that corresponds to nothing in the "real world" similarly has no serious content.

Once again, some might insist that 11.c "really" means something like one or more of the following:

15.a. No important regularities exist in human behavior.

15.b. Men never act machine-like.

15.c. We could never know enough to predict important, detailed aspects of human behavior.

15.d. We cannot predict some aspects of human behavior.

15.e. Some aspects of human behavior seem more predictable than others.

Clearly, the statements given in 15 could provide a better basis for serious discussion than 11.c. In the writer's opinion, this proceeds from the fact that the sentences in 11 give an excessively abbreviated form for a potentially interesting and possibly valid set of statements (12 and 15). But 11 basically has the form of a quasi-symbol.

It seems worth emphasizing that some hold that 11.b constitutes the fundamental, though tacit, assumption of the Bloomfieldian paradigm, while 11.c gives the fundamental, though tacit, assumption of the Chomskian paradigm. The foregoing analysis shows that both assertions as given do not "make sense" and, if changed to more reasonable forms, both may lead to the same third position (namely, 12.f and 15.e). That one can allegedly capture the basic distinction between the Bloomfieldian and Chomskian paradigms so pithily seems to illustrate once again the common Aristotelian nature of those two paradigms.

To turn now to a second example of interactions between semantic structure and syntactic structure, let us consider the syntactic construction known as the "pseudo-cleft sentence,"recently analyzed by Grosu (1973). Sentences 16.a, 16.b, and 16.c illustrate a cleft sentence, a pseudo-cleft sentence, and their non-pseudo-cleft counterpart respectively:

16.a. It *was* an apple that John ate.

16.b. What John ate *was* an apple.

16.c. John ate an apple.

We must recognize that not all idiolects make use of cleft and pseudo-cleft constructions, but evidently many do. Despite their allegedly interesting syntactic properties, it seems clear that 16.a and 16.b provide extremely awkward representations for 16.c, with the latter furnishing a much better basis for investigating the pertinent semantic aspects.

H. Statement of the Premises

The previous sections of this chapter have provided definitions and discussions of the dimensions of signs. In this section we will present the premises that underlie this theory. The first three premises consist of Sign Theory analogues to Korzybski's non-Aristotelian premises (1943):

Premise I (Non-identity). We must distinguish clearly between a sign, which some organisms use conditionally for something else, and the "something else." (This "something else" consists of the "meaning" of the sign.)

Premise II (Non-allness). A sign cannot incorporate in its dimensions all the characteristics of whatever the organisms use the sign for.

Premise III (Self-reflexiveness). One may use $sign_2$ for another sign, $sign_1$, but the resulting $sign_2$ belongs to a higher order of abstraction than $sign_1$.

Premise IV. Adequate sign analysis involves the following steps: (1) determination of which of the four types of signs (signal, symbol, quasi-symbol, or symbolism) one must deal with; (2) study of the dimensions of the sign to determine the nature of each of the eight dimensions as presented above; (3) inquiry into the significant interactions of the dimensions; (4) evaluation of the adequacy of the type determination; (5) iteration of the subsequent steps if necessary.

Premise V. Partial analysis of a sign (consideration of less than the whole sign) may readily lead to inaccurate, elementalistic, and misleading results.

I. Consequences of the Premises

The premises stated above overlap in a variety of areas and, as such, may not seem to constitute the basis for a tightly reasoned system. Future efforts may sort these matters out somewhat differently. At the present it seems enough to indicate their interrelated nature, particularly Premises I and II, and Premises IV and V. Nevertheless, the distinct aspects treated in those different premises seem at the present to make them all necessary.

This Sign Theory will not receive further treatment here in general terms. The following chapter presents the consequences of the premises just stated for those signs that consist of symbols. We define linguistics as precisely this: *the scientific study of signs that consist of symbols.*

VI. NON-ARISTOTELIAN LINGUISTICS

A. General

This chapter presents a discussion of a variety of linguistic issues using the definitions and assumptions developed in the previous chapters. Consequently, this material provides a part of the answer to "So what?"

The results exhibited here suffer from precisely the difficulties discussed by Kuhn (1962), but they also seem to promise much:

> The early versions of most new paradigms are crude. . . . When a new candidate for paradigm is first proposed, it has seldom solved more than a few of the problems that confront it, and most of those solutions are still far from perfect. . . . But paradigm debates are not really about relative problem-solving ability, though for good reasons they are usually couched in those terms. Instead, the issue is which paradigm should in the future guide research on problems many of which neither competitor can yet claim to resolve completely (pp. 155–56).

B. The "Charter"

A basically important function of any paradigm consists of a more or less explicit design of interesting analyses that require attention. The primary guide for non-Aristotelian linguistics consists of the call to develop the system-function for linguistics, as discussed in Section D of Chapter IV. In a sense this generalizes the well-known quest of historical linguistics for the steps that may have taken place between the "then" and "now" with emphasis on the phonological characteristics of the Indo-European languages.

From another viewpoint, the system-function approach, which would work inductively from a variety of language-specific studies, rises from the ashes of disappointment of the Chomskian paradigm, which held that one could strike *directly* to general features of language (unfortunately and insensitively labeled "linguistic universals," as discussed in Section F of Chapter II). Despite the initial claims, after ten years or so the Chomskian paradigm has produced very few "linguistic universals," and these have a decidedly trivial nature. For example, one such "universal" consists of the following: "All languages have consonants." One can readily recognize the yearnings for "linguistic universals" as a consequence of, or as compatible with, the "rationalist" approach of Descartes. However, the method of searching for such generalizations used by those who follow the Chomskian paradigm seems in basic conflict with the orientation of the older sciences that linguistics needs to emulate: build higher-order generalizations on the basis of lower-order descriptions, then higher-order descriptions, then inferences, etc., up to the higher-order generalizations. By consciously working toward a system-function for language, we would follow just such a procedure.

C. Discovery Procedures

Linguistic paradigms demonstrate their power and characteristics most clearly when applied to some language that supposedly has not previously received linguistic attention. Let us first consider the discovery procedures of non-Aristotelian linguistics in general.

The discovery procedures for this paradigm stem directly from Premise I of the Sign Theory outlined in the preceding chapter. That premise reflects our best understanding of the general nature of the physical characteristics of the world in which we live. On the submicroscopic level we can find only nonverbal processes, which we may characterize as dynamic aspects of space-time curvature. Consequently, when studying how humans linguistically segment the nonverbal world about them, we first need to acquire an understanding of the way the given speech community deals with such processes. Usually (but not with Hopi, as discussed by Whorf [1956]), the culture elementalistically splits "space" and "time." One needs to find out *how* the speech community deals with this split.

Next, one may address the problem of how those who use the given language separate out various facets of "time." These may become expressed formally in subsequent summaries in terms of time expressions (yesterday, today, etc.), tenses, modality, aspect considerations (perfectivity, progressivity, habituality, etc.), and perhaps interactions of the foregoing.

Next, one can proceed to inquire into the partitioning of "space." This may generate approximate equivalents for such English notions as "here," "there," "this," "that," "near (the speaker)," etc.

Premise II states, in effect, that no sign can contain or reflect all the characteristics of the real or potential space-time event that it ultimately represents. In a sense this consists of an incorporation into this non-Aristotelian sign theory of Werner Heisenberg's well-known Principle of Uncertainty in physics (according to which we can determine either the position or the velocity of an electron, but not both). Hence from the highly limited but exceedingly precise formulations of mathematical physics to the potentially limitless but mainly imprecise languages of discourse we can anticipate the need to deal with uncertainty in some way. In studying a language anew we need to probe to ascertain the manner in which the given language deals with this pervasive problem. Standard procedures for dealing with this matter consist of using something analogous to the subjunctive mood, modals, aspect markers, and the explicit use of the "etc."

Premise III incorporates a general semantic mechanism that Korzybski referred to as the theory of multiordinality, which has its roots in the theory of types due to Whitehead and Russell. On the level of present interest, multiordinality accounts for the fact that we use most important symbols on a variety of different orders of abstraction, and this (relative) difference in orders of abstraction consists of the origin of differences in "meaning." This accounts, in terms of the present paradigm, for the problem raised by Lakoff and quoted by McCawley (1968, p. 131) as illustrated by:

17.a. John has memorized the score of the Ninth Symphony.

17.b. The score of the Ninth Symphony *is* lying on the piano.

Whoever allegedly made (or makes) such sentences as 17.a and 17.b uses the noun phrase "the score of the Ninth Symphony" on two different orders of abstraction. McCawley stated that Lakoff called this process *reification*. Such a labeling seems inappropriate for two reasons: (1) it amounts to a misuse of a term long employed in philosophy, where "reification" refers to the fallacious treatment of the name for a high-order abstraction as the name for an object; and (2) Lakoff's label obscures a more general process probably present in many languages—multiordinality. The latter accounts for the differences in "meaning" of the "same" noun phrase "the score of the Ninth Symphony" in sentences 17.a and 17.b and also in the following examples:

17.c. John studies the complex acoustic phenomena produced by the score of the Ninth Symphony.

17.d. John heard the score of the Ninth Symphony.

17.e. The score of the Ninth Symphony typifies one stage in the development of Western music.

The speaker of 17.c uses "the score of the Ninth Symphony" as a label for a structure on the event level, in 17.d as a label for a structure on the object level, and in 17.e as a label for a high-order abstraction on the symbolic level (for a clarification of this use of the terms "event," "object," and "symbolic" levels, if needed, see Korzybski [1933] and Bourland [1952, 1963]).

After obtaining a grasp of the general semantic considerations presented above, one can begin to inquire more deeply into the segments of utterances, as used in the actual conduct of life within a specific culture.

Since we must begin with the primacy of dynamic processes varying in specific ways in a space-time continuum, eventually a linguistic analysis should relate both the "lexical items" and "structural items" to this fact. To the best of the writer's knowledge, no one has conducted this type of analysis since the death of Whorf, whose work the followers of the Chomskian paradigm hold in disdain (see the gratuitous comment in Bach [1968, p. 122]).

D. The Indivisibility of "Semantics" and "Syntax"

As a consequence of reflecting upon the epistemological implications of Einstein's General Theory of Relativity, people eventually brought to conscious awareness what they had "known" all along: among other things, one cannot have in isolation "matter" without "space" and "time." In fact, no *one* of those three Newtonian formulations can exist without the other two. In a directly analogous manner, the sign theory proposed in Chapter V directs our attention to another consideration that becomes evident upon reflection: we cannot have a set of symbols that have solely either "semantic" *or* "syntactic" dimensions. Accordingly, we must recognize the essentially elementalistic nature of the terms "semantic(s)" and "syntax" or "syntactic." The writer proposes the abandonment of "semantics" and "syntax" and their related forms as misleading, since we cannot have the one without the other. In their place we would do better to use the more unitary term "linguistics" (or "linguistic") .

Before proceeding, it seems necessary to mention an important matter. Only in the instances of linguistics ("Consider the sentence: 'Colorless green ideas sleep furiously' . . . ") and second language learning ("Make up a sentence using the words 'even though' . . . ") do we find utterances that do not appear in a real-life situation with at least the dimensions discussed in previous chapters. These contexts almost always disambiguate the allegedly ambiguous sentences that have intrigued many linguists in recent years. With the recognition of the artificiality of this problem, it should vanish as an important linguistic issue .

Let us return to the central problem of the deep and essential interrelatedness of "semantic" and "syntactic" matters. From the point of view of this paradigm, the interrelatedness of these two aspects of linguistics accounts for the great advances made by the Chomskian paradigm. Evidently the traditional linguistic training of the Chomskians led them to believe (1) in the separateness of "semantics" *versus* "syntax," and (2) that "semantics" consists of something murky and undefinable, while (3) syntax consists of something more definite and, indeed, more respectable. Nevertheless, despite what the Chomskians *said* about what they did, the features that appear at crucial places in a Chomskian explication have, in my view, joint semantic/syntactic roles. Hence the power of generative-transformational grammars: they can explicitly and straightforwardly combine "semantic" features and "syntactic" features, in the phrase structure rules as well as in the lexicon.

For a concrete example of these combinations, let us consider the phrase marker shown in Figure 2, on page 179, which duplicates an example given by Chomsky (1965, pp. 108f). Despite Chomsky's

A Non-Aristotelian Paradigm for Linguistics

FIGURE 2:
A Chomskian Phrase-Marker

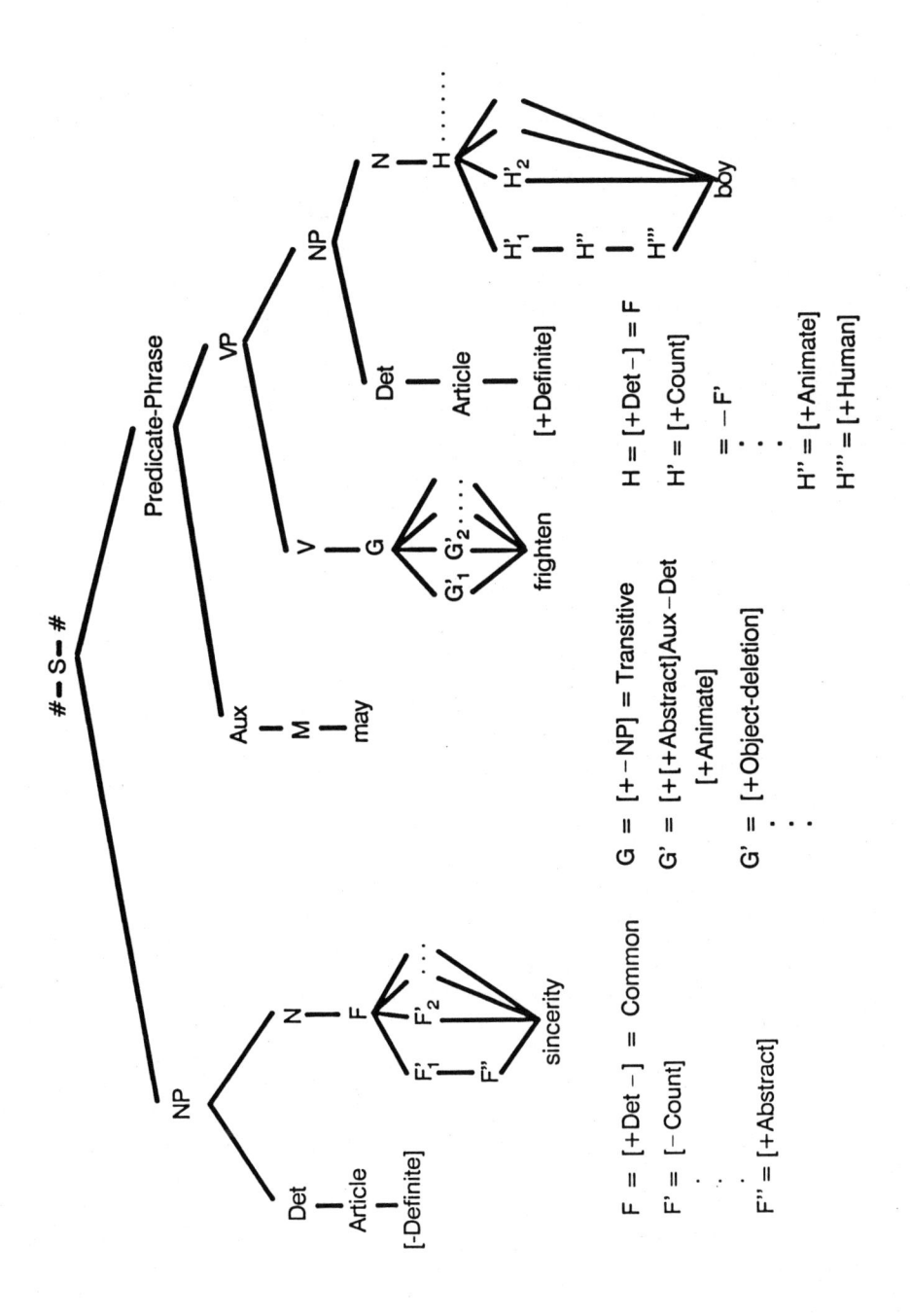

denial (p. 110) that he has given any "semantic" features in either the lexicon or the phrase-marker (in our Figure 2) that depends on that lexicon, it seems apparent that in fact such features as [± Animate], [±Human], [±Abstract], [±Count], and others not explicitly stated there, such as [±Singular], [±Present], [±Stative], etc., all play both "syntactic" *and* "semantic" roles. Such features function "syntactically" in ensuring compliance of the elements of the terminal string with the so-called rules of strict subcategorization and rules of selection; they function "semantically" in joining the utterance with the alleged intent of the alleged originator. We must add "alleged" in the preceding sentence, to recognize explicitly that the case discussed consists of a hypothetical example, rather than an utterance taken from a real-world situation.

In his penetrating critique of the semantic theory of Katz and Fodor (1963), the late Uriel Weinreich (1966; p. 415) came to essentially the same position as presented above, but from a quite different theoretical position. In discussing sentences with various grammatical and "semantical" oddities, Weinreich made the following observations:

> The customary approach is to say that [some sentences] are deviant on grammatical grounds, while [those of another set] are deviant on semantic grounds. This judgment can be made, however, only in relation to a given grammar G(L) of the language L; one may then cite the specific rules of G(L) which are violated in each [case], and indicate what the violation consists of. Whatever rules are violated by the second set, on the other hand, are not in G(L); presumably they are in the semantic description of the language, S(L). But . . . the demarcation between G(L) and S(L) proposed by Katz and Fodor is spurious, and no viable criterion has yet been proposed (p. 415).

Weinreich goes on to say:

> The absence of a criterion is all the clearer in a syntax formulated in feature terms. Chomsky (1965) suggests that syntactic features may be those semantic features which are mentioned in the grammar (p. 415n).

And finally,

> One of the sources of difficulty of [the theory of] Katz and Fodor, it seems, was its assumption that semantics begins where syntax ends. . . . On the contrary, we have argued for their deep interpretation (p. 468).

E. The Depth of Deep Structure

As work in the development of the Chomskian paradigm has progressed, attention has seemed to turn from the development of generative-transformational grammars of given languages to the consideration of increasingly abstract underlying structures that stem from the consideration of specific interesting sentences. These increasingly abstract developments have come particularly from the work of Ross (e.g., 1967) and Lakoff (e.g., 1967).

Bach and Harms (1968, p. viii) cited an interesting and illuminating example of the search for ever-deeper structure, based upon the surface sentence given below:

> 18.a. Floyd broke the glass.

They stated that "the form of this underlying structure may be indicated by a quasi-paraphrase" given below:

> 18.b. I declare to you that it past that it happen that Floyd do cause it to come about that it BE the glass broken.

Applying the dimensional procedures presented in Chapters IV and V to this case, we hold it necessary and now possible to push the form of the underlying structure to:

> 18.c. I declare to you (with an intension not stated, in a specific nonverbal and specific verbal environment) that it past that it happen that Floyd do cause it to come about that it happen that the glass break.

The determination of the value of going to the extreme of 18.c, if any, must await future elaborations of the present paradigm.

VII. Conclusion

This study has pointed out a variety of inadequacies in the assumptions said to underly the Chomskian paradigm for linguistics and has demonstrated that the (on the surface) contrary approaches offered by the Bloomfieldian and Chomskian paradigms share an underlying Aristotelian orientation.

In an effort to improve upon the known shortcomings of an Aristotelian orientation (characterized by the fallacious assumption of identity, two-valued orientations, elementalism, etc.), this study has presented a set of assumptions for a non-Aristotelian linguistics, based upon a more general sign theory.

Some of the more important and immediate consequences of this beginning effort, which could lead to a fully-developed non-Aristotelian paradigm for linguistics, consist of the following:

1. A general redefinition of the purpose of linguistic research: namely, the development of a linguistic system-function;

2. A recognition of the fact that one cannot validly separate "semantic" and "syntactic" considerations: we humans can only produce utterances that have these (and other) dimensions, and hence any grammar (however defined) that provides useful results (however defined) *must* present a semantic-syntactic mix;

3. On the basis of a reassessment of the nature of signs, a deepening of the semantic-syntactic structure of grammatical analysis;

4. A description of the effect of the preceding upon the procedure one should use in studying a specific language (discovery procedures); and

5. The relevance of Korzybski's theory of multiordinality for linguistics.

REFERENCES

Bach, Emmon. 1968. "Nouns and Noun Phrases." In E. Bach and R. T. Harms, eds., *Universals in Linguistics Theory.* New York: Holt, Rinehart and Winston.

———, and R. T. Harms. 1968. Preface to *Universals in Linguistic Theory.* New York: Holt, Rinehart and Winston.

Bloomfield, Leonard. 1933. *Language.* New York: Henry Holt.

Boole, George. 1847. "The Mathematical Analysis of Logic." In *Studies in Logic and Probability* by George Boole. London: Watts, 1952.

———. 1854. *The Laws of Thought.* Reprint. New York: Dover, 1958.

Bourland, D. David, Jr. 1952. "Introduction to a Structural Calculus: A Postulational Statement of Alfred Korzybski's Non-Aristotelian Linguistic System." *General Semantics Bulletin,* nos. 8 and 9.

———. 1963. "Semantic Construction: A Time-Binding Mechanism." *General Semantics Bulletin,* nos. 30 and 31.

———. 1965. "A Linguistic Note: Writing in E-Prime." *General Semantics Bulletin,* nos. 32 and 33.

———. 1968. "The Semantics of a Non-Aristotelian Language." *General Semantics Bulletin,* no. 35.

———. 1974. "The Language of E-Prime." In Washburn, D. E., and D. R. Smith, eds., *Coping with Increasing Complexity.* New York: Gordon and Breach.

———, and Robert P. McManus. 1965. "A General Model for Information Transfer Systems." *General Semantics Bulletin,* nos. 32 and 33.

Bourland, D. David, Jr., Charles H. Morgan, and Karen L. Ruskin. 1970. "A Semantic Experiment: Searching for Undefined Terms." In L. Thayer, ed., *Communication: General Semantics Perspectives.* New York: Spartan Books.

Campbell, Douglas G. 1943. "Neuropsychiatric Foundations and Clinical Applications of General Semantics." In *Papers from the Second American Congress on General Semantics,* ed. M. Kendig. Chicago: Institute of General Semantics.

Carmichael, R. D. 1923. *The Logic of Discovery.* Chicago: University of Chicago Press.

Carnap, Rudolf. 1946. *Introduction to Semantics*. Cambridge: Harvard University Press.
Chafe, Wallace L. 1970. *Meaning and the Structure of Language*. Chicago: University of Chicago Press.
Chomsky, Noam. 1957. *Syntactic Structures*. The Hague: Mouton.
———. 1959. "A Review of B. F. Skinner's *Verbal Behavior*." *Language*, 35 (26–58).
———. 1965. *Aspects of the Theory of Syntax*. Cambridge: MIT Press.
———. 1966. *Cartesian Linguistics*. New York: Harper & Row.
———. 1967. "The Formal Nature of Language." In *Biological Foundations of Language*, by E. H. Lenneberg. New York: Wiley.
———. 1969. "Deep Structure, Surface Structure, and Semantic Interpretation." *Semantics*, ed. by D. Steinberg and L. Jakobovits. Cambridge: University Press.
Cleckley, Hervey. 1942. "Semantic Dementia and Semi-Suicide: A Mask of Sanity." *Psychological Quarterly* 16 (July 1942): 521–29.
Dewey, John, and Arthur F. Bentley. 1949. *Knowing and the Known*. Boston: Beacon Press.
Ferrater-Mora, Jose. 1971. *Diccionario de filosofia*. Buenos Aires: Editorial Sudamericana.
Gleason, Harry A., Jr. 1965. *Linguistics and English Grammar*. New York: Holt, Rinehart & Winston.
Grosu, Alexander. 1973. "On the Status of the So-Called Right Roof Constraint." *Language* 49 (294–311).
Hayakawa, Samuel I. 1941. *Language in Action*. New York: Harcourt, Brace & World. Republished in expanded form as *Language in Thought and Action*, 1949.
Herrick, C. Judson. 1930. "Localization of Function in the Nervous System." *Proceedings of the National Academy of Science*, October 1930.
Hilbert, D., and W. Ackerman. 1928. *Gründzuge der Theoretischen Logik*. Reprinted as *Principles of Mathematical Logic*. New York: Chelsea Publishing Co. 1950.
Hobbes, Thomas. 1651. *Leviathan*.
Johnson, Wendell. 1946. *People in Quandaries*. New York: Harper & Row.
Katz, Jerrold J., and Jerry A. Fodor. 1963. "The Structure of a Semantic Theory." *Language* 39 (170–210).
Kelley, Douglas McG. 1951. "The Use of General Semantics and Korzybskian Principles as an Extensional Method of Group Psychotherapy in Traumatic Neuroses." *Journal of Nervous and Mental Disease* 114, n. 3.
Keyser, Cassius J. 1922. *Mathematical Philosophy*. New York: E. P. Dutton.
Kilpatrick, Franklin P. 1961. *Explorations in Transactional Psychology*. New York: New York University Press.
Koestler, Arthur. 1962. *The Ghost in the Machine*. London: Hutchinson Publishing Group.
Korzybski, Alfred. 1921. *The Manhood of Humanity*. New York: E. P. Dutton & Co.
———. 1933. *Science and Sanity: An Introduction to Non-Aristotelian Systems and General Semantics*. Lancaster, Pa.: Science Press.
———. 1941. "General Semantics, Psychiatry, Psychotherapy, and Prevention." *American Journal of Psychiatry* 98 (203–14).
———. 1946. "A Veteran's Readjustment and Extensional Methods." *Et cetera* 3, no. 4.
———. 1948. Seminar 1948. Tape recording of an intensive seminar on general semantics held at Lakeville, Conn., December 1948. Available from the Institute of General Semantics, Lakeville, Conn.
———. 1951. "The Role of Language in the Perceptual Process." In *Perception: An Approach to Personality*, ed. Robert R. Blake and Glenn V. Ramsey. New York: Ronald Press.
Kuhn, Thomas S. 1962. *The Structure of Scientific Revolutions*. Chicago: University of

Chicago Press.
Lakoff, George. 1967. *Instrumental Adverbs and the Concept of Deep Structure.* Duplicated. Cambridge, Mass.
Lancelot, C., and A. Arnauld, *et al.* 1660. *Grammaire générale et raisonnée.*
Lukasiewicz, Jan. 1918. Farewell lecture by Professor Lukasiewicz delivered in the Warsaw University Lecture Hall on March 7, 1918. Published in *Jan Lukasiewicz, Selected Works,* ed. L. Borowski, Amsterdam-London: North Holland, 1970.
———. 1920. *On Three-Valued Logic.* First published as "O logice trojwartosciowej" in *Ruch filozoficzny* 5 (17–171).
———. 1921. *Two-Valued Logic.* First published as "Logika dwuwartosciowa" in *Przeglad filozoficzny* 13 (189–205).
———. 1922. "A Numerical Interpretation of the Theory of Propositions." Delivered at the 232nd meeting of the Polish Philosophical Society in Lwow on October 14, 1922. First published in *Ruch filozoficny* 7 (92–93).
———. 1930. "Philosophical Remarks on Many-Valued Systems of Propositional Logic." Originally presented as "Philosophische Bemerkungen zu mehrwertigen Systemen des Aussagenkalkuls" in *Comptes rendus des seances de la Societe des Sciences et des Lettres de Varsovie* 23 (51–77).
———. 1931. "Comments on Nicod's Axiom and on 'Generalizing Deduction.' " First published as "Uwagi o aksjomacie Nicoda i 'dedukcji nogolniajacej' " in *Ksiega pamiatkowa Polskiego Towarzystwa Filozoficzuego,* Lwow.
McCawley, James D. 1968. "The Role of Semantics in a Grammar." In *Universals in Linguistic Theory,* ed. E. Bach and R. T. Harms. New York: Holt, Rinehart and Winston.
Mergener, John C. 1943. "General Semantics and the Problem of 'Rapport' in Psychiatry." In *Papers from the Second American Congress on General Semantics,* ed. M. Kendig. Chicago: Institute of General Semantics.
Mill, John Stuart. 1872. *A System of Logic, Ratiocinative and Inductive.* London: Longmans (reissued 1961).
de Morgan, Augustus. 1847. *Formal Logic.* London: Open Court (reprinted 1926).
Morris, Charles W. 1946. *Signs, Language and Behavior.* New York: George Bragriller.
Nida, Eugene A. 1960. *A Synopsis of English Syntax.* Norman, Okla.: Summer Institute of Linguistics.
Ogden, C. K., and I. A. Richards. 1923. 7th ed. *The Meaning of Meaning.* London: Kegan Paul, Trench, Trubner, 1945.
Otero, Carlos P. 1970. *Introducción a la linguistica transformacional.* Mexico, D.F.: Siglo XXI Editores.
Peirce, Charles S. 1903. *Collected Papers.* V. "Pragmatism and Pragmaticism." Ed. C. Hartshorn and P. Weiss. Cambridge: Harvard University Press (edition of 1965).
Pike, Kenneth L. 1967. *Language in Relation to a Unified Theory of the Structure of Human Behavior.* 2nd rev. ed. The Hague: Mouton, 1971.
Quine, Willard V. O. 1940. *Mathematical Logic.* Cambridge, Mass.: Harvard University Press.
Reichenbach, Hans. 1947. *Elements of Symbolic Logic.* New York: Macmillan.
Ross, John R. 1967. "On the Cyclic Nature of English Pronominalization." In *To Honor Roman Jakobson III.* The Hague: Mouton.
Russell, Bertrand. 1914. *Our Kowledge of the External World.* Chicago: University of Chicago Press.
Santayana, George. 1923. *Scepticism and Animal Faith.* New York: Scribner.
Sheffer, Henry M. 1921. "The General Theory of Notational Relativity." *Proceedings of the Sixth International Congress of Philosophy.* Cambridge: Harvard University Press.

Trager, G. L., and H. L. Smith, Jr. 1951. *An Outline of English Structure.* Reprint. Washington, D.C.: American Council of Learned Societies.

Weinreich, Uriel. 1966. "Explorations in Semantic Theory. *Current Trends in Linguistics* 3 (395–477).

Whitehead, Alfred North. 1929? *The Principle of Relativity with Applications to Physical Science.* Cambridge: Cambridge University Press. Reprinted in part in F. S. C. Northrop and Mason W. Gross, eds., *Alfred North Whitehead: An Anthology.* New York: Macmillan, 1961.

———, and Bertrand Russell. 1913. *Principia Mathematica.* Cambridge: Cambridge University Press (paperback ed. to 56, 1962).

Whorf, Benjamin Lee. 1956. *Language, Thought, and Reality.* Ed. John B. Carroll. Cambridge: MIT Press.

Yerkes, R. M., and A. W. Yerkes. 1929. *The Great Apes.* New Haven: Yale University Press.

Zipf, George K. 1949. *Human Behavior and the Principle of Least Effort.* Cambridge: Addison-Wesley.

THE EDITORS

D. DAVID BOURLAND, JR., graduated from Culver Military Academy (1946), Harvard College (A.B. Mathematics, 1951), Harvard Graduate School of Business Administration (M.B.A. 1953), and the Universidad de Costa Rica (Licenciatura in English Linguistics, 1973). He held a fellowship for study at the Institute for General Semantics, 1949–1950; attended IGS Seminars IX/47, IX/48, II/49, IX/49, XII/49, IX/68; edited the *General Semantics Bulletin*, 1964–1970; acted as a trustee of the Institute of General Semantics, 1964–1989. He served on the Staff, Commander Naval Forces Far East, as a Lieutenant, Junior Grade, 1953–1955, and worked in the field of naval operations research, 1955–1971. He taught at the Universidad de Costa Rica from 1971 to 1980, retiring as Associate Professor of Linguistics.

PAUL DENNITHORNE JOHNSTON serves as Executive Director of the International Society for General Semantics. He has worked as newspaper reporter and editor, and has published short stories and novels, and had four of his one-act plays produced. He received a B.A. in Philosophy, Sociology, and Politics in England from the City of London Polytechnic. He studied art at Malvern College in England, has illustrated books and magazines, and has exhibited and sold paintings in the United States, Britain, and the Bahamas.